Campus Sexual Assault

Sexual assault on college campuses has drawn tremendous public attention and colleges are under great pressure to respond. In many cases, the result has been a system of sexual assault tribunals that violates the rights of alleged assailants and assault survivors. Gerstmann shows how colleges are often punishing students as sex offenders without a fair hearing and are defining sexual offenses in an unconstitutionally broad manner. Using unbiased and accessible language, this book avoids easy answers and asks: How are colleges failing to assess accusations in a fair manner? Why are "affirmative consent" laws unconstitutional? How can we do a better job preventing sexual assault? The author argues that colleges are too often making poor choices in terms of how they respond to allegations of sexual assault and, in doing so, they are depriving students of due process, while failing to protect victims of assault.

Evan Gerstmann is Professor of Political Science at Loyola Marymount University. He is a widely cited, widely reviewed scholar of constitutional law. His work on same-sex marriage has been cited by courts, law reviews, and scholarly journals.

Campus Sexual Assault

Constitutional Rights and Fundamental Fairness

EVAN GERSTMANN
Loyola Marymount University, California

CAMBRIDGE
UNIVERSITY PRESS

CAMBRIDGE
UNIVERSITY PRESS

University Printing House, Cambridge CB2 8BS, United Kingdom

One Liberty Plaza, 20th Floor, New York, NY 10006, USA

477 Williamstown Road, Port Melbourne, VIC 3207, Australia

314-321, 3rd Floor, Plot 3, Splendor Forum, Jasola District Centre, New Delhi - 110025, India

79 Anson Road, #06-04/06, Singapore 079906

Cambridge University Press is part of the University of Cambridge.

It furthers the University's mission by disseminating knowledge in the pursuit of education, learning and research at the highest international levels of excellence.

www.cambridge.org
Information on this title: www.cambridge.org/9781108497923
DOI: 10.1017/9781108671255

© Evan Gerstmann 2019

First published 2019

A catalogue record for this publication is available from the British Library

Library of Congress Cataloging in Publication data
NAMES: Gerstmann, Evan, author.
TITLE: Campus sexual assault : constitutional rights and fundamental fairness / Evan Gerstmann, Loyola Marymount University, California.
DESCRIPTION: Cambridge, United Kingdom ; New York, NY : Cambridge University Press, [2019]
IDENTIFIERS: LCCN 2018029230 | ISBN 9781108497923
SUBJECTS: LCSH: Campus violence – Law and legislation – United States. | Rape in universities and colleges – United States. | Universities and colleges – Law and legislation – United States. | Private universities and colleges – Law and legislation – United States. | College students – Crimes against – United States. | Due process of law – United States. | Civil rights – United States. | Fairness.
CLASSIFICATION: LCC KF4225 .G47 2019 | DDC 345.73/02532–dc23
LC record available at https://lccn.loc.gov/2018029230

ISBN 978-1-108-49792-3 Hardback
ISBN 978-1-108-70931-6 Paperback

For my sons Isaac and Sam. May they continue growing into fine young men who listen to all and think for themselves.
And, as always, for Lauren.

Contents

Acknowledgments

First and foremost, I want to thank my wife Lauren who read every chapter, gave advice and perspective, and edited the first drafts. This is a much better book than it would have been without her.

My gratitude also goes to my colleagues and friends who read various parts of the manuscript or discussed the ideas therein with me. These include Judge Robert Gordon, Donald Downs, Jennifer Jones, Liza Taylor, Mark Graber, Jonathan Rauch, Anna On Ya Law, Robert Hume, Matthew Bosworth, Amir Hussein, Brian Treanor, and Christopher Kaczor.

All scholarly books depend in part on the work that came before them, but the work of some scholars and journalists, which included persons with very different points of view on the issues discussed in this book, were especially important. This group includes, but is not limited to, Nancy Chi Cantalupo, Aya Gruber, K. C. Johnson, Stuart Taylor, and Emily Yoffe.

I am also grateful for the support my dean, Robbin Crabtree, my department chair, Janie Steckenrider, my editor, Robert Dreesen, my research assistant, Nisha Bajania, and the institutional support of Loyola Marymount University.

Introduction

In 2009 the Center for Public Integrity began an investigation into how colleges handle allegations of peer-to-peer sexual assault. They found that colleges often gave little institutional support to victims even when college investigations found that the students had indeed been assaulted. Punishments often were perceived by victims as little more than a slap on the wrist, and victims did not feel protected from future assaults.

As the issue gained wider attention, other problems surfaced. Many colleges appeared to discourage reporting of such assaults out of fear of bad publicity or liability. It was too often unclear what conduct was against university rules and what the consequences for such conduct were. Complaining students were subjected to clumsy and insensitive questioning. Many victims did not feel heard, respected, or safe. Research indicates that underreporting of college sexual assault remains a serious problem.

Under the Obama administration, the Department of Education's Office of Civil Rights (the OCR) strongly acted on the position that peer-to-peer sexual assault of college students violates Title IX, the federal law barring gender discrimination that inhibits equal access to higher education. There was a significant increase in federal investigations of colleges for failure to properly respond to sexual assault allegations and the targets of such investigations were made public regardless of whether the OCR found any wrongdoing. In 2011, the OCR issued to all colleges a "Dear Colleague" letter giving unusually detailed instructions on how to handle allegations of sexual assault and threatened to withhold federal funding – which would be a virtual death sentence – from any college that did not follow the rules laid down. Even apart from the substance of the letter, it was controversial because the OCR did not follow any of the normal procedures for issuing these sorts of rules, such as allowing a period for public comment.[1] The letter was rescinded by the Trump administration, but at the time of this writing, only interim instructions have replaced it.

Apart from government pressure, college administrations resolved to respond more aggressively to complaints of peer-to-peer sexual assault. Colleges have developed large and growing bureaucratic apparatuses, often led by former OCR officials, to investigate and punish sexual assault. As described by Harvard law professors Jacob Gersen and Jeannie Suk Gersen:

> The federal bureaucracy interprets federal law to require colleges and universities to have internal bureaucracies that regulate sexual conduct. An effect of this development is the replication of bureaucracy by bureaucracy. Schools must employ Title IX coordinators to oversee their compliance and their processes of responding to individual complaints ... Former OCR governmental bureaucrats often lead or staff the extra-governmental bureaucracies, which makes sense from the perspective of schools seeking expert knowledge of what OCR wants schools to do ... the sex bureaucracy has managed to plant seeds of its own replication within the parties it regulates, and the plants are blossoming.[2]

The first argument of this book is that these bureaucratic apparatuses have too often done a poor job of providing fair process to students accused of sexual assault. We will see examples of students denied the most basic information they would need to mount an effective defense; colleges deliberately hiding exculpatory evidence and even discouraging exculpatory witnesses from testifying; colleges failing to inform students of the specific charges against them; and colleges changing the charges mid-process without informing the students among many other denials of fair process. These flawed procedures violate the constitutional rights of public university students and other legal rights of private university students.

This book also argues that many, perhaps most, universities are regulating consensual sexual activity in violation of students' constitutional rights. We will see that "affirmative consent" laws not only violate students' right to sexual autonomy, but also do not offer any extra protection to students against sexual assault.

To be clear, the argument of this book is not that "the pendulum has swung too far," in terms of combatting college sexual assault. In fact, colleges still need to do a better job of protecting victims of sexual assault, especially in terms of eliminating barriers to reporting and implementing empirically tested approaches to lowering rates of sexual assault. This is discussed in the last chapter of the book.

I reject the pendulum metaphor because it wrongly implies that colleges are now somehow doing *too much* to combat sexual assault, which is certainly not

---

[1] The OCR took the position that despite the detailed nature of the letter it was merely clarifying existing law and was not subject to the procedural requirements for legal rule making by a federal agency.

[2] Jacob Gersen and Jeannie Suk Gersen, "The Sex Bureaucracy," 104 *California Law Review* 881–948, 904–905 (2016) (citations omitted).

the argument of this book. The argument here is that colleges are too often making poor choices in terms of how they respond to allegations of sexual assault. As will be discussed at length, depriving students of due process does nothing to protect victims of sexual assault and is almost undoubtedly counterproductive as well as unconstitutional.

In fairness to college administrators, preventing sexual assault of college students is something that they cannot be reasonably expected to do alone. As discussed in the first and last chapters, legislators and police departments can and should do more to help colleges. Expecting colleges to run their own investigation, adjudication, and enforcement systems in jurisdictions with poorly drafted sexual assault laws or uncooperative police departments is a great deal to ask.

College Title IX Coordinators are like sailors buffeted by powerful winds and tides pulling their boats in opposite directions. Demands for swift action are not always compatible with the need to be thoughtful and thorough. Imperatives to "believe the women"[3] can conflict with legal obligations to presume innocence. As Brett Sokolow, one of the nation's leading consultants on college sexual assault, writes:

Caught in the middle of all this is the campus Title IX Coordinator (TIXC) who receives a complaint from a victim who is in pain. The TIXC pursues the complaint with diligent investigation within the requisite +/- 60 days, and then calls us in puzzlement over why they have now found text messages from the complainant both before and after the incident, describing it as consensual. It's easy for media outlets to paint uncaring campuses as the bad guys over and over again, but reality is often far more complex than that. Worse, FERPA – the federal student privacy law – leaves colleges unable to explain and defend the backstory to the cases they process.[4]

Universities[5] are ill-equipped to balance these competing concerns on their own. This area, which deeply impacts the constitutional rights and other rights of college students, is an obvious area for strong judicial involvement. Fair process is at the core of the courts' expertise. As we will see in Chapter 2, courts have been too reluctant to enforce constitutional due process protections for a variety of reasons, although this appears to be changing as more and more egregious cases reach the courts. This book attempts to move the process along by laying out an argument for what procedural protections are required and why the Constitution and other laws require them. This sort of clarity would benefit everybody – victims, accused students, and the higher education system.

---

[3] See, e.g., Bari Weiss, "The Limits of 'Believe All Women,'" *New York Times* (November 28, 2017), www.nytimes.com/2017/11/28/opinion/metoo-sexual-harassment-believe-women.html.
[4] An Open Letter to Higher Education about Sexual Violence from Brett A. Sokolow, Esq. and The NCHERM Group Partners (May 27, 2014). www.ncherm.org/wordpress/wp-content/uploads/2012/01/An-Open-Letter-from-The-NCHERM-Group.pdf.
[5] This book uses *colleges* and *universities* interchangeably.

WHY THIS BOOK AND WHY NOW?

I have spent the great majority of my academic career pressing for legal reforms that are considered liberal/progressive.[6] My first two books were on same-sex equality issues, and I am proud to say that I was strongly advocating for the constitutional right to same-sex marriage well before that issue was in the public eye. My previous work seeks to make sure that constitutional rights are applied equally to all. This book continues and extends that goal. I know that a great many bright, well-informed, progressive people are concerned that defending the constitutional rights of people accused of sexual assault is a type of "backlash" against the movement to fight sexual violence. I respectfully disagree – legal reform to ensure due process generally brings about positive change. But, I want to directly address the concerns I have heard from some of my friends and colleagues who have been generous enough to share their thoughts with me.

WHY WRITE A BOOK PRIMARILY ABOUT THE RIGHTS OF THE
ACCUSED RATHER THAN THE VICTIMS?

This is a question I have been asked a number of times, and it is a very fair question. There are several answers. First and foremost, I have seen absolutely no evidence that the types of severe deprivations of due process I discuss in this book do anything to protect victims of sexual assault. Due process protects the innocent. University administrators and professors should not adopt the rhetoric of self-described "law and order" politicians and paint due process as gauntlet of technicalities favored only by those who are soft on crime.

I have also been asked whether this is really the right time to write this book. My answer is that it is always a good time to write a book defending due process. When the public is afraid or angry, due process is often portrayed as an unaffordable impediment to justice and public safety. As explained in "Without Due Process: Lynching in North Carolina 1880–1890," lynchings were justified as necessary responses to the state's insufficiently conviction-oriented legal systems.[7] In the 1940s, the majority of the Supreme Court rejected Justice Frank Murphy's call for due process for Japanese Americans accused of disloyalty. In the 1980s, Attorney General Ed Meese argued against Miranda rights for criminal suspects because: "Suspects who are innocent of a crime should [get due process]. But the thing is, you don't have many suspects who are innocent of a crime. That's contradictory. If a person is innocent of a

---

[6] I utilize the first person only for the introduction where it seems appropriate for my goals. The remainder of the book is written in the traditional academic third person.

[7] Sarah Burke, Elias Carr Paper (#160), East Carolina Manuscript Collection, J. Y. Joyner Library, East Carolina University, Greenville, North Carolina, https://uncw.edu/csurf/Explorations/documents/withoutdueprocess.pdf.

crime, then he is not a suspect."[8] At the turn of the twenty-first century, our government argued that normal protections of due process were not always possible. As the Editorial Board of the *New York Times* put it after the 9/11 attacks:

Mr. Bush argued that the attacks changed everything: Due process and privacy were luxuries the country could no longer afford. Far too many members of Congress bought this argument. Others, afraid of being painted as soft on terror, refused to push back.[9]

In our zeal to combat sexual assault, we should not make the same mistake yet again and conflate concern for due process with being tolerant of sexual violence. The idea that due process is an impediment to public safety or that support for due process conflicts with protecting victims is an old trope and is without empirical support. In *Hamdi v. Rumsfeld*, "[T]he Government also argued at some length that its interests in reducing the process available to alleged enemy combatants are heightened by the practical difficulties that would accompany a system of trial-like process."[10] In fact, it turned out the civilian courts, even with all their supposedly impractical due process protections, were far more effective at convicting terrorists than President George W. Bush's military tribunals, which had far fewer due process protections for the accused.[11]

Quite the opposite, lack of due process can harm the victim as well as the accused. In the next two chapters we will see cases in which victims were denied justice by college sexual assault panels that gave them insufficient opportunity to produce and review evidence and to pose questions to the accused students about their shifting stories, and that fell short in various other ways.

More generally, victims are unlikely to be helped by a process in which people lack confidence. A process that violates peoples' rights and lacks peoples' trust leads to lawsuits, and fear of lawsuits scares people away. According to the *New York Times*:

School officials are being named in individual lawsuits, so fewer agree to serve on Title IX panels; self-identified victims increasingly need lawyers of their own, because they risk being sued. Advocates on both sides suspect that schools are hedging their bets as they adjudicate, fearing both lawsuits and Office for Civil Rights sanctions.[12]

---

[8] Howard Kurtz, "Meese Says Few Suspects Are Innocent of Crime," *Washington Post* (October 11, 1985), www.washingtonpost.com/archive/politics/1985/10/11/meese-says-few-suspects-are-inno cent-of-crime/272c4d16-f627-4ce4-896e-7faf8632a526/?utm_term=.32470d486886.

[9] Editorial Board, "We Can't Tell You," *New York Times* (April 3, 2010), www.nytimes.com/ 2010/04/04/opinion/04sun1.html.

[10] 542 U.S. 507 (2004).

[11] Dashiell Bennett, "Civilian Courts Are Way Better Than Military Courts at Convicting Terrorists," *The Atlantic* (April 23, 2013), www.theatlantic.com/politics/archive/2013/04/civilians-courts-vs -military-courts-terrorism/315994/</ac.

[12] Kathryn Joyce, "The Takedown of Title IX," *New York Times* (December 5, 2017).

It is also always important to be careful with the facts. The progressive left often accuses the political right of playing fast and loose with the facts. On issues such as global warming, evolution, and the prevalence of voter fraud, I tend to agree. But we all have feet of clay, and this is an area where I believe that too many progressives have been careless with the facts. The media is inundated with the claim that "1 in 4" or "1 in 5" women are sexually assaulted in campus. As is discussed in Chapter 8, these studies are rife with extremely serious methodological shortcomings. They do not sample representative populations. They have low response rates and are therefore highly vulnerable to "response bias," meaning that they are getting responses from an unrepresentative subset of an already unrepresentative sample. They have significant time-frame problems. Perhaps most importantly, they frame their questions using very broad language that calls for highly subjective responses that likely exaggerate the number of alleged sexual assaults on campuses. Several of the authors of these studies have publically stated that they are uncomfortable with the ways their studies are being used by politicians and the way they are being discussed in the media.

To be fair, these studies have their defenders, and reasonable people can disagree on the numbers. However, politicians and the media very rarely discuss these numbers in a fair or clear way and are prone to use these studies to promote panic and sensationalism rather than reason. To take one of many possible examples, in 2017, *The Dallas Morning News* ran a headline that read: "15 Percent of Female Undergraduates at the UT [University of Texas] Have Been Raped, Survey Says."[13] Many other news outlets ran the same or a very similar headline. However, one would have to read all the way down to the tenth paragraph of the article to find that "rape" included "the use of verbal pressure." One would have to find the survey instrument and read down to page 121 of the 124-page report to find that "rape" included procuring oral sex by "[s]howing displeasure, criticizing your sexuality or attractiveness, getting angry but not using physical force, after you said you didn't want to."[14]

There was no information provided about how many of the positive respondents were referring to verbal pressure such as "showing displeasure," but assuming that many more people would show displeasure at being turned down for sex than would resort to physical violence, it is likely that including verbal pressure in the question significantly affected the responses.

Especially in this time of "#MeToo" and "Times Up" there is an important conversation to be had about when verbal pressure to engage in sex crosses the line, either legally or ethically. But it is irresponsible to write headlines that simply conflate showing displeasure at being turned down for sexual activity with rape this way.

[13] www.dallasnews.com/news/higher-education/2017/03/23/survey-15-percent-female-undergra duatesat-ut-raped.
[14] www.utsystem.edu/sites/default/files/sites/clase/files/2017-10/health-aggregate-R11-V4.pdf.

Sensationalistic headlines that scream of huge numbers of sexual assault at colleges also have a negative impact beyond the issues discussed in this book. Public faith in institutions of higher education is failing badly. As *the New York Times*'s Frank Bruni writes:

A Gallup poll found that only 44 percent of all Americans had a "great deal" or "quite a lot" of confidence in the country's colleges and universities, while 56 percent had only "some" or "very little." College – once a great aspiration – was now a polarizing question mark. That's not so surprising, given Americans' intensifying resentment of anything that smacks of elitism and given Republicans' attacks on science and intellectuals. As Ron Daniels, the president of Johns Hopkins University, recently told me, "Even if we were completely unblemished in the way in which we pursued our mission, it would be hard to imagine that in Trump's America, we wouldn't be targets for scorn."[15]

Uncritically publicizing questionable numbers that paint colleges as dens of sexual iniquity feeds into anti-intellectual narratives and the view of liberal institutions as promoting moral laxity. As we will see, the evidence indicates that today's college students are no more sexually active than their parents were. The progressive left should not be helping anti-intellectual forces undermine confidence in our nation's universities.

The political left has just as much obligation as the political right to stay away from "alternative facts," and there has been too little fidelity to the facts in this debate. As we will see in Chapter 2, it has been commonplace to claim that it has been shown that only 2 percent of rape claims are false. But when one looks at the footnotes supporting this claim, they invariably lead to other articles whose footnotes lead to yet more articles, none of which ever cite an empirical study, or they cite a study that makes no such claim. When skeptical academics chased down the original citation, it appeared that the 2 percent figure originated in a speech given a long time ago by a police official. No record remains to tell how that statistic was derived or whether it was anything more than an offhand, subjective estimate.

Similarly, as we will see in Chapter 8, it is oft-claimed that sexual assault is more prevalent on campus than off campus. But there do not appear to be *any* supporting studies that come to this conclusion by administering the same survey to students and nonstudents. In fact, the only study I have seen that asked the same questions to both populations concluded that students are in *less* danger of being sexually assaulted than equivalently aged nonstudents. As it turns out, nonstudents of college age living in rural areas are the population that, by a significant margin, are most at risk of being sexually assaulted. Yet this population has drawn only a tiny fraction of the attention that has been devoted to college students.

We see the same thing with the oft-made claim that most college sexual assault is committed by repeat "predators," the same term that was used to vilify young African American men in the 1990s. These claims are based on a single study of a single campus that utilized highly questionable methodology such as "convenience sampling" rather than random sampling.

Also, the discussion about sexual assault overwhelmingly assumes female victims and male perpetrators. In fact, the empirical evidence points to far higher numbers of male victims and female perpetrators than the prevailing public discourse would suggest. This issue produced perhaps the most interesting conversations with my friends and colleagues regardless of whether they are progressive or conservative. Although I cited research on this point from perfectly reputable sources, most of the people with whom I spoke simply refused to believe that this could be true. Readers can judge the evidence for themselves after reading Chapter 3. The pull of the female victim/male perpetrator narrative is very strong, and, especially because our language makes writing in gender-neutral terms awkward, I generally use female pronouns in describing victims throughout this book. (This is also partially due to the fact that – despite the fact that this might not accurately reflect the gender balance of offenses – the vast majority of complainants in college are female and virtually all the accused students are male.)

Another reason that I felt compelled to write this book is that this country has a history of dealing poorly with sexual offenses once those offenses achieve a high level of political salience, and politicians become eager to show that they are tough and uncompromising. As I was finishing this book, Senator Kirsten Gillibrand, who spearheaded the successful effort to pressure Al Franken into resigning from the US Senate, was asked about the fact that the accusations against Franken were significantly less serious than the accusations against Roy Moore, an alleged child molester who was running for the Senate at the time with the support of his party. Senator Gillibrand argued that any line drawing was inappropriate:

I think when we start having to talk about the differences between sexual assault and sexual harassment and unwanted groping, you are having the wrong conversation. You need to draw a line in the sand and say none of it is O.K. None of it is acceptable.[16]

But there are heavy costs to refusing to draw lines, even in the area of sexual offenses. Sarah Stillman has written a chilling piece in *the New Yorker* about children who end up on sex-offender registration lists. One of the young people whose story she tells is Charla Roberts:

In Charla Roberts's living room, not far from Paris, Texas, I learned how, at the age of ten, Roberts had pulled down the pants of a male classmate at her public elementary school. She was prosecuted for "indecency with a child," and added to the state's online offender database for the next ten years. The terms of her probation barred her from leaving her mother's house after six in the evening, leaving the county, or living in

---

[16] Bret Stephens, "When #MeToo Goes Too Far," *New York Times* (December 20, 2017), www.nytimes.com/2017/12/20/opinion/metoo-damon-too-far.html.

proximity to "minor children," which ruled out most apartments. When I spoke to the victim, he was shocked to learn of Roberts's fate. He described the playground offense as an act of "public humiliation, instead of a sexual act" – a hurtful prank, but hardly a sex crime. Roberts can still be found on a commercial database online, her photo featured below a banner that reads, *"protect your child from sex offenders."*[17]

In researching this book, I have seen too many examples of school officials refusing to draw lines that should have been drawn. Writing in the *Harvard Law Review Forum*, law professor Janet Halley tells of a student she represented who lost his student housing and campus job just because he *reminded* another student of the man who assaulted her:

> I recently assisted a young man who was subjected by administrators at his small liberal arts university in Oregon to a month-long investigation into all his campus relationships, seeking information about his possible sexual misconduct in them (an immense invasion of his and his friends' privacy), and who was ordered to stay away from a fellow student (cutting him off from his housing, his campus job, and educational opportunity) – all because he *reminded her* of the man who had raped her months before and thousands of miles away. He was found to be completely innocent of any sexual misconduct and was informed of the basis of the complaint against him only by accident and off-hand. But the stay-away order remained in place, and was so broadly drawn up that he was at constant risk of violating it and coming under discipline for *that.*[18]

Another motivation for writing this book is that I am concerned about the frequent invocation of terms such as *epidemic* and *crisis* to describe sexual assault in America. They imply a problem that has suddenly come upon us and that is worsening, justifying emergency responses. It is the language of fear and alarmism. In fact, the overwhelming trend for sexual violence is that it is down sharply. As the *Washington Post* reported in 2006: "The number of rapes per capita in the United States has plunged by more than 85 percent since the 1970s."[19]

As with so many of the statistical issues discussed in this book, reasonable people can differ about how to properly interpret data, and this is an especially tricky issue because sexual violence is likely underreported. But it seems doubtful that these statistics are completely illusory. The then-president of the National Organization of Women said: "Overall, there has clearly been a decline over the last 10 to 20 years. It's very liberating for women, in terms of now being able to be more free and more safe." The president of the Rape, Abuse and Incest National Network (RAINN) said: "The decline has been steady and consistent, which gives us a lot of confidence that it's a real occurrence, not a statistical anomaly."[20]

---

[17] Sarah Stillman, "The List," *New Yorker* (March 14, 2016).

[18] Janet Halley, *Trading the Gavel for Megaphone in Title IX Enforcement*, 128 Harvard Law Review Forum 103 (February 18, 2015).

[19] David A. Fahrenthold, "Statistics Show a Drop in U.S. Rape Cases," *Washington Post* (2006), www.washingtonpost.com/wp-dyn/content/article/2006/06/18/AR2006061800610.html.

[20] Id.

Similarly, there is good evidence that incidents of workplace sexual harassment are also more likely significantly down than up. In 2017, *the New York Times* reported:

Workplace sexual harassment may be decreasing. In surveys of federal government employees the percentage of women who said they had experienced one of eight harassing behaviors in the last two years was 18 percent, less than half of the percentage it was in 1994.[21]

The point here is not, of course, that 18 percent, or any nonzero number, is acceptable. Half of a big number can still be a pretty big number. The point is that we should avoid the rhetoric of crisis, which has so often been used to promote panic rather than reason and to erode constitutional protections. Interestingly, in the same piece *the Times* reported that "women were only somewhat less likely than men to admit to harassing behavior, even though men, in polls and in formal complaints, are far less likely to say they've been sexually harassed."

WHAT'S WRONG WITH AFFIRMATIVE CONSENT?

Several states and a great many individual colleges have adopted legislation or policies implementing affirmative consent. (I refer to these states and schools as implementing "affirmative consent regimes.") In these regimes any sexual touching without clear, overt, contemporaneous consent for each specific act of sexual touching is sexual assault. What's wrong with that? This issue is covered in Chapters 6 through 8. While affirmative consent is well intentioned, it is a far more sweeping regime of sexual regulation than its proponents acknowledge. First, we will see that it does not reflect the way that most college students behave (and there is also the question of why adults in power are applying it only to college students and not to themselves as well). This means that vast numbers of college students are now defined as sex offenders. Defenders of affirmative consent often argue that it will change norms and that affirmative consent won't punish innocent students because it only matters when someone files a complaint. We will see that these responses are not as reassuring as they might initially seem to some.

We will also see that affirmative consent is a major deviation from how the law usually looks at consent. The general rule is that the law asks whether a reasonable person would have believed that they had been given consent. The reasonable person test is ubiquitous in the law. You can kill a person if a reasonable person in your position would have believed that they were acting in self-defense. No one who meets the "reasonable person" standard in their belief that they had been given consent should be considered a sex offender. And, as we will see, there is no empirical evidence to indicate that affirmative consent

---

[21] Jugal K. Patel et al., "The Upshot: We Asked 615 Men How They Conduct Themselves at Work," *New York Times* (December 28, 2017), www.nytimes.com/interactive/2017/12/28/upshot/sexual-harassment-survey-600-men.html.

does more to protect students from sexual assault than the reasonable person test. To the contrary, the one study I found that looked at the impact of various jury instructions on willingness to convict found that the reasonable person test with a "no means no" instruction was more likely to lead a jury to declare a situation to be a rape than an affirmative consent instruction. Further, affirmative consent does nothing to address the situations, which were extremely common in the cases I looked at, where the accusing student says that her consent was negated by alcohol, undue verbal pressure, or fear of what the accused student might do if she said no.

Most importantly, affirmative consent violates the constitutional right to sexual autonomy of college students. Students, like all persons, are at liberty to develop their own means of expressing sexual consent, and they should not have to follow a government-approved method of doing so. This is discussed at length in Chapter 7.

HOW REPRESENTATIVE ARE THE CASES DISCUSSED IN THIS BOOK?

This book largely discusses cases in which students who were accused of sexual assault were not given a fair opportunity to defend themselves. In some of the cases, the accused students seemed clearly to be innocent and in other cases there are not enough facts to tell. As always, reasonable people might disagree about the fairness of this or that case, but readers are also entitled to ask whether these cases are representative of the larger picture.

That question is hard to answer. The cases discussed in this book are not meant to be representative. They are meant to be illustrative of what can go wrong when due process is not protected. In some cases, the lack of process is the result of published procedures of large universities, so we know that many people are affected by them. But there is no way to tell how representative any given case is because the specifics of sexual assault cases are confidential pursuant to the federal law the Family Educational Rights and Privacy Act (FERPA). Because of FERPA:

> We don't know how many [sexual assault] hearings are held every year; how many of those hearings find the accused responsible; how many appeals there are; how frequently the hearings are before a panel, as opposed to a single investigator (an individual who questions witnesses and writes a report without a hearing); for panels how many require unanimous findings; how the definitions of offense vary from place; or how many cases are overturned on appeal.[22]

The cases discussed in this book are the litigated cases, which are the cases about which there is publically available information. Presumably many of the unlitigated cases were not litigated because they achieved a fair and just result. But there is getting to be *a great deal* of litigation, and in many of those

---

[22] Adam Goldstein, "What They're Not Talking About with Title IX That Really Matters," *Washington Post* (December 20, 2017), www.washingtonpost.com/news/grade-point/wp/2017/12/20/what-theyre-not-talking-about-with-title-ix-that-really-matters/?utm_term=.2d39087e37d9.

cases the courts have been finding that colleges are denying basic due process to students accused of sexual assault. According the 2017 Report of NCHERM, a major college safety consulting group:

The field is losing case after case in federal court on what should be very basic due process protections. Never before have colleges been losing more cases than they are winning, but that is the trend as we write this. The courts are not expanding due process yet, but are insisting that colleges provide the full measure of college-based due process that has been required over almost 60 years of litigation by students.[23]

NCHERM warns its clients that the situation will only get worse because the courts have always been deferential (I will argue in Chapter 2 that they have been far too deferential) to college disciplinary decisions but "that historical deference is eroding as judges lose patience with skewed proceedings."[24] Given the high barriers to litigation, it is likely that many due process cases that could have been brought on their merits were not brought because the students lacked the resources.

In sum, the cases discussed in this book are hopefully not typical, but they are hardly likely to be complete outliers either. According to the 2016 report of the National Association of College and University Attorneys, the pace of litigation since 2014 has been "unprecedented" and with a heavy trend toward suits by the accused students rather than the accusing students.[25] As noted previously, accused students have been winning these suits to an increasing degree. Clearly something is happening at universities that extends beyond a few anomalous cases.

WHAT WILL THE IMPACT OF THE TRUMP ADMINISTRATION BE?

After Donald Trump was elected president, many feared that the OCR would abandon victims of campus sexual assault. Fears were further inflamed when the new head of the OCR, Candace Jackson, was quoted as saying that most accusations of sexual assault were unfounded:

Investigative processes have not been "fairly balanced between the accusing victim and the accused student," Ms. Jackson argued, and students have been branded rapists "when the facts just don't back that up." In most investigations, she said, there's "not even an accusation that these accused students overrode the will of a young woman. Rather, the accusations – 90 percent of them – fall into the category of 'we were both drunk,' 'we broke

[23] Nedda Black et al., "The 2017 NCHERM Group Whitepaper: Due Process and the Sex Police," www.ncherm.org/wordpress/wp-content/uploads/2017/04/TNG-Whitepaper-Final-Electronic-Version.pdf.
[24] Id.
[25] Craig Wood et al., "Between a Rock and a Hard Place: A Discussion of Issues That Frequently Arise in Sexual Misconduct-Related Litigation Colleges and Universities," National Association of College and University Attorney, vol. 14, no. 4 (May 18, 2016), http://counsel.cua.edu/res/docs/titleixlitigation.pdf.

up, and six months later I found myself under a Title IX investigation because she just decided that our last sleeping together was not quite right,'" Ms. Jackson said.[26]

Trump's Secretary of Education, Betsy DeVos, rescinded the 2011 Dear Colleague Letter and replaced it with a new 2017 "Q&A on Campus Sexual Misconduct." However, despite the fears of her critics, these changes are unlikely, in and of themselves, to have much of an impact on how colleges adjudicate sexual assault cases. The most explicit change in policy is that colleges are no longer forbidden from using the standard of requiring clear and convincing evidence of sexual assault to adjudicate accusations. The 2011 guidance letter required the lower standard of "preponderance of the evidence." Simply put, the preponderance of the evidence standard makes it easier for the college to rule against the accused student than the clear and convincing evidence standard. But, as we will see, the great majority of colleges already used the preponderance standard, and even among those that did not, there is little reason to believe that those colleges will jump at the chance to reinstitute the clear and convincing standard.

Under Trump, the OCR also rescinded its policy under which a single complaint would automatically trigger an investigation of at least three prior years' worth of complaints to determine if there was a systemic problem. This change of policy is more likely to help victims of sexual assault as to hurt them. Although the policy was well intentioned, the Republican-led Congress was unwilling to accede to the Obama administration's requests for the resources to implement such an ambitious program, so the policy produced a huge backlog of cases and delays in investigations.

Furthermore, the 2011 letter did not call for the type of due process violations that are criticized in this book. In fact, the letter stated: "[T]he parties must have an equal opportunity to present relevant witnesses and other evidence. The complainant and the alleged perpetrator must be afforded similar and timely access to any information that will be used at the hearing." The due process violations have been occurring as a result of how the letter was implemented, not based upon any explicit directions to do so. For example, the 2011 letter only discouraged universities from allowing accused students from directly cross-examining their accusers. This seems like an obviously sensible policy, but in no way did it mandate processes, like those criticized in this book, where the accused students cannot pose questions even to adult witnesses such as the professional investigators who found them responsible for sexual assault. Meanwhile, university administrators are under heavy pressure to maintain Obama-era policies.[27]

---

[26] Erica Greene and Sheryl Gay Stolberg, "Campus Rape Policies Get a New Look as the Accused Get DeVos's Ear," *New York Times* (July 12, 2017), www.nytimes.com/2017/07/12/us/politics/campus-rape-betsy-devos-title-iv-education-trump-candice-jackson.html?mtrref=www.google.com&gwh=07C37001911FCCAAB7A370CCC52280oF&gwt=pay.

[27] Anemona Hartocollis, "Universities Face Pressure to Hold the Line on Title IX," *New York Times* (February 18, 2007), www.nytimes.com/2017/02/18/us/college-campuses-title-ix-sexual-assault.html?mtrref=www.google.com&gwh=1C12C65DBBE5012D4B7F4E4F55816E73&gwt=pay.

As the director of the Center for Higher Education Law and Policy writes in the *Chronicle of Higher Education*, most of the pre-Trump OCR guidance has remained in place and, so far, very little has changed under the Trump administration:

[F]or all the fanfare, at this point very little has changed. A great deal of the rescinded 2011 and 2014 guidance, was based on earlier, nonrescinded guidance (especially, but not exclusively, from 2001). And Obama-era guidance from 2015 has not been rescinded; some of it relies on previous guidance, including aspects of the rescinded guidance. Crucially, most major aspects of previous Title IX guidance – like the role of the Title IX coordinator – remain intact.[28]

Perhaps the most significant change coming out of the Trump administration is the OCR no longer discourages mediation for sexual assault claims if both parties desire it. This opens the door to more colleges and universities offering restorative justice options on a purely voluntary basis. In Chapter 9, this book argues that in certain cases restorative justice is a far better approach than traditional adversary, punitive models for adjudicating sexual assault allegations.

Finally, just as this book was going to press, the New York Times reported that the Department of Education had drafted new proposed permanent rules governing Title IX investigations. Some of these proposals are reasonable but others are egregiously harmful to victims of sexual assault. Notably, the proposed rules reportedly state that sexual assaults between students at off-campus events, including fraternities, are outside the scope of Title IX. This could place the majority of peer to peer sexual assaults outside the purview of Title IX. There will be a lengthy public comment period before these rules go into effect and they could be significantly changed. Progressives are doing themselves no favors by denying the problems with how colleges handle sexual assault. If progressives are not proactive in dealing with these problems, the reform process will be left to those who might not have the best interests of survivors of sexual violence at heart.

CONCLUSION

Americans are having a fierce and important debate about how to most effectively deal with sexual assault. This is a good thing, but we can do better. This book argues that we must avoid false dichotomies between protecting victims and providing due process. We must be careful with the facts and should not rush to judgment. We should heed the lessons of history and not repeat our mistakes. We must respect everyone's right to feel safe and everyone's right to be treated fairly. We must adhere to the Constitution's limitations on government power. This book offers suggestions for the path forward.

---

[28] Peter F. Lake, "'Interim' Guidance on Title IX Creates Confusion, Not Clarity," *Chronicle of Higher Education* (September 24, 2017), www.chronicle.com/article/Interim-Guidance-on/241282.

PART I

THE NEED FOR DUE PROCESS

I

The Due Process Deficit and the Importance of College Adjudication

THE DUE PROCESS DEFICIT

> *The history of liberty has largely been the history of observance of procedural safeguards.*
>
> Justice Felix Frankfurter[1]

Our society is in the midst of an intense debate regarding how to best handle allegations of sexual assault. This book addresses one of the most pressing aspects of this debate – how colleges can keep their campuses safe while providing fair procedures for accused students. It argues that, in too many instances, colleges are failing to meet what should be considered the minimal constitutional requirements for due process:

- Accused students can have as little as one day's notice to prepare for the hearing and cannot be represented by an attorney during the hearing;
- They have no right to see the evidence against them, produce their own evidence, or call witnesses on their own behalf;
- They have no right to directly question the witnesses against them;
- In some cases, anonymous accusations are allowed;
- The university has no obligation to reveal exculpatory evidence;
- The student can end up being found guilty of charges other than the ones at issue during the hearing, with no opportunity to defend themselves against those charges;
- The person investigating the alleged crime is also the person who effectively decides guilt or innocence; and
- The university is pressured or even required by the government to define terms such as *assault* far more broadly than those terms are understood either popularly or legally outside of the university context.

---

[1] McNabb v. United States, 318 U.S. 332, 347 (1943).

Of course, not all colleges fail in all of these ways. However, as numerous examples throughout this book will show, these problems exist at many colleges. The Obama administration pushed universities hard on this issue. It required that colleges use a relatively low standard of proof in adjudicating allegations of sexual assault, which Chapter 4 will argue is problematic but not necessarily a violation of due process.[2] It also warned universities against any sort of mediation. Chapter 9 will argue that this was a mistake. Many cases would be better served by a restorative justice approach, if both parties agree to it, than by the traditional punitive approach.[3]

Nonetheless, none of the violations described in the preceding text were specifically mandated by the federal government. As with most complex issues, a number of factors have been at play. Some campuses overreacted to the Obama administration's exhortations. The tendency to overreact was likely worsened by the threat of being publicly listed by the OCR as a university under investigation for violating Title IX.[4] As will be discussed, the federal government has also threatened to end federal funding for noncompliant schools. While the Trump administration has struck a different tone on this issue, it has not changed either policy.

Also, as will be discussed in Chapter 4, many universities fear student backlash or bad publicity if they are seen as failing to respond strongly to allegations of sexual assault. Colleges are also responding to advice that they receive from advisory groups. The Association of Title IX Administrators has warned universities that they can be found inequitable and noncompliant if they have "built [their] investigation and resolution mechanisms into castles of due process."[5] Importantly, colleges are not court rooms, and the persons tasked with adjudicating college sexual assault are generally not lawyers and have not had the importance of due process issues at the core of their education or training. They wish to be victim centered. As the President of Davidson College, Carol Quillen, has written: "Nothing about due process says to a rape survivor, 'I believe you.'"[6]

To be fair, Quillen also expressed her commitment to due process, and none of the cases in this book involve her college. However, it would be difficult to overstate the lack of due process in many campus tribunals tasked with

[2] The Trump administration reversed this requirement but, as noted in the introduction, few colleges have adopted a higher standard of proof as a result.
[3] The Trump administration also reversed this policy. As we will see in Chapter 9, this opens the door to greater use of restorative justice approaches to appropriate cases.
[4] As of June 2016, there were 246 ongoing investigations by the US Department of Education into how 195 colleges and universities handle sexual assault reports under the gender equity law. www.huffingtonpost.com/entry/title-ix-investigations-sexual-haras sment_us_575f4boee4bo53d433061b3d.
[5] Jacob Gersen and Jeannie Suk, *The Sex Bureaucracy*, 104 Cal. L. Rev. 881–948, 934–935 (2016).
[6] Carol Quillen, "Solutions to Campus Sexual Assault Start with Culture Change," *Charlotte Observer* (February 12, 2017).

adjudicating allegations of sexual assault. Twenty-eight Harvard Law School professors, including professors with strong records of feminist scholarship, signed an open letter stating that "Harvard has adopted procedures for deciding cases of alleged sexual misconduct which *lack the most basic elements of fairness and due process [and] are overwhelmingly stacked against the accused.*" [7]

Sixteen faculty members of the University of Pennsylvania Law School reached similar conclusions about that university's lack of fundamental fairness and about the federal government's improper pressure:

> Although we appreciate the efforts by Penn and other universities to implement fair procedures, particularly in light of the financial sanctions threatened by OCR *we believe that OCR's approach exerts improper pressure upon universities to adopt procedures that do not afford fundamental fairness.* We do not believe that providing justice for victims of sexual assault requires subordinating so many protections long deemed necessary to protect from injustice those accused of serious offenses. We also believe that, given the complexities of the problem, OCR's process has sacrificed the basic safeguards of the lawmaking process and that those safeguards are critically necessary to formulate sound regulatory policy. [8]

This chapter argues that the courts have been far too timid about protecting the rights of students accused of sexual misconduct. In the name of judicial restraint, they have upheld procedures that they have conceded are biased and lacking in procedural safeguards. A good illustration of this is the case of *John Doe v. University of California San Diego* (UCSD) in which a California appellate court unanimously upheld a process that all three judges described as a "kangaroo court" during oral argument.

In addition to the procedural issues, the UCSD case is informative because of the facts. Very few of the cases of alleged college sexual assault that have been litigated involve violent attacks by strangers. They are often cases in which the accuser and accused have been in a sexual relationship or were in the midst of sexual acts, and the charges turn on whether the accuser's consent was sufficiently "ongoing" or "overt" when the accused attempted to perform a certain sexual act or turn on whether the complaining student was unable to give effective consent as a result of alcohol consumption. In this case, both of the parties were in bed together after having engaged in sexual activity the previous night. The female student ("Jane") accused the male student ("Doe") of either attempting or actually touching her in a sexual manner that morning without her "effective consent." [9]

---

[7] www.bostonglobe.com/opinion/2014/10/14/rethink-harvard-sexual-harassment-policy/HFDDiZN7 nU2UwuUuWMnqbM/story.html (emphasis added).
[8] www.washingtonpost.com/news/volokh-conspiracy/wp/2015/02/19/open-letter-from-16-penn-law-school-professors-about-title-ix-and-sexual-assault-complaints/?utm_term=.50ce98e79130.
[9] Doe v. Regents of the University of California (4th Circuit Ct. of Appeals, November 22, 2016).

In the UCSD case, the facts were especially difficult to determine because it involved many of the complicating factors discussed previously. Both students had been in a relationship and Jane stated that she would "gladly spend the night" with Doe but did not want to have sex.[10] They did end up spending the night together and having sex, and Jane argued that she was too drunk that night to consent. Jane also accused Doe of sexually assaulting her that morning when they woke up together. She also accused Doe of retaliating against her for complaining about him to the university.

The university's investigator interviewed 14 witnesses and found "insufficient evidence" for both the claim of the evening assault and of retaliation. The panel therefore only reviewed the morning assault charges.[11] Doe was found responsible for those charges and was suspended by UCSD, with the suspension increasing in length each time he appealed the ruling.[12] By the end of the process his length of suspension had been increased to a year and a quarter, with additional punishments such as nonacademic probation for the duration of his time as a student as UCSD.[13] He challenged the university's decision in state superior court.

The superior court found numerous severe violations of Doe's due process rights and ruled that "the hearing against petitioner was unfair."[14] At the university hearing, the sole witness against Doe was Jane who was shielded from Doe by a screen. (It was not clear whether she was also shielded from the panel.) Doe was accompanied by counsel, but that counsel was not allowed to participate in the hearing. All Doe's questions to Jane were screened by the panel chair, who disallowed the great majority of his questions, but the questions written by the university representative making the case against Doe were not screened. All questions were posed by the panel chair, who did not allow follow-up when answers were evasive or unresponsive.[15] When Jane testified that she "physically wanted to have sex but mentally wouldn't," Doe was not allowed to ask follow-up questions to clarify that ambiguous statement.[16] When Jane was asked about the fact that she engaged in what she admitted was voluntary sexual activity with Doe later that same day as the morning in question, she was allowed to reply that she did not see why that was relevant, with no follow-up questions.

In addition, no witnesses other than Doe and Jane appeared before the panel. The panel relied heavily upon the findings of the investigator who found it more likely than not that Doe violated the Student Sexual Offense Policy during the morning in question. However, the investigator did not appear at the hearing,

[10] Id. at 9.   [11] Id. at 60.
[12] Technically, Doe's first objection to the panel's ruling, which he made to the dean, was not an appeal because the panel only recommends the sanction and the dean imposes it. In this case, the dean imposed a greater sanction than the panel recommended. When Doe appealed that decision to the Council of Provosts, his term of suspension was increased again. Id. at pp. 77–80.
[13] Id. at 77.   [14] Doe v. Regents of UCSD (Sup. Ct. San Diego 7/10/15) at p. 2.   [15] Id. at 3–4.
[16] Id. at 5.

which means that Doe had no opportunity to question her about her methods or evidence. Further, Doe was not allowed access to the basis of her conclusions, such as her interview notes with the 14 witnesses she interviewed.[17] Nor was he allowed access to the notes of the investigator's interviews with Jane – a fact that particularly troubled the appellate court.

The superior court concluded: "The hearing deprived the petitioner of the opportunity to examine anything about the summary conclusions relied upon by the hearing panel. At no time is the petitioner given the opportunity to confront the [investigator's] report or [the investigator] because she was not present at the hearing."[18]

The university appealed the ruling and, based upon the oral argument, it appeared that the superior court's ruling would be upheld. During that argument, all three judges appeared appalled at the lack of due process at UCSD. Presiding Judge Richard Huffman told the university's attorney:

One of us [Judge Gilbert Nares, interjecting]: two of us; [Judge Joan Irion interjecting]: three of us; [Judge Huffman continuing]: have really grave concerns about this system ... when I finished reading all the briefs my comment was *"where's the kangaroo?"*[19]

Regarding the university's refusal to allow Doe access to the investigator's notes of her interviews with the witnesses, Huffman scolded the university's attorney for UCSD's apparent indifference to the fairness of the hearing:

I am at a total loss why anybody interested in a fair and accurate outcome would do something like that ... Why not [give access]? "Because you are not entitled to them!" Well, why not? "Because I don't have to give them to you!"[20]

When the university attorney tried to argue that there was no evidence that the interview notes contained exonerating evidence, Judge Orion cut him off: "There is no evidence on the record because we don't have the statements ... we don't know how they impact – we don't know what they said and neither did the accused."[21] Indeed, as will be discussed in Chapter 4, even if there was exonerating evidence in the interview notes, universities have absolutely no obligation to turn such evidence over to the accused.

Despite the court's "grave concerns" about the process and the university's seeming lack of concern over its fairness, the appellate court unanimously overturned the superior court judgment and sided with the university. The decision was based upon the extremely low level of protection for a student's due process rights, even when facing suspension or expulsion by a public university for a sexual assault. The appellate court wrote that while the

[17] Id. at 3.   [18] Id. at 3.
[19] K. C. Johnson, https://academicwonderland.com/2016/11/05/at-ucsd-where-is-the-kangaroo/ (provides link to recording of oral argument) (emphasis added).
[20] K. C. Johnson, At UCSD, "Where Is the Kangaroo." *Academic Wonderland* 0:37, https://academicwonderland.com/2016/11/05/at-ucsd-where-is-the-kangaroo/.
[21] Id. at 0:31.

investigator's failure to give anybody access to the notes of her interview with Jane "gives us pause," the law was clear that Doe had no right to any potential exonerating evidence even if he directly asked for it. "There is no formal right to discovery in student conduct review hearings ... courts have held that a fair hearing only requires that the respondent be aware of what he or she is accused of doing and the basis of that accusation."[22]

Regarding the interview notes, the appellate court acknowledged that "an investigator's notes of her interviews with the complainant could be critical in the respondent's ability to propose questions for complainant. That said, we are hesitant to prescribe such a bright line rule on the record before us, especially when [Doe] has not shown that he was prejudiced by the absence of the interview notes."[23]

But as the court pointed out during oral argument, it is virtually impossible to prove anything about the notes if one has never seen them. Prior to Jane's filing of the complaint against Doe with USCD, she had been arrested for public intoxication. Doe wanted to argue that when Jane's parents, who were devout Mormons, found out about the arrest and about her sexual relationship with Doe, she felt pressured into placing the blame on him. He wanted to know why the investigator found that two of Jane's three allegations against him were without merit and whether the arrest or parental pressure played a role in that determination. Without access to either the notes or the investigator, and only very limited ability to indirectly ask questions to Jane, he had no real way to determine whether the notes shed any light on this.

The appellate court stated: "Here, we are concerned that the procedure employed by UCSD has great potential to be unfair to a student accused of violating the Sex Offense Policy ... that said, on the record before us, we cannot say that the procedure used by UCSD violates due process."[24]

This judicial tolerance of what the judges described as a "kangaroo" court with "great potential to be unfair," and for which it was "at a total loss why anybody interested in a fair and accurate outcome would do something like that" is deeply troubling.

It is important to note that lack of due process in college sexual assault hearings can negatively impact women as well as men. Stories about false findings of guilt and kangaroo-type college tribunals are mainstays of the conservative press and antifeminist bloggers and websites, and they lend credence to whose first instinct is to doubt the credibility and motives of women who have been sexually assaulted.

Further, lack of due process can utterly undermine the case of even women who have been brutally assaulted in front of multiple witnesses. In 2014 the *New York Times* reported on a case in which Anna, a first-year student at

[22] Doe v. Regents of the University of California (4th Circuit Ct. of Appeals, November 22, 2016) at p. 60.
[23] Id. at 61.   [24] Id. at 73.

Hobart and William Smith Colleges, was apparently gang raped by members of the college football team. The young woman went missing around midnight and texted her friend that she was "scared" and didn't know what to do. The friend searched for her and found her a few hours later bent over a pool table being sexually assaulted from the rear with six or seven people watching and laughing. The sexual assault nurse assessed that Anna had experienced "blunt force trauma" from "either multiple partners, multiple times or that the intercourse was very forceful."[25]

As is often the case in college sexual assault cases, alcohol was involved. Anna had twice the legal limit for blood alcohol and her memory of the event was vague.[26] She filed a complaint against two of the students with the college and a hearing was held. As with the UCSD case, there were severe detriments in terms of due process. Neither side could bring an attorney to the hearing, just nonspeaking advisors. Without an advocate to protect her interests, she was run roughshod over:

- Panelists interrupted her answers and asked her about a campus police report she had never seen before;
- The hearing proceeded before her rape-kit results were known; and
- The medical records indicating blunt force trauma were not reviewed by two of the three panelists.[27]

The panelists also did not seem to always correctly recall the testimony of witnesses. One witness had testified that one of the football players had wanted to go upstairs and have sex, but a panelist said the witness had testified that it was Anna who wanted to go upstairs for that reason. When both accused football players changed their stories in significant ways, they were not asked to explain the discrepancies.[28]

Both students were cleared just 12 days after Anna filed her complaint. She would have been immeasurably helped by being afforded basic due process rights such as representation by an attorney, the right to present evidence and to examine evidence in a timely fashion, and the right to have her attorney cross-examine witnesses. Yet, as we have seen, none of these essential rights are considered by the courts to be guaranteed by the due process clause of the US Constitution even in public universities, let alone private ones.[29]

---

[25] Walt Bogdanich, "Reporting a Rape and Wishing She Hadn't," *New York Times* (July 12, 2014).

[26] Emily Bazalon, "New York Times Reports Another Campus Sexual Assault Horror Story: Now We Need the Data," Slate.com/XX Factor (July 14, 2014), www.slate.com/blogs/xx_factor/2014/07/14/new_york_times_story_on_hobart_and_william_smith_rape_case_proves_one_thing.html.

[27] Bogdanich, "Reporting a Rape and Wishing She Hadn't."

[28] Bazalon, "New York Times Reports Another Campus Sexual Assault Horror Story."

[29] In Chapter 3 I argue that due process rights should apply equally to private universities as well as public ones for several reasons.

WHY SEXUAL ASSAULT INVESTIGATION AND ADJUDICATION CANNOT BE LEFT ENTIRELY TO POLICE AND PROSECUTORS

Given these sorts of gross violations of due process, some have understandably argued that these matters should be left to the police and that colleges should focus solely on education, prevention, and support services for survivors of sexual assault. The open letter from the University of Pennsylvania law faculty members suggests:

[W]e support effective enforcement of Title IX at universities, as all agree that sexual assaults seriously interfere with students' rights to equal educational opportunities. It is not altogether clear, however, why the federal government requires such serious cases to be handled by campus tribunals staffed by academics, instead of by professional judges and lawyers. Perhaps it is time to funnel the more serious cases through the criminal justice process and to make that process much more accessible to and supportive of sexual assault complainants.[30]

Janet Napolitano, who served as Barack Obama's Secretary of Homeland Security before going on to serve as the president of the University of California, also wonders whether universities are institutionally capable of handling these sorts of issues and whether efforts would be better spent at improving police response:

Are these roles that are well suited for our nation's institutions of higher education? Survivors are choosing not to report to law enforcement because of their lack of faith and confidence in the criminal justice system. If that is the case, it can be argued that rather than pushing institutions to become surrogates for the criminal justice system, more work should be done to improve that system's handling and prosecution of sexual assault cases.[31]

Napolitano also points out that law enforcement has important resources for the investigation and punishment of sexual assault that colleges lack:

Law enforcement has the tools to effectively investigate these crimes. The criminal justice process has the authority to impose serious punishments on offenders, including incarceration. The most serious sanction that a college can impose is dismissal, which is wholly inadequate where a crime has been committed. Having law enforcement conduct investigations ensures, if properly done, that effective investigations will be conducted and that there will be appropriate punishments that have a strong deterrent effect, all to the ultimate benefit of the survivors and the safety of the university community as a whole.[32]

Yale Law Professor Jed Rubenfeld points out that until 2005 the OCR had interpreted Title IX as *not* requiring an independent university investigation of

---

[30] Open letter at p. 2.
[31] Janet Napolitano, *"Only Yes Means Yes": An Essay on University Policies Regarding Sexual Violence and Sexual Assault*, 33 Yale L. & Pol'y Rev. 387, 400–401 (2015).
[32] Id. at 401.

"a possible violation of the penal law, the determination of which is the exclusive province of the police and the office of the District Attorney."[33] He also points out that if a serious crime such a murder took place on campus "it would be extremely rare for a school to conduct its own murder trial and unheard of to fail to bring in the police."[34]

Several states are considering bills that require students to report sexual assault to law enforcement authorities before colleges launch their own investigation.[35] Critics of these proposed laws point out that they would conflict with the Violence Against Women Reauthorization Act of 2013, which requires colleges to tell sexual assault complainants that they have a right to not file a complaint with law enforcement. However, Congress may create a federal mandatory reporting requirement that would override the Violence Against Women Act on this point. In fact, the proposed Campus Safe Act would prohibit colleges from taking even interim measures to protect sexual assault complainants until they had reported the crime to the police.[36]

While there is a certain commonsense appeal to leaving campus sexual assault to the police and district attorneys, there are even stronger reasons that point in the opposite direction. Indeed, such a policy would leave millions of students significantly less protected and, in some cases, largely unprotected from sexual assault.

An oft-made argument for proactive college involvement is their ability to provide immediate protection to victims of sexual assault. After all, the primary purpose of Title IX is to provide equal access to education, and it is easy to see how a rape victim could be denied such access if the rapist is in the same class or dormitory as the victim. Colleges can quickly move to separate the two parties helping the victim continue her or his education by reducing the threat to the victim's safety and preventing further psychological trauma caused by repeated proximity to the assailant. "Unlike the criminal justice system, universities have the power to separate the victim from her attacker once a report is received, thus minimizing the risk that the victim will be deprived of access to education and the ability to succeed at her school."[37]

---

[33] Jeb Rubenfeld, "Privatization, State Action, and Title IX: Do Campus Sexual Assault Hearings Violate Due Process?," Yale Law School, Public Law Research Paper No. 588 (2016), 5.

[34] Id.

[35] Allie Bidwell, "'Mandatory Reporting' Bills Hinder Fight against Sexual Assault Critics Say," *U.S. News & World Report* (February 19, 2015), www.usnews.com/news/articles/2015/02/19/mandatory-reporting-bills-hinder-fight-against-sexual-assault-critics-say.

[36] H.R. 3403 – Safe Campus Act of 2015 would require students to report sexual assault to the police before Institutions of Higher Education (IHEs) could undertake an investigation or any protective measures: "The requirement to report and refer a sexual violence allegation does not apply if an alleged victim provides written notification to an IHE declining law enforcement involvement. In such case, an IHE may not initiate a disciplinary proceeding, including to impose interim sanctions." www.congress.gov/bill/114th-congress/house-bill/3403.

[37] Sarah Edwards, *The Case in Favor of Tougher Title IX Policies: Pushing Back Against the Pushback*, 43 Duke Journal of Gender Law and Policy 121–144, 137 (2015).

Indeed, because "sexual assault is a traumatizing event that bears lifelong consequences ... [that] may be exacerbated if the assailant remains on campus ... an accuser's primary goal when initiating proceedings may be to remove the accused from campus."[38] Thus, forcing the student to go directly to the police may be contrary to the wishes and needs of sexual assault victims.

Powerful political actors have made this argument as well. Senator Kirsten Gillibrand, a leading advocate for victims of sexual assault, has argued: "So the reason why there is a dual system is so that you can have a way to handle this case if the survivor doesn't feel comfortable going through a criminal trial – that could take a year or two or three."[39]

Professor K. C. Johnson and journalist Stuart Taylor dispute this reasoning. They point out that universities can and do suspend students who have been charged with felonies. If a student files a complaint with the police that results in the charging or arrest of her assailant for a serious crime, universities routinely suspend that student and bar him from campus.[40]

Johnson and Taylor make a good point, but it is not a completely satisfactory response. For one thing, it assumes that the police and district attorneys will act in an effective and timely fashion. This is not always the case. One high-profile example is the response to the rape of a University of Montana student by a University of Montana football player. The case was made famous by writer Jon Krakauer in his book *Missoula: Rape and Justice System in a College Town*.[41] In her *Washington Post* review of the book, Caitlin Flanagan chides Krakauer for being unfair to the university and other parties, but concedes that his description of the ineffectiveness of the prosecutor's office and police hits home:

More compelling are Krakauer's descriptions of problems within the Missoula County Attorney's Office, an operation apparently overly concerned with maintaining a high percentage of convictions, thus leaving more-difficult cases untried. He describes insensitive police interviews with victims, as well as an egregious incident in which the office waited a full five weeks before interviewing four football players accused of gang rape, by which point all four "had had ample opportunity to rehearse their stories." Charges were never filed.[42]

---

[38] Emily D. Safko, *Are Campus Sexual Assault Tribunals Fair? The Need for Judicial Review and Additional Due Process Protections in Light of the New Case Law*, 84 Fordham Law Review 2289–2333, 2302–2303 (2016).

[39] Cited in Ashe Schowe, "Kirsten Gillibrand's Assault on Reality," *Washington Examiner* (2015), www.washingtonexaminer.com/kirsten-gillibrands-assault-on-reality/article/2566958.

[40] K. C. Johnson and *Stuart* Taylor, *The Campus Rape Frenzy: The Attack on Due Process at America's Universities* (New York: Encounter Books, 2017), 156–157.

[41] Jon Krakauer, Missoula: Rape and Justice System in a College Town (New York: Doubleday, 2015).

[42] Caitlin Flanagan, "An Investigation of Campus Rape Finds No Easy Solutions," *Washington Post* (April 20, 2015), www.washingtonpost.com/opinions/an-investigation-of-campus-rape -reveals-no-easy-solutions/2015/04/20/95d2625a-c82c-11e4-a199-6cb5e63819d2_story.html? utm_term=.f4a39dbea15a.

Moreover, these problems go well beyond a few high-profile cases. Unfortunately, there is ample evidence of widespread (although by no means uniform) unwillingness by police to aggressively pursue nonviolent, nonstranger rapes that are exactly the kind of sexual assaults most common on campus. City University of New York Law School Dean Michelle Anderson has described the breadth and depth of the problem in the *Yale Law Journal*:

> Despite substantial progressive reform of rape law, the criminal justice system continues to fail to address the most common form of rape: non-stranger rape without traditional physical force. Even today, there is little chance of obtaining a conviction in an acquaintance rape case without extrinsic physical injury. Disbelief and disregard are common . . . For example, over the past couple of decades in cities across the country, police have refused to take complaints, recoded rape complaints as non-crimes, and labeled legitimate complaints as unfounded. From Philadelphia – where police demoted one-third of reported sex crimes to non-crimes that they did not investigate – to Cleveland, Baltimore, New York, St. Louis, and Milwaukee, law enforcement officers disbelieved victims, blamed them for their assaults, and refused to act on complaints. The U.S. Department of Justice's Civil Rights Division has found discriminatory law enforcement responses to sexual violence in places as diverse as New Orleans, Louisiana; Missoula, Montana; and Maricopa County, Arizona.[43]

It would be difficult to exaggerate the scope of this problem. Rape victims across the country have often been unable to get the police to even examine their rape kits and many thousands of such kits lay unexamined:

> Information from cities large and small paints an appalling picture. According to Human Rights Watch, Los Angeles County had the largest backlog in 2009, with at least 12,500 untested kits. In 2015, Houston had 6,600 untested kits; Cleveland had about 4,000 untested kits; and there were substantial backlogs in cities as diverse as Muncie, Indiana; Reno, Nevada; and Green Bay, Wisconsin. In 2014, an inspector general found that a group of New Orleans detectives buried more than a thousand rape cases in three years, ignored or misrepresented DNA findings, and covered up their actions by backdating reports. After more than ten thousand untested kits were discovered in Detroit, a Justice Department study identified victim-blaming attitudes as the reason the kits were not tested, noting, "Rape survivors were often assumed to be prostitutes and therefore what happened to them was considered their fault."[44]

In fairness to the police, they are sometimes blamed for problems that may be beyond their control. For example, after an investigation, the *Atlanta Constitution Journal* ran a story with the headline "At Georgia colleges, allegations of rape but no prosecutions," that read: "Campus police at nine of Georgia's largest universities logged 152 allegations of rapes and sodomies since 2010, according to law enforcement documents obtained by The Atlanta

---

[43] Michelle J. Anderson, *Campus Sexual Assault Adjudication and Resistance to Reform*, 125 Yale Law Journal 1940–1978 (May 2016).
[44] Id.

Journal-Constitution. Not one resulted in criminal prosecution."[45] However, a bit further down in the article, the reader learned that in nearly all the cases, the alleged victims declined to provide the police with the basic information they would need to even consider pursuing a prosecution:

> In the vast majority of cases reviewed by the AJC [*Atlanta Journal-Constitution*], the victim either didn't come forward to authorities or chose not to pursue charges. In nearly half of those sex assaults, police didn't even know the name of the victim and only learned of the attack through counselors or health center reports. In the cases that remained, most of the victims declined to pursue charges.[46]

There is a certain "the chicken or the egg" quality to trying to determine why there is a such a disparity between the number of sexual assaults reported on campus and those prosecuted by police. The police naturally argue that they cannot pursue cases that are not reported to them in the first place or where the victim can't or won't provide them with the name of the alleged assailant. Advocates for sexual assault victims often argue that poor police responsiveness to sexual assault victims is the reason that such victims do not come forward in the first place. "Women often don't come forward because they fear they won't be believed and the lack of prosecution for the few who do try bolsters that view, experts said."[47]

A fair response to all this may be to say, as Janet Napolitano does, that it still might make more sense to focus on police reform than to have colleges do their job for them. However, to be effective such an effort would require more than police reform – it would also require significant reform of many states' rape laws. In many, sometimes most, states, rape laws are drawn much more narrowly than one might expect. While I argue in Chapters 6–8 that sexual assault is being defined in an unconstitutionally broad and vague fashion when it pertains to college students, the opposite is true for many state's rape laws – they are drawn so narrowly as to fail to protect many victims of what most people would understand to be rape.

A relatively minor example of this is that a small number of states still define rape as a crime that can only be perpetrated against a member of the opposite sex.[48] Approximately 6 percent of reported college sexual assault victims are men, and virtually all accused assailants are also men,[49] so these students would not be covered by these laws. However, this is true only in a small minority of

---

[45] www.myajc.com/news/georgia-colleges-allegations-rape-but-prosecutions/gSBkgfxrYjGtZ4urWN6 OnJ/.

[46] Id. at 1.

[47] www.myajc.com/news/georgia-colleges-allegations-rape-but-prosecutions/gSBkgfxrYjGtZ4urWN6 OnJ/.

[48] See, e.g., Alabama Code Sec. 13A-6-61.

[49] Report of United Educators, "Confronting Campus Sexual Assault: An Examination of Higher Education Claims" (2014), 4, www.ncdsv.org/ERS_Confronting-Campus-Sexual-Assault_2015 .pdf.

states, and even in those states there are laws against forcing "deviate sexual conduct," which, putting aside the insult of a victim needing to proceed under such a statute, would likely cover same-sex sexual assault.[50] Also, in a small minority of states, including Texas, sexual groping of a nonminor is Class C misdemeanor, which is roughly the equivalent of a speeding ticket.[51]

Much more significantly, an absolute majority of states still retain a force requirement in their rape statutes:

> Even today, a majority of jurisdictions rely on the concept of force in defining rape. State statutory schemes are more varied than ever, meaning that cross-jurisdictional comparisons are necessarily inexact. That said, a survey of rape laws shows that many states expressly define rape as requiring force, while others define rape as sex without consent but then include force as a component of non-consent.[52]

This means that in many states a burglar could break into a person's house while that person slept, sexually penetrate them, and not be guilty of rape. This may sound to some like a fanciful example, yet those are the facts of a 2013 case, *State v. Elias*. As the Idaho Supreme Court described the facts:

> On the night of the crime, Elias entered the victim's home and then her bedroom where she was sleeping with her two small children lying next to her. The victim slept in only a t-shirt and awoke around 3:30 a.m. because Elias had his fingers inside of her vagina. She rolled over onto her side and felt a razor-cut-like burning in her vagina. Her rolling over had caused Elias's hand to move . . . Elias asked if the victim wanted him to leave. She said she did, and after Elias left her bedroom, she immediately called both a friend and the police to report what had just occurred.[53]

In a decision that defies common sense, but not the law of Idaho and of many other states, the state high court ruled that Elias was *not* guilty of sexual assault: "[E]ven accepting the State's version of the evidence, the surrounding circumstances here do not constitute force within the meaning of [the statute]."[54]

This is far from an isolated example. In a Pennsylvania case a man was acquitted of rape by an appellate court even though he sexually penetrated a twelve-year-old girl in her sleep and, after waking, she was unable to push him off. Although she was pinned down by her assailant the court opined that the girl's "inability to get up immediately was merely the result of the force of gravity . . . was not that 'force' contemplated under the statute."[55]

---

[50] Alabama Code Sec. 13A-6-63.

[51] www.weatherforddemocrat.com/news/local_news/some-types-of-groping-not-a-crime/article_1b2c113c-456b-5329-a17e-a11ebd1a0f52.html.

[52] Deborah Tuerkheimer, *Rape On and Off of Campus*, 65 Emory Law Journal 1–45, 15 (2015).

[53] No. 39139, 2013 WL 3480737, at 1(Idaho Ct. App. July 12, 2013).   [54] Id. at 6.

[55] Commonwealth v. Thompson, 2 Pa. D. & C. 4th 632 (C.P. Cty. 1989) at p. 653. (Both *Elias* and *Thompson* are cited and discussed in Tuerkheimer, which also discusses several other similar cases.) Obviously in *Thompson* there is the separate issue of statutory rape, which is not germane to this discussion as college students are almost invariably above the age of sexual consent.

Another serious shortcoming in most state rape statutes concerns the role of alcohol in a victim's incapacitation. The great majority of college sexual assault cases involve alcohol consumption by one or both parties,[56] so how the law treats alcohol-induced incapacitation is crucial.

To appreciate this issue, it is important to understand the distinction between intoxication and incapacitation. Later in this book, we will see that many colleges have either intentionally or unintentionally blurred this distinction, resulting in a situation in which vast numbers of college students could be found guilty of sexual assault for the sort of drunken hookups that are commonplace on college campuses. Most state laws, though, veer the other way and do not protect victims from being taken advantage of even when they are truly incapacitated and are utterly unable to either consent to sexual activity or to defend themselves against unwanted sexual behavior.

To be intoxicated is merely to be under the influence of alcohol. A couple who spend a romantic evening together over a few drinks would be considered intoxicated. "Incapacitation" involves much stronger detrimental effects and is generally defined in terms such as being "physically helpless" and "rendered temporarily incapable of understanding or controlling [her] conduct."[57]

In the majority of states, it is not rape to initiate sexual activity with an incapacitated person unless the initiator got the victim to *involuntarily* consume a narcotic, anesthetic, or intoxicant. The paradigm case would be when someone surreptitiously spikes the victim's drink with a "date rape" drug such as Rohypnol. But if someone voluntarily drinks to the point of incapacitation, most states consider them fair game for sexual predators. A person can sexually penetrate another person who is passed out or so drunk that they cannot stand up or walk or even know where they are, even if the perpetrator is completely aware of the victim's helpless condition. This is a huge problem in terms of protecting college students.

Some might say that the solution is for college students not to drink so much, and that would certainly be a good idea. Ideas for how to gain some sort of control over college drinking are discussed in the Chapter 9. However, it is also true that students, especially first-year students, are vulnerable to pressure to over drink and that some groups of men purposely take advantage of that fact in an organized fashion. In Jon Krakauer's book on rape at the University of Montana, he describes through the words of fraternity brother, "Frank," how young women at fraternity parties are singled out and rendered vulnerable:

We'd be on the lookout for the good-looking girls, especially the freshman, the really young ones. They were the easiest ... then we'd get them drinking right away ... they'd

[56] Report of United Educators, "Confronting Campus Sexual Assault," 6, www.ncdsv.org /ERS_Confronting-Campus-Sexual-Assault_2015.pdf.
[57] Valerie M. Ryan, *Intoxicating Encounters: Allocating Responsibility in the Law of Rape*, 40 California Law Review 407–429, 414–415 (2004).

be guzzling it, you know, because they were freshmen, kind of nervous ... I mean she so plastered that she probably did not know what was going on anyway.[58]

In another example of this sort of behavior, in 2013, an e-mail surfaced in which the "social chair of Phi Kappa Tau instructed his fraternity brothers how to lure 'rapebait' by getting female party guests intoxicated."[59] Again, common sense tells us that this sort predatory sexual behavior should not be tolerated on college campuses. Yet if colleges were to leave such matters to law enforcement, these practices would go unsanctioned in the majority of states.

Yet another reason that colleges cannot simply get out of the business of investigating and adjudicating sexual assaults is the issue of standard of proof. As will be discussed in Chapter 4, there are three commonly used levels of standards of proof. The highest, which is used by the criminal justice system, is guilt "beyond a reasonable doubt." The lowest is "preponderance of the evidence,"[60] which means that the finder of fact merely has to decide if it more likely than not that a student committed an act such as sexual assault. Between these two standards is "clear and convincing evidence." A rough way to characterize these three standards is to say "preponderance of the evidence" means that the fact finder must be 50.1 percent certain of the person's guilt, while "beyond a reasonable doubt" requires 90 percent or more certainty, and the middle standard, "clear and convincing evidence" requires something like 75 percent certainty.

Were college sexual assault cases left entirely to criminal justice authorities, guilt would have to be proven beyond a reasonable doubt. While there are good reasons for applying this standard to the criminal justice system, this high standard of proof can be especially difficult to meet in situations with no witnesses other than the parties, who often have hazy memories after a night of alcohol consumption. I will argue later that reasonable people can disagree about which standard best suits college sexual assault hearings, but it is certainly reasonable for colleges to decide to keep a student off of their campuses if college authorities are "clearly convinced" that the student sexually assaulted another student.

This means that colleges, for all their problems and deficiencies, have an obligation to independently investigate and adjudicate sexual assault allegations that occur on their campuses. Of course, having a lower standard of proof, by definition, makes it more likely that they will wrongly determine

[58] Quoted in Nicholas Kristof, "When the Rapist Doesn't See It as Rape," *New York Times* (May 24, 2015), www.nytimes.com/2015/05/24/opinion/sunday/nicholas-kristof-when-the-rapist-doesnt-see-it-as-rape.html.
[59] www.myajc.com/news/local/wrongly-accused-rape-students-question-their-expulsions-from-tech/BBvnT55EBWtaCHbhunSxON/.
[60] There are standards of proof lower than preponderance of the evidence, such as "supported by substantial evidence," but those are generally reserved for review of a previous determination, not for initial determination of guilt or innocence.

that an innocent student committed sexual assault. As we will see in Chapter 2, such mistakes can have devastating consequences for students ranging from expulsion to deportation, as well as a lifetime of greatly diminished opportunity. Therefore, it is of the utmost importance that colleges afford students the due process rights that guard against false findings of sexual assault.

DUE PROCESS AND THE COMMONALITY OF INTERESTS

Unfortunately, a good deal of the debate seems to implicitly assume that sexual assault investigations and adjudications are a zero-sum game. The more protections we have for the accused, the less protection we provide for the victim.[61] In fact, the opposite is true. As we saw in the Hobart and William Smith College case, weak procedural safeguards can undermine the victim's case as well as the accused's case. Even more importantly, the main effect of due process is to ensure that the innocent are exonerated, not to provide loopholes for the guilty. Requiring universities to provide the accused student with a clear statement of the charges and of the facts supporting those charges, or to reveal exonerating evidence, or to provide a written statement of the basis for the panel's determination, do nothing to undermine a sexual assault victim's right to safety and equality on college campuses.

It is true that there are a few specific due processes issues that can fairly be described as posing some sort of conflict of interest between the accusing and accused students. One such issue is the standard of proof. A lower standard of proof makes it less likely that a panel will inaccurately exonerate a guilty student who then remains on campus posing a possible threat to the accusing student's physical safety and exacerbating her or his trauma. However, it also makes it more likely that an innocent student will be expelled with a mark on his record for sexual violence that will likely damage him for the rest of his life.

The other major due process issue that poses a true conflict of interest between the accusing and accused students is that of cross-examining the accusing students. Cross-examination is universally recognized as crucial tool in defending the innocent and separating truth from fiction. However, the prospect of being aggressively questioned about the details of a traumatic experience may keep students from reporting the assault in the first place.

These two tricky and important issues will be discussed at length in Chapters 4 and 5. For now, it suffices to point out that they are the

---

[61] E.g., Michelle Anderson writing in the *Yale Law Review* equates arguments for stronger due process rights in campus sexual assault tribunals with the resistance to progressive reform of rape law. "In general, the resistance to progressive reform of campus sexual assault has mirrored the backlash to the progressive reform of rape law, in that it favors unique procedures to benefit the accused." Anderson, *Campus Sexual Assault Adjudication and Resistance to Reform*, 1981–1982.

exceptions, not the rule. For the most part, due process is designed to help fact-finding tribunals make accurate findings. Far from being in conflict, men and women both have a strong interest in a process that produces fair and accurate results. As the iconic feminist law professor Catherine MacKinnon has pointed out: "It is not in women's interest to have men convicted of rape who did not do it . . . Lives are destroyed both by wrongful convictions and the lack of rightful ones, as the law and the credibility of women – that rare commodity – are also undermined."[62]

Surprisingly, some college administrators and political officials in positions of power see positive value even in false accusations of rape or in expelling even innocent students. For example, the assistant dean of student life at Vassar College made waves when she said:

To use the word [rape] carefully would be to be careful for the sake of the violator, and the survivors don't care a hoot about them . . . [wrongly accused students] have a lot of pain, but it [is] not a pain that I would necessarily have spared them. I think it ideally initiates a process of self-exploration. "How do I see women?" "If I didn't violate her, could I have"? "Do I have the potential to do to her what they say I did?" Those are good questions.[63]

More recently, Congressman Jared Polis argued for expelling innocent students as a "better safe than sorry" strategy: "If there's ten people that have been accused and under a reasonable likelihood standard maybe one or two did it, seems better to get rid of all of ten people."[64]

This view that is acceptable, even desirable, to punish the innocent is at odds with the values of a constitutional democracy. It also runs counter to the values of progressive feminism. As we will see in Chapter 7, what is sometimes called "carceral feminism"[65] – an enthusiasm for harsh punishment of sex-related crimes – is far more a movement of mainstream conservatism than it is of feminism, which has focused more on reform of the sort myopic rape law discussed earlier than it has on punishment.[66]

It is certainly true that we must carefully balance other important interests against the benefits of each element of due process, and the next several chapters

---

[62] Catherine MacKinnon, *Women's Lives, Men's Laws* (Cambridge, MA: Harvard University Press, 2005), 131.

[63] Quoted in Nancy Gibbs, "Cover Stories Behavior: When Is It Rape?," *Time.com* (June 24, 2001), http://content.time.com/time/magazine/article/0,9171,157165,00.html.

[64] Quoted in Ashe Schow, "Campus Sexual Assault Hearings Applaud Witch Hunt Mentality," Washington Examiner, September 10, 2015, www.washingtonexaminer.com/campus-sexual-assault-hearing-applauds-witch-hunt-mentality/article/2571784. Polis later took this comment back after criticism.

[65] See, e.g., JoAnn Wypijewski, "Liberals and Feminists, Stop Enabling the Police State," *The Nation* (September 10, 2014), www.thenation.com/article/how-feminists-and-liberals-enabled-modern-police-state/.

[66] Anderson, *Campus Sexual Assault Adjudication and Resistance to Reform.*

do exactly that. However, we cannot forget that everyone benefits from the protection of the innocent as well from the punishment of the guilty.

Therefore, it is vitally important that courts take their constitutional responsibilities seriously and ensure that colleges and universities investigate and adjudicate these matters with respect for the due process rights of all students. The next chapter will set out the foundational principles of constitutional due process as they apply to public universities. Chapter 3 will argue that these same principles also apply to private universities under Title IX and contract principles. Chapters 4 and 5 will look at specific issues such as the right to counsel, burden of proof, the right to review evidence and to present evidence, protections against self-incrimination and double jeopardy, the right to examine witnesses, and many other central issues of due process. Chapters 6 through 8 will look at how many universities substantively define sexual assault, and the final chapter will discuss suggestions for reform.

2

Due Process and the Constitution

As we saw in the previous chapter, powerful and influential institutions such as Harvard University have designed procedures for investigating sexual assault that many of their own faculty say "lack the most basic elements of fairness and due process [and] are overwhelmingly stacked against the accused." Even a school that sets up what a court described as a kangaroo court lacking fair process can survive appellate judicial review. Something is not right here.

While there are many complexities here, two things are clear. Colleges must act vigorously to protect students against sexual assault and must respect the due process rights of all students when this happens. When public universities fail to respect due process rights, courts should enforce those rights as a matter of constitutional law. The next chapter will argue that the same is true for private universities, utilizing a variety of legal theories.

This chapter argues that the Constitution and the due process clause require much better and fairer processes than are now often the case. The first section will discuss the foundational cases in this area. It will argue that the courts are relying too much on those cases' relatively narrow formulations of due process rather than on their groundbreaking rulings that due process applies to college and K–12 public education disciplinary processes in the first place. The second part applies the Supreme Court's three-part balancing test for due process to college tribunals in the modern context and demonstrates that all parts of the test point firmly in the direction of robust protection of students' due process rights.

THE FOUNDATIONAL CASES

The first question some might ask is why due process applies at all to the internal deliberations of universities. After all, college sexual assault tribunals are not criminal courts of law, or even courts of civil law. The answer is that any time a governmental body deprives a person of a liberty or property interest, this invokes the Constitution's due process clause, which is part of both the Fifth

Amendment (pertaining to the federal government) and the Fourteenth
Amendment (pertaining to state and local government). Public universities are
covered by the Fourteenth Amendment so the factor determining whether due
process applies is whether one has a liberty or property interest in remaining in
college or whether a college education is merely an unprotected "privilege."

This was the first question at issue in the important civil rights era case *Dixon
v. Alabama State Board of Education.*[1] The case was brought by "six
Negroes ... [who] were students in good standing at the Alabama State
College and remained so until they entered a publicly owned [segregated]
lunchroom in the Montgomery County Courthouse on or about February 25,
1960, after which and because of which the defendant State Board of Education
expelled each of them from the college."[2]

The expulsions were enacted with utter disregard for the basic protections of
due process. There were no formal charges, no hearing and:

the President of the College testified that he did not know why the plaintiffs and three
additional students were expelled and twenty other students were placed on probation.
The notice of expulsion which [the president] mailed to each of the plaintiffs assigned no
specific ground for expulsion, but referred in general terms to "this problem of Alabama
State College."[3]

The district court sided with the university, holding that "The right to attend
a public college or university is not in and of itself a constitutional right."[4]
In a groundbreaking decision, the appellate court overruled the district court
holding that even if the students were able to transfer to another school, the
interruption of their education was a constitutionally recognizable injury:

The precise nature of the private interest involved in this case is the right to remain at
a public institution of higher learning in which the plaintiffs were students in good
standing. It requires no argument to demonstrate that education is vital and, indeed,
basic to civilized society. Without sufficient education the plaintiffs would not be able to
earn an adequate livelihood, to enjoy life to the fullest, or to fulfill as completely as
possible the duties and responsibilities of good citizens.... Surely no one can question
that the right to remain at the college in which the plaintiffs were students in good
standing is an interest of extremely great value.[5]

The question is, then, to which what sort of process the students were entitled.
The *Dixon* Court went into significant detail about that, but it should be
stressed that the court clearly did not intend this to be a sweeping ruling
about the limits of due process. It was what is called *dicta* – a statement by
the court that is not essential to its ruling. Because the students had received
virtually no process, the court's holding that they were entitled to *some* process
was sufficient to rule in the students' favor. The *Dixon* Court's specific
statements were to guide the parties to the case in the event that the university

[1] 294 F. 2d 150 (5th Cir. 1961).   [2] 186 F. Supp. 945, 947 (1960).   [3] 294 F. 2d at 151–152.
[4] 186 F. Supp. at 950.   [5] 294 F. 2d at 157.

continued its efforts to expel the students: "For the guidance of the parties in the event of further proceedings, we state our views on the nature of the notice and hearing required by due process prior to expulsion from a state college or university. They should, we think, comply with the following standards."[6] The *Dixon* Court then laid out certain specifics on due process. The Court began by discussing the need for some type of hearing, the specifics of which would vary with the circumstance of each case:

The notice should contain a statement of the specific charges and grounds which, if proven, would justify expulsion under the regulations of the Board of Education. The nature of the hearing should vary depending upon the circumstances of the particular case. The case before us requires something more than an informal interview with an administrative authority of the college. By its nature, a charge of misconduct, as opposed to a failure to meet the scholastic standards of the college, depends upon a collection of the facts concerning the charged misconduct, easily colored by the point of view of the witnesses. In such circumstances, a hearing that gives the board or the administrative authorities of the college an opportunity to hear both sides in considerable detail is best suited to protect the rights of all involved.[7]

In oft-quoted language the *Dixon* Court added that the hearing did not need to be "full-dress" or allow cross-examination of witnesses:

This is not to imply that a full-dress judicial hearing, with the right to cross-examine witnesses, is required. Such a hearing, with the attending publicity and disturbance of college activities, might be detrimental to the college's educational atmosphere and impractical to carry out. Nevertheless, the rudiments of an adversary proceeding may be preserved without encroaching upon the interests of the college. In the instant case, the student should be given the names of the witnesses against him and an oral or written report on the facts to which each witness testifies. He should also be given the opportunity to present to the Board, or at least to an administrative official of the college, his own defense against the charges and to produce either oral testimony or written affidavits of witnesses in his behalf. If the hearing is not before the Board directly, the results and findings of the hearing should be presented in a report open to the student's inspection. If these rudimentary elements of fair play are followed in a case of misconduct of this particular type, we feel that the requirements of due process of law will have been fulfilled.[8]

Dixon was a courageous decision. In 1961, racial segregation was an enormously controversial issue that many courts were still afraid to touch. At that time, the Supreme Court was still purposely ducking the issue of bans on interracial marriage and would not hold them unconstitutional until six years later in *Loving v. Virginia*.[9] So it was bold for a Southern court to decide that the due process clause required Alabama to reinstate students who had been expelled for protesting segregation. Unfortunately, the case is cited less for

[6] 294 F. 2d. at 158.   [7] 294 F. 2d at 158–159.   [8] Id. at 159.
[9] See Evan Gerstmann, *Same-Sex Marriage and the Constitution*, 3rd ed. (Cambridge: Cambridge University Press, 2017), 89.

its groundbreaking ruling that the due process clause applies to college disciplinary proceedings than it is for its dicta *limiting* due process protections, especially its statements that:

"This is not to imply that a full-dress judicial hearing, with the right to cross-examine witnesses, is required"; and

"If these rudimentary elements of fair play are followed in a case of misconduct of this particular type, we feel that the requirements of due process of law will have been fulfilled."

Written at a time of tremendous backlash against *Brown v. Board of Education* and against racial desegregation, *Dixon* should be seen as setting a floor on due process rights, not a ceiling. The case represented a great leap forward in terms of due process for African American students protesting segregation and should be applied in light of that protective spirit rather than being diluted by its understandable caution about overplaying the court's hand in a hostile environment.

The other foundational case did not involve college at all, but rather due process rights for public high school students. In *Goss v. Lopez*, a student was suspended for 10 days for his alleged participation in a lunch room disruption in which there was no evidence that he participated. He was not given the benefit of a hearing prior to his suspension.[10] The Supreme Court held that even a 10-day suspension, which interrupted his education and damaged his reputation, was sufficient injury to trigger due process protections:

A short suspension is, of course, a far milder deprivation than expulsion. But, "education is perhaps the most important function of state and local governments," *Brown v. Board of Education*, 347 U. S. 483 (1954), and the total exclusion from the educational process for more than a trivial period, and certainly if the suspension is for 10 days, is a serious event in the life of the suspended child. Neither the property interest in educational benefits temporarily denied nor the liberty interest in reputation, which is also implicated, is so insubstantial that suspensions may constitutionally be imposed by any procedure the school chooses, no matter how arbitrary.[11]

In terms of what sort of process is due, the Court held: "*At the very minimum*, therefore, students facing suspension and the consequent interference with a protected property interest must be given some kind of notice and afforded *some* kind of hearing."[12] The *Goss* Court added:

Students facing temporary suspension have interests qualifying for protection of the Due Process Clause, and due process requires, in connection with a suspension of 10 days or less, that the student be given oral or written notice of the charges against him and, if he denies them, an explanation of the evidence the authorities have and an opportunity to present his side of the story. The Clause requires *at least* these rudimentary precautions against unfair or mistaken findings of misconduct and arbitrary exclusion from school.[13]

---

[10] Goss v. Lopez, 419 U.S. 565 (1975).   [11] 419 U.S. at 576 (emphasis added).
[12] 419 U.S. at 579 (emphasis added).   [13] 419 U.S. at 581 (emphasis added).

It should be emphasized that the *Goss* Court used language such as "at the very minimum" and "at least." Like *Dixon*, this case should be read as a floor rather than a ceiling on due process rights. As explained in the following text, the Supreme Court has held that due process is a balancing test. The greater the liberty or property interest that is being taken away, the more process to which the person is entitled. Obviously, a student who is being expelled or given a lengthy suspension from college for a sex offense that will be part of his permanent academic record has far more at stake than the high school student in *Goss* and deserves significantly more protection from inaccurate outcomes.

It should also be noted that both *Dixon* and *Goss* occurred in what could be called the "premodern" era of procedural due process. As we will see in the following text, the Supreme Court's seminal decision setting out today's constitutional standards for due process was decided after these two decisions.

Unfortunately, many courts have cited *Dixon* and *Goss*, not for their groundbreaking holdings that due process applies to students, but as decisions *limiting* the due process rights of students. Recall from the last chapter that an appellate court in California upheld a college tribunal that it described as a "kangaroo court" lacking any sense of fairness. The court cited *Goss* for the proposition that "a fair hearing only requires that the respondent be aware of what he or she is accused of doing and the basis of that accusation."[14] Although, at oral argument, the appellate court's presiding judge said "I am at a total loss why anybody interested in a fair and accurate outcome would do something like that [refuse to allow the accused student access to the investigator's notes or to pose questions to their investigator]," the same judge wrote the opinion siding with the university, citing *Dixon* for the proposition that "the student should be given [only] the names of the witnesses against him and an oral or written report on the facts to which each witness testifies."[15]

While the California Court stated that the college's procedure "has great potential to be unfair to a student accused of violating the Sex Offense Policy," the court could not say that the college violated the student's due process rights because the *Dixon* Court "set forth somewhat comprehensive parameters in the event that a student is facing disciplinary sanctions."[16]

The California court is far from alone in applying *Dixon* and *Goss* in this fashion as we will see in the cases discussed in the next three chapters. The courts have especially relied on the dicta from *Dixon* to limit an accused student's right to examine witnesses against them, even witnesses who are not the complainant and for whom the risk of being retraumatized is not at issue.

What then, are the appropriate parameters of due process? The next section will take this question up by applying the three-part balancing test used by the

---

[14] Doe v. Regents of the University of California (4th Circuit Ct. of Appeals, November 22, 2016) at 60.
[15] Id. at 60.   [16] Id. at 71.

Supreme Court to make such judgments. It will argue that all three parts of the test point to far stronger due process protections than currently are enforced.

DUE PROCESS IN THE BALANCE

The Supreme Court case *Mathews v. Eldridge*[17] is one of the most important cases in all constitutional law. It sets out the test for what sort of due process protection a person is entitled to when the government seeks to deprive him or her of an important interest. It applies to situations as varied as termination of disability benefits (which was the issue in *Eldridge*) to the nature and rules of military tribunals determining if a citizen is an enemy combatant.[18] It is the Court's "general approach" for determining the requirements of procedural due process for any particular situation:

Mathews had an impact far beyond the narrow question presented in that case. According to the Supreme Court, Mathews offers "a general approach" for testing challenged procedures under a due process claim. The Court has subsequently applied Mathews three-factor analysis in a variety of contexts unrelated to public benefits fits terminations, including terminations of parental rights, involuntary civil commitments to mental hospitals, civil forfeitures, detention of citizens as enemy combatants, immigration deportation proceedings, and terminations of public employment. The Court has even used the Mathews balancing approach to analyze claims under the Constitution's Suspension Clause.[19]

Because it applies to such a broad range of circumstances, it stresses flexibility in its particulars:

These decisions underscore the truism that "[d]ue process," unlike some legal rules, is not a technical conception with a fixed content unrelated to time, place and circumstances. [D]ue process is flexible and calls for such procedural protections as the particular situation demands.[20]

To achieve this flexibility, the Court set out a three-part balancing test, called the *Mathews* test:

[T]he specific dictates of due process generally requires consideration of three distinct factors: First, the private interest that will be affected by the official action; second, the risk of an erroneous deprivation of such interest through the procedures used, and the probable value, if any, of additional or substitute procedural safeguards; and finally, the Government's interest, including the function involved and the fiscal and administrative burdens that the additional or substitute procedural requirement would entail.[21]

So, to determine the due process rights of students accused of sexual assault, the *Mathews* test requires that the courts balance those three factors. For each

---

[17] 424 U.S. 319 (1976).   [18] Hamdi v. Rumsfeld, 542 U.S. 507 (2004).
[19] Jason Parkin, *Adaptable Due Process*, 160, no. 5 University of Pennsylvania Law Review 1309–1377, 1325–1326 (April 2012) (citations omitted).
[20] 424 U.S. at 334 (citations omitted).   [21] 424 U.S. at 335.

element of due process, for example the right to direct questions to witnesses against the accused, the courts should weigh:

1. The importance of the student's interest in not erroneously being found responsible for committing a sex offense;
2. The likelihood of an erroneous decision if a student cannot examine witnesses against him and the degree to which allowing the accused student to direct questions to witnesses makes an erroneous decision less likely; and
3. The government's interest in not allowing the student to directly examine witnesses against him, including the fiscal and administrative burdens that would entail.

The next three sections will argue that all three *Mathews* factors weigh heavily in favor of greater due process rights. The accused student's interests are very substantial; the risk of inaccurate fact finding by college tribunals is also very substantial under the current way of doing things, and the college's interest in not allowing so many basic elements of due process is more minor than most courts seem to suppose. The discussion will consider the college's very strong interest in protecting students from sexual assault and promoting an atmosphere of gender equality as well as the limited resources available to many colleges.

The Importance of the Interest

Disruption of Education and Damage to Reputation
Goss recognized the disruptive impact of even a 10-day suspension from high school. A suspension from college, even one that only lasts until the end of the semester, is far more disruptive. It delays graduation and likely means the loss of a semester's tuition – a tremendous burden for students who are already struggling to pay for the costs of college. Their eligibility for financial aid and scholarships could also be affected.

    Goss also recognized the reputational damage from a suspension.[22] The reputational damage is far worse for a student found responsible for sexual assault. As Nancy Gertner, a former federal judge and a self-described "unrepentant feminist [and] longtime litigator on behalf of women's rights," points out, even the accusation will deeply impact the life of the accused. As a defense attorney she learned to appreciate "the stigma of the very accusation, which persists – especially today on the Internet – even if the accused is exonerated."[23]

---

[22] 417 U.S. at 574.

[23] Nancy Gertner, "Sex, Lies and Justice," *The American Prospect* (Winter 2015), http://prospect .org/article/sex-lies-and-justice. This also shows that, even from the accused student's perspective, it is crucial that the process be fair to the accusing student as well. If people lack faith in the

Courts have recognized that "[i]t goes without saying, and needs no elaboration, that a record of expulsion from high school constitutes a lifetime stigma,"[24] and that would certainly be true of expulsion from college. As University of Chicago Law School Professor Geoffrey Stone puts it: An expulsion for sexual assault "will haunt the student for the rest of his days."[25]

Even apart from the widespread publicity that sometimes accompanies these cases,[26] state laws are increasingly mandating that universities "place a notation on a student's transcript when the student is found responsible for sexual assault."[27] Thus, a finding of responsibility for sexual assault will have a profound impact on a student's ability to transfer, find employment, or pursue graduate education.

Further, if a student is found responsible for sexual assault, expulsion is a likely possibility, especially because colleges face the possibility of monetary liability should they allow a sex offender to remain on campus.[28] Universities are increasingly enacting policies that make expulsion the preferred or even mandatory consequence of finding a student guilty of sexual assault.[29] As a federal court has held: "The interests of students in completing their education, as well as avoiding unfair or mistaken exclusion from the educational environment, and the accompanying stigma are, of course, paramount."[30]

If a student is expelled after a finding that he committed sexual assault, he may never be able to get a college degree from any school. Even in states that don't mandate that universities mark the student's record, colleges virtually always require a student who seeks to transfer into them to demonstrate that he

---

fairness of the process, even an exonerated student will suffer continued damage to his reputation.

[24] Givens v. Poe, 346 F. Supp. 202, 208 (W.D. N.C. 1972) (quoting Vought v. Van Buren Public Schools, 306 F. Supp. 1388, 1393 [E.D. Mich. 1969]).

[25] Geoffrey Stone, "Campus Sexual Assault" (January 31, 2015), www.law.uchicago.edu/news/geoffrey-stone-university-responses-campus-sexual-assault.

[26] Sometimes the publicity results from the athletic status of the accused student such as football quarterback Jameis Winston, who was a central figure in the widely viewed documentary "The Hunting Ground." Other times it can result from the high profile of the accusing student as in the case of Emma Sulkowicz whose protest of Columbia University's sexual assault procedures received widespread publicity.

[27] Craig Wood et al., NACUA (National Association of College and University Attorneys) Notes: "Between a Rock and Hard Place: A Discussion of Issues That Frequently Arise in Sexual Misconduct-Related Litigation Against Colleges and Universities" (May 18, 2016), http://counsel.cua.edu/res/docs/titleixlitigation.pdf.

[28] Id.

[29] Jake New, "Expulsion Presumed," *Inside Higher Ed* (June 27, 2014), www.insidehighered.com /news/2014/06/27/should-expulsion-be-default-discipline-policy-students-accused-sexual-assault.

[30] Gorman v. University of Rhode Island, 837 F. 2d. 714 (1988).

left in good standing.[31] Failure to graduate from college usually means a lifetime of greatly diminished earnings: "Young adults with just a high-school diploma earned 62 percent of the typical salary of college graduates. That's down from 81 percent in 1965, the earliest year for which comparable data are available."[32] As important as a college education was in 1961, when *Dixon* was decided, it is far more important now.

Loss of Career Opportunities

Even for students who somehow manage to graduate from college, a finding that a student committed sexual assault will make it extremely difficult for him to find employment. While it is true that a student's records are protected by federal privacy laws, this does not realistically mean that prospective employers won't see them. As a federal judge has observed:

> To be sure, plaintiff's disciplinary records are considered confidential under the Family Educational Rights and Privacy Act, 20 U.S.C. § 1232g, but this information can be shared with plaintiff's authorization. Thus, if plaintiff seeks education or employment with institutions or organizations that require disclosure of such records, plaintiff's only options are to forgo opportunities with those institutions or organizations or to author- ize the dissemination of records that would likely foreclose plaintiff's ability to pursue such opportunities because of the allegedly defamatory nature of the records.[33]

Further, a student who is expelled for a sexual offense, even if they manage to graduate from college, would be unlikely get admitted to professional schools such as education, medicine, or law. The student's life would be forever altered by an inaccurate finding of responsibility for such an offense.

Deportation

As of 2016, there were more than one million foreign students enrolled in American higher education.[34] If a college expels a noncitizen student, that student is at serious risk for deportation. Foreign students who are expelled are required by the federal government to leave the United States immediately.[35]

[31] James M. Piccozi, *University Disciplinary Policy: What's Fair, What's Due and What You Don't Get*, 96 Yale Law Journal 2132–2161, 2138 (July 1987).

[32] Hope Yen, "New Study Shows the Value of a College Education," Associated Press (February 11, 2014), www.bostonglobe.com/news/nation/2014/02/11/new-study-shows-value-college-education/3IWWEOXwQEAcMFSyo9msOK/story.html.

[33] Doe v. Rectors of George Mason University, 149 F. Supp. 3d 602, 616 n. 9 (E.D. Virginia 2016). Cited in Johnson and Taylor, *The Campus Rape Frenzy*, 169.

[34] Rosanna Xia, "Number of International Students in U.S. Colleges at an All-Time High, and California Is Their Top Destination," *Los Angeles Times* (November 25, 2016), www.latimes .com/local/lanow/la-me-study-abroad-students-20161124-story.html.

[35] "Expulsion from the school which has issued you the most current Form I-20 would cause you to lose the status of Foreign Student and the right to legally remain in the United States. Under such circumstances, the student is expected to depart the United States immediately." www .f1studentvisa.com/maintaining-status.html.

A good illustration of this issue is the Washington State case *Abdullatif Arishi v. Washington State University*.[36] A college panel found Arishi responsible for sex with an underage female who had listed her age as 19 on a dating website. (She was not a student at Washington State University.) The college concluded that Arishi should have realized that she was underage from her appearance even though the college investigator had never personally met or spoken with the girl in question. The student was forced to return to Saudi Arabia just one year short of completing his degree. Eventually, the college's decision was vacated by the courts. Applying Washington State administrative law, an appellate court found that the college panel procedures were so lacking in due process that Arishi had demonstrated "a reasonable probability that had he been provided with all of the rights and safeguards available in full adjudication, the result of the proceeding would have been different."[37]

In some cases, deportation can threaten the life of the accused student. A Penn State student was only spared deportation to Syria, where nearly half a million people have been killed in the ongoing war, when a federal judge blocked the deportation order. Penn State then rescinded the student's suspension.[38] Had the student not had the resources to seek a court order, he could have been placed in mortal danger.

Undocumented students would be even more at risk for deportation if they were, correctly or incorrectly, found responsible for a sexual offense by a college panel. There are anywhere from 7,000 to 13,000 undocumented college students in the United States, mostly in California. Under the Trump regime, it is difficult to imagine that such students, if found to have committed sexual assault by a college panel, would not be quickly deported.

Criminal Incarceration

Lack of due process in college hearings is often defended on the grounds that the consequences of an adverse finding do not include criminal incarceration. As mentioned in the previous chapter, Congressman Jared Polis has argued that students should be expelled even if there is just a small possibility that they committed a sexual offense. Polis justified this statement by saying: "We're not talking about depriving them of life or liberty, we're talking about their transfer to another university."[39]

But it is not that simple. In fact, lack of due process in college hearings can indeed put students in serious danger of criminal incarceration. Since 1997, the federal government has made it clear that it expects universities to investigate and adjudicate sexual assault allegations even when there is already an ongoing

---

[36] Court of Appeals of Washington, Division 3 (December 21, 2016).
[37] Id. at 72. As the ruling was based on state law, it has no effect outside of Washington State.
[38] Johnson and Taylor, *The Campus Rape Frenzy*, 94.
[39] Schow, "Campus Sexual Assault Hearing Applauds Witch Hunt Mentality." It should be noted that the congressman eventually tried to walk back these remarks in the face of criticism.

criminal investigation.[40] Any statement made by a student during the college investigation, adjudication, or appeal can be used by police and prosecutors. Because colleges usually don't allow representation by an attorney at hearings and are allowed to hold a student's failure to answer questions against him, students are effectively waiving their right against self-incrimination in a parallel criminal investigation. This is especially true because the federal government encourages universities to work cooperatively with police in such matters.

Further, if a student appeals an adverse decision by a college panel, his punishment can be increased if he fails to show remorse for his transgression, so he is virtually forced to admit sexual misconduct. Recall that in the case of *Doe v. University of California San Diego*, one of the complaints of unfair process by Doe was that his penalty was increased on appeal and that no explanation was given for this increased sanction. The appellate court rejected this argument, holding that it was reasonable to assume that the enhanced penalty was a result of a lack of contrition:

Although the council of provosts did not provide a reasoned explanation for increasing John's suspension, we do not have to scour the record to find possible justifications for the slight increase. For example, in John's posthearing statement to Mallory, which he provided to the council of provosts as part of his appeal, he did not take responsibility for the sexual misconduct the Panel found he committed.[41]

Recall also, that the appellate court was extremely critical of the university's process. Yet, once the college tribunal ruled, the university virtually required Doe to admit guilt lest his punishment be increased, as it in fact was. Crucially, *any such admissions can then be used by the police.* At a 2015 meeting of the International Association of College Law Enforcement Administrators, Susan Riseling, the chief of police and associate vice chancellor at the University of Wisconsin at Madison, gave an illustrative example of how the police can take advantage of the student's need to admit guilt to the university to circumvent the student's constitutional rights:

[Riseling] also described a case at Wisconsin, in which the Title IX investigation was the only reason police were able to arrest a student accused of raping his roommate's girlfriend.

The accused student denied the charges when interviewed by police, Riseling said. In his disciplinary hearing, however, he changed his story in an apparent attempt to receive a lesser punishment by admitting he regretted what had occurred. That version of events was "in direct conflict with what he told police," Riseling said. Police subpoenaed the Title IX records of the hearing and were able to use that as evidence against the student.

---

[40] Stephen Henrick, *A Hostile Environment for Student Defendants: Title IX and Sexual Assault on College Campuses*, 40 Northern Kentucky Law Review 49–92, 58(2013).

[41] Doe v. University of California San Diego at 80.

"It's Title IX, not Miranda," Riseling said. "Use what you can."[42]

Riseling also suggested that "Title IX investigators should watch the police's interview through a television feed, and prompt the detective to ask any additional questions." This close cooperation between Title IX investigators and police makes it clear that lack of due process in college hearings and investigations threaten the accused student's core liberty interest in avoiding criminal incarceration.

In sum, many very important interests are at stake here. The student's ability to graduate, find employment, attend graduate or professional school, avoid tremendous reputational damage, avoid deportation in some cases, and avoid coerced confessions that can lead to criminal prosecutions and prison time are all at stake. Therefore, the first prong of the *Mathews* test, the strength of the interest at stake, weighs heavily in favor of strong due process protection. The next section will examine the second prong of the *Mathews* test.

The Likelihood of Error and Value of Additional Procedures in Avoiding Error

Having determined the strength of the interests involved in college sexual assault hearings, the Supreme Court requires that we next look at the likelihood of erroneous decisions by campus tribunals as they are currently run. Chapters 4 and 5 discuss the many elements of due process missing from many college tribunals.[43] This section argues that absent substantially greater due process protections, the risk of erroneous decision making is quite high.

Senator Claire McCaskill, a leading voice on the issue of campus sexual assault, has expressed skepticism about the idea that students might be erroneously found responsible for sexual assault. "I don't think we are anywhere near the tipping point where the people being accused of this are somehow being treated unfairly."[44]

This section argues that this confidence is misplaced. In fact, it would be difficult to think of a more challenging subject to adjudicate confidently than peer-to-peer sexual assault on college campuses. The behavior usually takes

---

[42] Jake New, "Making Title IX Work," *Inside Higher Education* (July 15, 2015), www .insidehighered.com/news/2015/07/06/college-law-enforcement-administrators-hear-approach-make-title-ix-more-effective (emphasis added).

[43] It is, of course, impossible to make universally true generalizations about what sort of due process is given by each of the thousands of colleges and universities in our highly diversified system of higher education. In some cases, it is likely that colleges and universities have stronger due process protections than the ones discussed in this book. The argument of this book is that *all* public colleges and universities should be held to a higher *constitutional* standard of due process. In addition, Chapter 3 argues that private colleges and universities should be held to this higher standard as well.

[44] Quoted in Emily Yoffe, "The College Rape Overcorrection," *Slate* (December 7, 2014), www .slate.com/articles/double_x/doublex/2014/12/college_rape_campus_sexual_assault_is_a_serious_problem_but_the_efforts.html.

place in private with few witnesses besides the two students, whose memories are often dulled or altogether erased by heavy consumption of alcohol. In addition, there are many other confounding factors:

[S]tudent-on-student sexual misconduct cases are difficult from an evidentiary perspective. In cases of student-on-student sexual misconduct, the fact of sexual contact is often not in dispute and consent is the principal – and perhaps only – issue. Moreover, these incidents typically occur in dormitory rooms, and third-party eyewitnesses are rare. Because alcohol is often involved and consensual foreplay typically precedes an acquaintance rape, physical evidence of an assault is often unavailable. Even the presence of physical evidence of intercourse may not be dispositive of misconduct if consent is at issue. Thus, such disciplinary hearings are susceptible to being reduced to a "he said/she said" credibility contest.[45]

Further, the hearings often take place well after the incident at issue, with no preservation of evidence. The panels are generally composed of academics and administrators with no relevant professional expertise.[46] Throughout this book we will see that the fact-finding processes can allow crucial evidence to remain unexamined, testimony by witnesses to be relayed secondhand, ambiguities in what exactly the student is being charged with, and many other problems.

The Prevalence of False Accusations

One source of some people's confidence that the panels are unlikely to make mistakes is the belief in some quarters that accusers almost never lie about sexual assault. For example, writing for *Vox*, the *Washington Post* and *Bloomberg* columnist Ezra Klein has defended a very broad college sexual assault bill that he admits is a "terrible law" largely on the basis that women almost never make false accusations of sexual assault. He writes: "I don't want to say these kinds of false accusations never happen because they do happen and they're awful. *But they happen very, very rarely.*"[47]

This belief that women almost never lie about sexual assault leads some to argue that we should invert the usual presumption of innocence when it comes to such allegations. Jon Krakauer, whose work is discussed in the previous chapter, argues for "a mandatory belief by police in the truth of the complaining witness's accusation unless otherwise proven false."[48] In a similar vein, presidential

---

[45] Lisa Tenerowicz, *Student Misconduct at Private Colleges and Universities: A Roadmap for 'Fundamental Fairness' in Disciplinary Proceedings*, 42 Boston College Law Review 653–693, 661 (2001) (citations omitted).

[46] The panel members usually do receive training although the training process usually lacks transparency. The problems with panel training are discussed in Chapter 4.

[47] Ezra Klein, "'Yes Means Yes' Is a Terrible Law and I Support It Completely," *Vox* (October 13, 2014) (emphasis in original; citation omitted), www.vox.com/2014/10/13/6966847/yes-means-yes-is-a-terrible-bill-and-i-completely-support-it.

[48] Cited in Emily Safko, *Are Campus Sexual Assault Tribunals Fair? The Need for Judicial Review and Additional Due Process Protections in Light of New Case Law*, 84 Fordham Law Review 2289–2333, 2298 (2016).

candidate Hillary Clinton's director of progressive media, Zerlina Maxwell, stated that in the college context "we should believe as a matter of default, what an accuser says [as] false accusations are exceedingly rare and errors can be undone by an investigation that clears the accused."[49] Discussing the controversy over sexual assault at Harvard, Jeannie Suk Gersen, a Harvard Law professor, writes: "It is a near-religious teaching among many people today that if you are against sexual assault, then you must always believe individuals who say they have been assaulted."[50]

Different studies have produced widely varying estimates on the prevalence of false accusations of sexual assault. Nonetheless, "Recently, it has become commonplace to assert that a 2–8% false reporting rate is the 'accepted' figure."[51] The lower figure of 2 percent is cited particularly frequently: "The 2% figure ... has become so ingrained that claims regarding the rarity of false complaints are sometimes made without any reference to supporting evidence."[52]

In fact, studies vary widely in their conclusions about false reports, with estimates ranging from 8 percent to 41 percent, and some estimates significantly higher, although the very high-end studies have some obvious flaws.[53] Yet, we know very little despite the numerous studies. For each study there are equally good reasons to assume that their estimates are either far too low or far too high.

In terms of assuming that many studies exaggerate the number of false reports, it is important to remember that the studies are relying on police determinations for their data. As discussed in the previous chapter, police are sometimes overly inclined to dismiss reports of sexual assault as unfounded. As one army attorney and former prosecutor puts it:

False reports have an incredibly corrosive impact on how sexual assault accusations are policed. Police treat sexual assault accusers badly – much worse than the lawyers do – much worse than the courtroom does. Forget what you see on "Law and Order SVU," the police end absolutely discourages victims from reporting. Why is this so? Because cops suspect just about every victim is another false accuser, because either he/she has personally dealt with such a problem, or has heard stories from his or her cop buddies to

[49] Johnson and Taylor, *The Campus Rape Frenzy*, 229.
[50] "Shutting Down Conversations about Rape at Harvard Law," *New Yorker* (December 11, 2015), www.newyorker.com/news/news-desk/argument-sexual-assault-race-harvard-law-school.
[51] Rubenfeld, "Privatization, State Action, and Title IX," 44.
[52] Philip N. S. Rumney, *False Allegations of Rape*, 65 *Cambridge Law Journal* 128–158, 143 (2006). *See also*, Edward Greer, *The Truth behind Legal Dominance Feminism's Two Percent False Rape Claim Figure*, 33 Loy. L.A. L. Rev. 947 (2000). Available at: http://digitalcommons.lmu.edu/llr/vol33/iss3/3 for multiple citations to authors stating that only two percent of rape claims are false.
[53] See Rumney, *False Allegations of Rape*, for a discussion of these studies as well as their conclusions and methods.

this effect (and yes, in my experience female cops can be even worse offenders). This police behavior is bad, and counterproductive – but it's real.[54]

For those who wish to argue that the studies *underestimate* the percentage of false reports, there are ample grounds as well. Most of the studies ask what percentage of allegations is determined to be "unfounded," which means that the allegation "has [been] determined through investigation to be false."[55] So the percentage of claims that are labeled as "unfounded" does not include most cases in which the police declined to prosecute or grand juries declined to indict due to lack of evidence. How many of these cases involve untrue claims and how many involve real crimes in which there was an unfortunate lack of evidence is therefore a matter of utter speculation. But if in a significant number of cases the insufficiency of the evidence is the result of there not being a crime, then the number of false reports is significantly higher than the studies show.

Of course, it is possible to argue that even when no crime occurred, that does not mean that there was not a rape or sexual assault as many would understand it. As we saw in the previous chapter, there are many states where actions that should be considered rape or sexual assault are not considered crimes.

Because the studies vary so widely in their conclusions, because the studies depend upon police and prosecutors of widely varying attitudes and levels of competence, because "unfounded" allegations is a much narrower category than false allegations, and because the laws of sexual assault vary so much, the only fair conclusion is that we really don't have good estimates of the percentage of false allegations.

As a result, this debate turns out to be more normative than empirical. Advocates for victims are understandably concerned about giving credence to the "myth of the lying woman." Unfortunately, there is good reason to believe that this myth is far from dead. One British survey found that 81 percent of men and 68 percent of women agreed with the statement that "women cry rape the next day when really they have just had second thoughts."[56] In America, one need look no further than the election of a president whom a dozen or so different women accused of sexual assault[57] to understand rape victim advocates' deep concern about a culture of not believing victims.

However, there are many people with understandable concerns about presumptively believing allegations of sexual assault. As will be discussed in

---

[54] Quoted in Emily Bazelon and Rachael Larimore, "How Often Do Women Falsely Cry Rape," Slate.com, www.slate.com/articles/news_and_politics/jurisprudence/2009/10/how_often_do_-women_falsely_cry_rape.html.

[55] Rumney, *False Allegations of Rape*, 138.

[56] S. Burton et al., "Young People's Attitudes Towards Violence, Sex and Relationships: A Survey and Focus Group Study" (Edinburgh: The Zero Tolerance Charitable Trust, 1998) (cited in Rumney, *False Allegations of Rape*, 129 n. 8).

[57] "An Exhaustive List of the Allegations Women Have Made Against Donald Trump," *The Cut* (October 27, 2016), http://nymag.com/thecut/2016/10/all-the-women-accusing-trump-of-rape-sexual-assault.html.

Chapter 6, there are reasons to believe that black men in college are being disproportionately targeted by such allegations, and the history of how white-power structures have dealt with allegations of sexual misconduct by black men, especially toward white women, certainly counsels caution. It is not hard to find students who are athletes, fraternity members, Muslims, or foreigners who also think that college authorities are all too ready to believe the worst about them. And throughout this book we will see numerous examples of students who were found responsible for sexual misconduct as a result of highly questionable hearings. In sum, we are dealing with a great deal of unknowns and cannot responsibly conclude that untrue claims of sexual assault are so extremely rare that we do not need to worry about due process.

Due Process and Likelihood of Error

College sexual assault tribunals, then, are operating on uncertain ground. Distinguishing outright lies from truth is difficult enough, but they also face extremely difficult questions of *interpretation*. Sometimes both the accuser and the accused may be telling the absolute truth as they see it, but the question of whether a sexual assault occurred remains unclear.

A case that well illustrates the degree that cases can turn on interpretation of events, often by people in an intoxicated state, is *Doe v. University of Southern California*.[58] This complicated case will be used to illustrate a variety of points throughout this book. It involved two University of Southern California (USC) students, "John" and "Jane," who were at an off-campus party where both were drinking heavily. Earlier in the evening both had gone to a third party's bedroom and engaged in consensual sexual activity. Also at the party were two male students from an out-of-state university, "Student 1" and "Student 2," who were friends of John's teammates on the USC football team.

Forty-five minutes after the initial sexual encounter, John and Jane returned to the bedroom where Jane began to perform oral sex on John. During this second encounter, which was voluntary up to this point, Student 1 and Student 2 entered the room and began to digitally penetrate Jane from behind. According to the court: "At some point during this encounter, other men present in the room – not including John – exceeded the scope of Jane's consent."[59]

Either Student 1 or Student 2 began penetrating her from behind in a rough manner causing her pain. Both Student 1 and Student 2 then struck Jane's

---

[58] Throughout this chapter I will discuss cases pertaining to both public and private universities. I will be arguing in the next chapter that due process applies to private and public universities. In any event, these cases illustrate the ways in which lack of due process can produce erroneous results.

[59] John Doe v. University of Southern California (Cal. 2nd Appellate District B262917 2016) at 3–5.

buttocks in a very hard manner, also causing her pain. At that point John said: "Is she crying – I can't believe she is crying," and all physical contact with Jane ceased.[60] All three men left the bedroom, but there was disagreement as to what order they left. Jane reported that she had been sexually assaulted and that "her memories of the night were foggy as a result of her intoxication."[61] She also said that the entire incident lasted between one and two minutes.

The resulting sexual assault hearing suffered from severe due process problems, especially the lack of clarity regarding what charges were alleged against John. The university's investigation focused on whether the sexual contact between Jane and John was consensual, and the college panel focused on whether John participated in a group sexual assault. However, in the end, John was found responsible by an appeals panel for "encouraging or permitting" the assault of Jane by Student 1 and Student 2 and of "endangering" her by leaving the room before the other two men did. He was suspended for two years, and it was not clear whether he would eventually be able to re-enroll. USC had no jurisdiction over Student 1 or Student 2, so the college panel had no impact on them.

On the second charge, the court found that the university lacked a factual basis for concluding that John left Jane in the room with the other two men. The "encouraging or permitting" charge was more difficult because it turned entirely upon interpreting ambiguous statements in an alcohol-infused, sexually charged, fast-evolving situation. Jane interpreted John's exclamation "Is she crying – I can't believe she is crying," as "mocking or ridiculing rather than compassionate."[62] As for John's other comments, which resulted in his being found responsible for encouraging the other two men, the court found that Jane was "extremely vague about what John actually said." Jane remembered that John "made comments about my body." She was also unclear about which person said certain things. When asked for clarification about who said what, she testified, "They were all saying it. Like, 'Look at her! Oh my god!' ... They were all kind of feeding off each other."[63] She did not claim that John ever told anyone to hit her or to penetrate her.

A case like this shows that the issue of sexual assault can be far more complex than asking how often accusations are false. There does not seem to be any question that Jane told the truth as she saw it. Whether John's comments were compassionate or mocking is a question of interpretation. The same is true for Jane's perception that John and the unidentified men were feeding off of each other. John's perception was that as soon as Jane indicated her distress he ceased all sexual activity, as did the two other men. Jane's perception was that John encouraged the abusive behavior of the other men.

Unfortunately, the college panel's lack of due process greatly increased the possibility of an erroneous finding. As will be discussed in later chapters, both the hearing panel and the appeals panel relied upon evidence that John had

---

[60] Id. at 5.   [61] Id. at 6.   [62] Id. at 5.   [63] Id. at 32–33.

never seen and gave him inadequate notice of what he was charged with. Jane, but not John, was provided with all of the witness statements prior to the hearing and was allowed to clarify inconsistencies. The appellate court set aside USC's findings as a result. Obviously, a student who could not afford to pay an attorney to challenge USC's finding, and further pay an attorney through an appeals process, would not have been so fortunate. It is also worth noting that the college panel may have been inclined to punish John as it was powerless over the two students who struck and penetrated Jane.

If the USC case shows how lack of due process increases the risk of an erroneous error in a case filled with ambiguities, *Doe v. Amherst*[64] demonstrates how a lack of due process can produce a likely erroneous result by missing crucial evidence. In this case "Doe" was a young man expelled from Amherst College after the college found that he forced a young woman "Sandra Jones" to have oral sex with him. The college investigation failed to discover a series of text messages between Jones and her friend "DR" that seemed to exonerate Doe:

SANDRA JONES: Ohmygod I jus did something so f-ckig stupid
DR: What did you do
SANDRA JONES: F-cked [Doe] . . . . F-ck
DR: No you didn't . . . .
SANDRA JONES: official story is he puked and I took care of him but yes. Yes I did. F-ck
DR: [Sandra] what are you doing????????
SANDRA JONES: Oh and apparently [another student i]s coming over so nothing happened everything's fine."[65]

In the text messages, Jones tells her friend that because Doe was her roommate's boyfriend, her roommate "would literally never speak to me again." Jones texted her friend that other students in the common area, where she and Doe were making out, were "not gonna believe that we left to NOT f-ck." She was also concerned that Doe was "too drunk to make a good lie out of shit."[66] She also texted that "It's pretty obvi [obvious] I wasn't an innocent bystander."[67]

Further, earlier that night Jones had invited another male student to come to her room to "entertain" her. She texted him again shortly after her encounter with Doe, telling him that she had just engaged in some "sophomore floor bonding" because she thought the second student was "a lost cause." The second student did come over, and Jones kept up a running text commentary to her friend complaining that the second male student was not being sexually aggressive enough:

[64] D.C. Mass. Case 3:15-cv-30097.
[65] Jessica Denis, "Title IX and College Rape: A Series of Injustice Part 4," www.huffingtonpost.com/jessica-denis/title-ix-and-college-rape_3_b_11976002.html.
[66] Johnson and Taylor, *The Campus Rape Frenzy*, 1.
[67] Walter Robinson, "Expelled under New Policy, Ex-Amherst College Student Files Suit," *Boston Globe* (May 29, 2015).

> Ok Why is he just talking to me?
> Like, hot girl in a slutty dress. Make. Your. Move. YEAH.
> Ohmygod action did not happen til 5 in the f-cking morning.[68]

The investigator hired by the college failed to obtain the texts and submitted a report stating that Jones "did not email, text, or otherwise reduce what happened with [Doe] to writing." According to the *Boston Globe* "During the 2013 hearing, Jones's roommate testified that she had learned Jones had exchanged text messages with a resident dorm counselor just after the alleged rape. But the school made no effort to contact the counselor or obtain the texts, according to the hearing record."[69] Doe had no opportunity to directly question Jones. Doe was expelled, and the texts only came to light when Doe brought a federal court action.[70] As in the previous case, a student who couldn't afford an attorney would not have had that opportunity.

So, we can see that whether the case involves genuinely different perspectives or crucial missing evidence, lack of due process creates a strong likelihood of erroneous results.

Finally, it should be noted that lack of due process can also produce erroneous results in the other direction – failing to protect students who have likely been sexually assaulted. In Chapter 1, we saw a case in which a woman, Anna, who had apparently been gang raped was forced to testify before a panel that did not have the results of her rape kit, most of whom had not read the report of the trauma nurse, and that asked her about a report she had never seen. Anna is certainly not the only alleged rape victim who sought help from her university only to find herself suddenly struggling to spontaneously respond to important evidence that she should have been allowed to examine well ahead of time. In a case at Stanford University, a sophomore who alleged that she was raped by a Stanford football player was not shown the player's statement until the night before the hearing. The document she first saw the night before the hearing also contained new statements from two of the player's teammates. She requested a postponement of the hearing to review the documents and to request a redaction of statements she believed were prejudicial against her, but the request was denied.

Furthermore, the accused student was allowed to make what she believed were speculative statements on why she might be "targeting" him. Her lawyer was not allowed to speak at the hearing or to object to speculative or prejudicial testimony, so she submitted follow-up questions to the panel to ask the accused student, but those were also denied.

---

[68] Johnson and Taylor, *The Campus Rape Frenzy*, 2.

[69] Walter Robinson, "Expelled under New Policy, Ex-Amherst College Student Files Suit," *Boston Globe* (May 29, 2015).

[70] Johnson and Taylor, *The Campus Rape Frenzy*, 5–7.

Despite all this, three of the five panelists concluded that she had in fact been raped by the accused student, but Stanford requires at least a 4–1 ruling. The accused has not received any punishment.[71]

In short, whether the accused student is seemingly guilty, seemingly innocent, or it all comes down to difficult interpretations of largely agreed upon facts, lack of due process greatly increases the possibility of erroneous decision making. As shown in the previous section, the liberty interests in these cases are very high. The strength of the student's interests at stake, and the likelihood of their erroneous deprivation are the first two prongs of the *Mathews* balancing test. The third prong is "the Government's interest, including the function involved and the fiscal and administrative burdens that the additional or substitute procedural requirement would entail." This last prong is discussed in the next section.

The Costs of Due Process

The fear that allowing accused students the right to legal representation or allowing them other due process rights could drive up college costs has been a major theme in relevant litigation. For example, in *Hart v. Ferris State College*, a student, Dorothy Hart was facing expulsion from a campus tribunal on charges of selling marijuana and argued that she was entitled to due process prior to expulsion.

Citing the *Dixon* case, the federal judge ruled in favor of Ferris State to limit due process, reasoning:

[T]he administrative burden would not be insubstantial. A more active role by counsel would inevitably be more intrusive from the College's point of view. If plaintiff's counsel were permitted to cross-examine witnesses, the College might well find it desirable to have counsel ready to represent its own interests in insuring that witnesses not be harassed and that plaintiff's witnesses be subjected to equally searching cross-examination. The entire character of the hearing could easily be escalated into a fully adversary proceeding. As the landmark *Dixon* decision recognized, a full-dress judicial hearing, including the right to cross-examine witnesses, "with the attending publicity and disturbance of college activities, might be detrimental to the college's educational atmosphere and impractical to carry out."[72]

In a federal appellate case, another court raised similar concerns about the "university's fisc."

[W]e do not think he is entitled to be represented in the sense of having a lawyer who is permitted to examine or cross-examine o witnesses, to submit and object to documents,

---

[71] All factual descriptions of this case are from Joe Trope and Marc Tracy, "A Majority Agreed She Was Raped by a Stanford Football Player: That Wasn't Enough," *New York Times* (December 29, 2016).

[72] 557 F. Supp. 1379, 1388 (W.D. Mich. 1983).

to address the tribunal, and otherwise to perform the traditional function of a trial lawyer. To recognize such a right would force student disciplinary proceedings into the mold of adversary litigation. The university would have to hire its own lawyer to prosecute these cases and no doubt lawyers would also be dragged in – from the law faculty or elsewhere – to serve as judges. The cost and complexity of such proceedings would be increased, to the detriment of discipline as well as of the university's fisc.[73]

This section argues that concerns over the cost associated with due process are greatly exaggerated and should not be seen as a reason to deny students due process rights to protect their vital interests. First, while the previously mentioned courts focus on legal representation and cross-examination, admittedly two very important rights, most elements of due process are not likely to impose significant costs on colleges and universities. Requiring universities to reveal exonerating evidence that they already have in their possession costs them little or nothing. The same is true for most of the due process issues discussed so far: granting access to investigator's notes, allowing accused students to review evidence prior to the hearing, giving the accused student a clear statement of the charges and evidence against him, requiring the panel to read the report of the trauma nurse, waiting until the results of the rape kit are available, and so forth.

As for due process rights that do impose costs, these costs are not unreasonable. Many universities have enormous budgets and any due process costs would represent only the tiniest sliver of those budgets. The annual budget of the University of Michigan, for example, was well more than eight billion dollars in 2017/2018.[74] Universities in smaller states have smaller budgets than the University of Michigan, but they are far from small. For example, the 2017–2018 operating budget for the University of Indiana was $3.5 billion.[75]

Of course, it is true that there are smaller colleges and universities with smaller budgets, but there is no reason that such schools have to bear all the costs incurred by instituting due process on their own. John Banzhaf, a public interest law professor at George Washington University, has proposed a very workable consortium approach:

Banzhaf's proposal, however, would be to set up an independent organization funded and shared by schools in a geographic area, akin to a consortium of universities that shares everything from library books to teaching staff. Colleges in a specific area, such as in and around the nation's capital, would pool funding to finance a team of experts fully trained in investigating campus sexual assault.

If adjudication is deemed necessary, the schools could refer a case to an independent arbitration panel set up to hear it and mete out punishments.

---

[73] Osteen v. Henley, 13 F.3d 221, 223 (7th Cir. 1993).

[74] University of Michigan FY 2017–2018 Budget, http://obp.umich.edu/wp-content/uploads/pub-data/budget/greybooksummary_fy18_allcamp.pdf.

[75] "Indiana University Trustees Approve Operating Budget for 2017–18," https://news.iu.edu/stories/2017/06/iu/releases/16-operating-budget.html.

"They could afford to have to keep on staff two or three or four people because they are covering 30 to 40 colleges. They would have the training, they would have the expertise, to interview the victims fairly and properly, to get and preserve the evidence, and to do so in a completely impartial way," Banzhaf said.[76]

Such an approach would be far preferable to denying students important due process rights. Also, as Banzhaf notes, allowing the consortium to hire the investigator and panel chair would avoid the conflict of interest problems that arise when university employees must decide if there has been wrongdoing by their own university.

Further, there is a strong likelihood that greater due process rights would *reduce* costs to colleges and universities by decreasing college litigation. There is an increasing trend of students suing universities over procedurally lacking sexual assault hearings, especially by students believing they were wrongly found responsible, but also by complainants who are dismayed at the university's process:

The unprecedented pace of sexual misconduct-related cases filed against colleges and universities shows no signs of abating. Since January 2014, 42 lawsuits involving student-on-student sexual misconduct have been filed against colleges and universities. Moreover, institutions are increasingly facing so-called "reverse Title IX" cases with respondents, or accused students, seeking to overturn an adverse disciplinary decision … . The prospect of these reverse Title IX cases further weighs in favor of institutions preparing themselves for possible litigation from the moment they receive a report of student-on-student sexual assault.[77]

The costs to a university found to have violated a student's due process rights can be enormous. In a 2018 decision, the magistrate assessed James Madison University $849,231.25 in legal costs for a case that was decided on the pleadings and did not even proceed to trial, which would have greatly increased those costs.[78]

In a better world, all this litigation might lead university attorneys to advise their clients to afford their students full due process rights. After all, allowing a student to examine a police report before demanding that she answer questions about it, or allowing an accused student access to the investigator's notes, is obviously far less expensive than litigating those issues after the college has ruled. Unfortunately, universities are getting some very different advice, including advice to destroy internal documents to make it harder for students to sue their schools. In 2016, the National Association of College and University Attorneys wrote:

[76] Tierney Sneed, "Is This the Solution to the Campus Rape Conundrum?," *USNews.com* (March 16, 2105), www.usnews.com/news/articles/2015/03/16/is-this-the-solution-to-the-campus-rape-conundrum.
[77] Wood et al., "Between a Rock and Hard Place," 2 (citations omitted, emphasis added).
[78] Doe v. Alger, www.vawd.uscourts.gov/OPINIONS/HOPPE/rrfees.pdf.

Against this backdrop is an oppositional question. General counsel and senior administrators should consider what the institution does not want to retain – unless and until the
institution is required to retain everything because litigation is now reasonably anticipated. Many e-mails – as well as staff notes that precede an investigation report, notes of
hearing participants during a disciplinary hearing, drafts of hearing outcome reports,
and other such working papers – might actually prove very useful to a plaintiff's lawyer
who may wish to argue that the institution acted in an inconsistent manner or that
assertions of institutional witnesses are inconsistent with contemporaneous working
drafts. *For that reason, it would be prudent to retain a "master set" of all final reports,
proceedings, and outcome documents, and promptly destroy the various preliminary
and personal documents.* That way, the institution will have a single, consistent record
that is not contradicted or undermined by the institution's own files.[79]

It is a mistake to view the interests of students and universities in such an
oppositional manner. Respecting due process is in the best interests of the
accusing and accused students and, as one court put it, of the "university's fisc."

Finally, any such costs should be regarded as a cost of doing business that
colleges and universities should be expected to bear. Protecting students from
sexual violence and wrongful expulsion or suspension is a core educational
responsibility. Colleges and universities spend vast sums on luxury amenities as
a result of market forces.[80] Due process rights are obviously not as visible to
prospective students as rock-climbing walls and lazy rivers,[81] so market forces
channel money to these sorts of amenities. Therefore, it is the responsibility of
the courts to ensure that colleges put some money aside not to cheat students of
their due process rights.

CONCLUSION

The courts should hold colleges and universities to a much higher standard for
due process in investigating and adjudicating accusations of sexual assault.
The current situation serves neither the accused nor accusing students, or even
the economic interests of the college. It leaves wrongly accused students
vulnerable to temporary or permanent disruption of their education, grave
economic and reputational damage, and, in some cases, deportation or
coerced confessions of criminal activity. Lack of due process can also result in
the bullying of and lack of justice for students who have been sexually assaulted,
and it can severely undermine the ability of panels to effectively adjudicate

[79] Wood et al., "Between a Rock and Hard Place," 6 (emphasis added).
[80] See Brian Jacob, Brian McCall, and Kevin M. Stange, "College as Country Club: Do Colleges
Cater to Students' Preferences for Consumption?," NBER Working Paper Series (2013), www
.nber.org/papers/w18745.pdf.
[81] See Cara Newlon, "The College Amenities Arms Race," *Forbes* (July 31, 2014), www.forbes
.com/sites/caranewlon/2014/07/31/the-college-amenities-arms-race/#513638674883 for numerous
examples of these sort of expensive, luxury amenities.

situations loaded with ambiguity and difficult questions of interpretation. Thus it hurts the victim and accused alike and undermines the panels.

Therefore it is clear that all three prongs of the *Mathews* balancing test weigh in favor of strengthening due process rights in campus sexual assault investigations and adjudications. The students' interests are extremely strong, the lack of due process undermines the college's ability to make correct determinations, and the costs are less burdensome than many courts seem to assume.

Chapters 4 and 5 will look at each major issue of due process individually, but first, Chapter 3 will examine the question of due process in private colleges and universities. It will argue that, under at least two different legal theories, these colleges should be held to the same high standards of due process as their public counterparts.

Two final points should be made here. This chapter discusses public universities much the way that it would discuss any other government entity. However, even without judicial intervention, universities should ask themselves whether they have an even greater obligation than other government actors to provide due process. What message does it send when colleges, much less law schools, fail to give students a full opportunity to present facts and arguments? Even should these arguments fail to convince, private universities should seriously consider whether the very nature of being a university obligates them to provide the same due process as public universities do, just as most private colleges protect academic freedom even though the First Amendment does not apply to them.

3

Due Process and Private Universities

The previous chapter argued that, under the Constitution, public universities should be held to a much higher standard than they are for due process when they investigate and adjudicate allegations of peer-to-peer sexual assault. Three-quarters of college students in America attend public universities.[1] But, with more than 20 million students attending American universities, this still means that millions of students are enrolled in private colleges and universities. This chapter argues that these students should be protected by the same, or at least very similar, due process rights as public university students. Two theories will be discussed: (1) universities' lack of due process should be read by the courts as a violation of Title IX, the federal law forbidding gender discrimination; and (2) due process should be legally incorporated into universities' contractual agreements with students under a doctrine called "contracts of adhesion."

LACK OF DUE PROCESS AS TITLE IX GENDER DISCRIMINATION

This section argues that because virtually all the students sanctioned by colleges for sexual assault are male,[2] lack of due process in this area amounts to Title IX gender discrimination. This is especially true because, as we will see, gender stereotypes pervade many aspects of the process, ranging from the underlying legislation, to the cultural norms and unsupported empirical assumptions that lead to only male students being charged with sexual assault, to the training materials relied upon by sexual assault panels.

Before beginning discussion on this issue, it is important to note that this section is not intended as an addition to the "gender wars" literature or to the archive of writings criticizing feminism and political correctness. There are a

---

[1] Lynn O'Shaughnessy, "20 Surprising Higher Education Facts," *US News* (September 6, 2011), www.usnews.com/education/blogs/the-college-solution/2011/09/06/20-surprising-higher-education-facts.

[2] Report of United Educators, "Confronting Campus Sexual Assault," 3.

great many barriers to survivors of sexual assault receiving the protection they need. As discussed in Chapter 1, too many police departments are insufficiently responsive, especially to nonviolent sexual assaults. We also saw that, in many states, rape laws are unconscionably narrow.

Nevertheless, none of these problems mean that lack of due process in college tribunals cannot be considered gender discrimination. As Laura Kipnis writes: "There are plenty of cases where unequivocal sexual assaults happen and the system fails to deal with it – especially when it comes to athletes and frats – even as there are shocking prosecutorial excesses in other situations. There's no coherence to the situation."[3]

The simple fact is that virtually all the accused students are men, so an unfair process, as a matter of common sense, discriminates against male students. Perhaps people are slow to recognize this because of an assumption that men are always the victimizer and women are overwhelmingly often the victim, which makes a system in which all the accused students are male seem natural. In fact, *it is not the case at all* that victims of sexual assault are nearly always female or that assaulters are nearly always male. This may sound surprising given the tenor of media coverage, but a review of the most reliable statistics available demonstrates that, when it comes to gender and sexual assault, the situation is far more complex than the public discussion would indicate.

Lara Stemple and Ilan Meyer reviewed the evidence from the Center for Disease Control and Prevention and the Bureau of Justice Statistics (the research arm of the Federal Department of Justice) and published their findings in the *American Journal of Public Health*, which is the leading public health journal in the country. They found that rates of sexual victimization among men and women are not as dramatically different as the popular discourse would suggest:

To explore patterns of sexual victimization and gender, we examined 5 sets of federal agency survey data on this topic (Table 1). In particular, we show that 12-month prevalence data from 2 new sets of surveys conducted, independently, by the Centers for Disease Control and Prevention (CDC) and the Bureau of Justice Statistics (BJS) *found widespread sexual victimization among men in the United States, with some forms of victimization roughly equal to those experienced by women.*[4]

Numerous other studies have found that male college students are sexually assaulted at a surprisingly high rate.[5]

[3] Laura Kipnis, *Unwanted Advances* (New York: HarperCollins, 2017), 17.
[4] Lara Stemple and Ilan H. Meyer, "The Sexual Victimization of Men in America: New Data Challenge Old Assumptions," *American Journal of Public Health* 104, no. 6 (June 2014),e19–e26. doi: 10.2105/AJPH.2014.301946 (emphasis added).
[5] See Denise Hines et al., "Gender Differences Sexual Assault Victimization among College Students," in Roland Maiuro, ed., *Perspectives on College Sexual Assault* (New York: Springer Publishing, 2015), 29–30 and studies cited therein (stating that while rates of sexual assault or women are twice that for men "the rates among men are concerning . . . [and] we found no gender

Given the prevailing narrative, one might expect that sexual violence against men is nearly always perpetrated by other men. However, when Meyer, a Williams Distinguished Senior Scholar for Public Policy at the Williams Institute for Sexual Orientation Law and Public Policy at UCLA School of Law, and Stemple, Director of the UCLA Health and Human Rights Law Project, looked at the data:

The results were surprising. For example, the CDC's nationally representative data revealed that over one year, men and women were equally likely to experience nonconsensual sex, and *most male victims reported female perpetrators*. Over their lifetime, 79 percent of men who were "made to penetrate" someone else (a form of rape, in the view of most researchers) reported female perpetrators. Likewise, *most men who experienced sexual coercion and unwanted sexual contact had female perpetrators*.

We also pooled four years of the National Crime Victimization Survey (NCVS) data and found that 35 percent of male victims who experienced rape or sexual assault reported at least one female perpetrator. Among those who were raped or sexually assaulted by a woman, 58 percent of male victims and 41 percent of female victims reported that the incident involved a violent attack, *meaning the female perpetrator hit, knocked down or otherwise attacked the victim, many of whom reported injuries.*[6]

It should be made clear that Stemple and Meyer's data were not limited to college students (although it does separate out data from juvenile and prison populations), so it does not rule out the possibility that college women might be less likely to be perpetrators than other women. It does mean that we should not simply assume that the fact that virtually all students punished by colleges for sexual assault are men reflects the reality of who is assaulting whom. It is significantly more likely to be the result of stereotypes about male sexual aggressiveness and female sexual passivity:

Despite such findings, contemporary depictions of sexual victimization reinforce the stereotypical sexual victimization paradigm, comprising male perpetrators and female victims. As we demonstrate, the reality concerning sexual victimization and gender is more complex.[7]

Sexual assault is a complicated issue and no single study is definitive. But the narrative of male perpetrators and female victims has been so widely accepted that it can cause researchers to simply build that assumption into their survey instruments. Until 2013, the Federal Bureau of Investigation's *Uniform Crime Report* defined rape as something that could only happen to females: "the carnal knowledge of a female forcibly and against her will."[8] The definition

---

differences in the prevalence of forced or threatened sexual intercourse or in the victims' reports that they were too intoxicated to consent to sexual intercourse").

[6] Lara Stemple and Ilan H. Meyer, "Sexual Victimization by Women Is More Common Than Previously Known," *Scientific American* (October 10, 2017), www.scientificamerican.com/article/sexual-victimization-by-women-is-more-common-than-previously-known/ (emphasis added).

[7] Stemple and Meyer, "The Sexual Victimization of Men in America," 31.

[8] https://ucr.fbi.gov/crime-in-the-u.s/2016/crime-in-the-u.s.-2016/topic-pages/rape.

was since updated but still requires "penetration." The *National Intimate Partner Sexual Violence Survey* also suffers from this problem. Thus, if a man forces a woman to have penile/vaginal sex that is defined as rape. So, if a woman forces a man to commit the very same act, logically that should also be defined as rape, but it isn't because the man was not penetrated. Because of this imbalance, the survey reports that if a man is raped, it is almost always by another man. This hides that fact that when a man is forced to do the penetrating, the perpetrator is most often a woman:

> The majority of male rape victims (93.3%) reported only male perpetrators. For three of the other forms of sexual violence, a majority of male victims reported only female perpetrators: being made to penetrate (79.2%), sexual coercion (83.6%), and unwanted sexual contact (53.1%).[9]

According to the data from the *National Intimate Partner Sexual Violence Survey 2010–2012 State Report*, the number of women forcing men to engage in sexual intercourse is shockingly similar to the number of men who force women to engage in sexual intercourse.[10] To be clear, the argument here is not that men and women commit sexual assault at the same rate. One could argue that a woman forcing sexual intercourse on a man is fundamentally different than a man forcing a woman. Further, there are disparities between reported data for "12-month prevalence" and "lifetime" numbers of sexual assault that are difficult to interpret. Nonetheless, it is indisputable that women commit a very significant amount of sexual assault against men. A variety of biases in public perception and the survey instruments means that we not in a position to making sweeping generalizations about gender and sexual assault. And most importantly for purposes of this discussion, we see that the fact that virtually all the accused students are male cannot simply be assumed to be the result of some sort of uniquely predatory aspect to male nature. Rather, the overwhelming perception of sexual assault victims as female and attackers as male is the result of bias in the survey instruments as well as cultural stereotypes such as male "invincibility" and men as "sexually insatiable."[11]

One might counter that the reason all the accused are men, even if significant numbers of men are sexually assaulted by women, is that men are just not bringing complaints to their colleges. However, it is very likely that this reluctance is a product of deeply sexist stereotypes that should not be countenanced by the law:

> Portraying male victimization as aberrant or harmless also adds to the stigmatization of men who face sexual victimization. Sexual victimization can be a stigmatizing experience for both men and women. However, through decades of feminist-led struggle, fallacies

---

[9] www.cdc.gov/ViolencePrevention/pdf/NISVS_Report2010-a.pdf, 24.

[10] Compare tables A.1 and A.5 in Appendix A, https://ucr.fbi.gov/crime-in-the-u.s/2016/crime-in-the-u.s.-2016/topic-pages/rape.

[11] Stemple and Meyer "The Sexual Victimization of Men in America" at 33.

described as "rape myths" have been largely discredited in American society .... For men, a similar discourse has not been developed ... Feelings of embarrassment, the victim's fear that he will not be believed, and the belief that reporting itself is unmasculine have all been cited as reasons for male resistance to reporting sexual victimization. Popular media also reflects insensitivity, if not callousness, toward male victims. For example, a 2009 CBS News report about a serial rapist who raped 4 men concluded, "No one has been seriously hurt."[12]

These stereotypes contribute to a system where male students are extremely unlikely to file complaints for sexual assault:

The minimization of male sexual victimization and the hesitancy of victims to come forward may also contribute to a paucity of legal action concerning male sexual victimization. Although state laws have become more gender neutral, criminal prosecution for the sexual victimization of men remains rare and has been attributed to a lack of concern for male victims. The faulty assertion that male victimization is uncommon has also been used to justify the exclusion of men and boys in scholarship on sexual victimization. Perhaps such widespread exclusion itself causes male victims to assume they are alone in their experience, thereby fueling underreporting.[13]

As Stemple and Meyer point out, society is awash with stereotypes that discourage men from reporting sexual victimization, ranging from jokes about "not bending over in the shower" to sweeping generalizations about male sexuality.

In fact, because many college sexual assault cases involve heavy use of alcohol, it is possible that sexual assault of men by women is especially unlikely to be taken seriously in a college context. There is a widespread assumption that sexual assault by incapacitation can never occur against a male because men who are drunk to the point of incapacitation cannot have erections:

Brett Sokolow, the man who's emerged as the country's leading consultant on campus rape adjudications [and] president and CEO of the risk management firm the NCHERM Group, is the guy that schools call when they need to figure out how to comply with Title IX and fend off civil rights lawsuits from students .... argues that the onus being put on men is not about gender bias, but about anatomy. His report says that "*courts operate on the presumption that if a man is able to engage in and complete the act of sexual intercourse, he is not incapacitated.*" Or as [Laura Dunn, founder and executive director of SurvJustice, a nonprofit that advocates for sexual assault survivors] put it: "*People who are truly incapacitated can't get erections.*"[14]

These assertions, which justify the assumption that if two very drunken students of different genders have sexual contact then the man must be the assailant, lack empirical foundation. "Despite initial evidence to the contrary, high blood

---

[12] Stemple and Meyer, "The Sexual Victimization of Men in America."
[13] Id. (citations omitted).
[14] Amanda Hess, "How Drunk Is Too Drunk to Have Sex," *The Slate* (February 11, 2015), www .slate.com/articles/double_x/doublex/2015/02/drunk_sex_on_campus_universities_are_struggling_ to_determine_when_intoxicated.html (emphasis added).

alcohol concentration (BAC) – particularly .08% and above does not seem to attenuate erectile tumescence reliably . . . . the attenuation effect is far from universal, having occurred in fewer than half of studies on alcohol and erectile response."[15]

Furthermore, not only is gender bias reflected in cultural stereotypes and unsupported empirical assumptions, it is also reflected in the very words of the relevant law. The main federal law mandating reporting of sexual assaults on college campuses, The Jeanne Clery Disclosure of Campus Security Policy and Campus Crime Statistics Act, is named after a female victim of sexual violence. It was most recently expanded by a law entitled The Violence Against Women Reauthorization Act. Note that such a law could have easily been more neutrally titled the "Gender Based Violence Act," but it wasn't.[16] The assumption that victims of sexual violence are women and not men is encoded in the very laws that require its measurement.

In addition, there is evidence that the materials used to train members of college sexual assault panels frequently contain sexually discriminatory material. Training materials are generally not made public so the following examples, which are the subjects of litigation, may not be fully representative. Nonetheless, the fact that major universities and colleges are relying on these materials is certainly a red flag.

For example, the training materials for Ohio State University, the third-largest university in the United States,[17] include the statements, "sex offenders are overwhelmingly white males," "in large study of college men, 8.8% admitted rape or attempted rape," and "22–57% of college men report perpetrating a form of sexually aggressive behavior."[18] The training materials at Stanford University tell panelists to be "very, very cautious in accepting a man's claim that he has been wrongly accused of abuse or violence."[19] Similarly, the training materials at Middlebury College are also rife with gender stereotypes and gender-based assumptions about whom the attackers and victims are. The accused may not be "who he says he is" and if the accusing student's account of the facts changes, panelists should not be deterred by "inconsistencies in her story."[20] Obviously, these training materials are loaded with presumptions about which gender is the attacker and which is the

---

[15] William H. George et al., "Alcohol and Erectile Response: The Effects of High Dosage in the Context of Demands to Maximize Sexual Arousal," *Exp Clin Psychopharmacol* 14, no. 4 (November 2006): 461–470 (citations omitted).

[16] The string of federal legislation mandating reporting of sexual assault is complicated, as federal mandates tend to be. The Campus Sexual Violence Act amended the Clery Act "to add new crime reporting requirements specifically related to sexual assault, domestic violence, dating violence and stalking" (Napolitano, *"Only Yes Means Yes"*). The Campus Sexual Violence Act is a provision of the Violence Against Women Reauthorization Act of 2013.

[17] www.worldatlas.com/articles/largest-universities-in-the-united-states.html.

[18] Doe v. the Ohio State University (S.D. Ohio 02/22/16) Case No. 2:15-cv-2830.

[19] Johnson and Taylor, *The Campus Rape Frenzy*, 148.   [20] Id. at 150.

victim. This is particular noteworthy in an academic context, where there is normally an admirable sensitivity to gender assumptions embedded in language.

Even high-level administrators at major universities can make astoundingly gendered claims and suffer no consequence or push back. Testifying in a lawsuit in 2014, Sue Wasiolek, Duke University's Dean of Students and Assistant Vice President for Student Affairs, was willing to state flat out: "Assuming it is a male and female, it is the responsibility of the male to gain consent before proceeding with sex."[21] Despite the fact that such a statement is blatantly gender discriminatory, Dean Wasiolek still held the same position at the time this book was written. There is no indication that Dean Wasiolek has ever been called upon to retract this statement, nor is there any record of any of her peers at other institutions publicly contradicting her. At Duke, highly gendered messages about who the victims of sexual assault are go beyond the comments of a single dean. Students "of any gender" who have experienced sexual assault are directed to the university's Women's Center.[22]

Universities, which are normally highly aware of gender diversity issues, can also have blind spots about lack of gender diversity in this context. In the 2015 "Annual Report of the Judicial Codes Counselor," Amanda Minikus, the Judicial Codes Counselor for Cornell University, reported that gender imbalances in the sexual assault adjudicatory process are so egregious that they threaten the fairness and accuracy of investigations. She noted, among other things:

- All lead investigators in the judicial administrator's office are women;
- The judicial administrator, who signs and approves every report, is also a woman;
- Although 3 of 15 available assistant investigators are men, none of them appear to have participated in a sexual assault investigation at Cornell;
- When a male student is asked by a room full of women to "describe graphic encounters or his sexual habits, as is often required … he may feel embarrassed, unable to candidly express himself, and feel compelled to describe events in a way that he believes female investigators will find less offensive."[23]

As noted, universities are generally sensitive to issues of diversity, power imbalances, and gender dynamics. Yet, in Cornell's case, it took an independent review to point out that it is not appropriate to have an all-female panel questioning a male student about intimate sexual details. It is

---

[21] John H. Tucker, "A Duke Senior Sues the University after Being Expelled over Allegations of Sexual Misconduct," *Indy Week* (May 28, 2014), www.indyweek.com/indyweek/a-duke-senior-sues-the-university-after-being-expelled-over-allegations-of-sexual-misconduct/Content?oid=4171302.

[22] https://studentaffairs.duke.edu/wc/gender-violence.

[23] Amanda L. Minikus, "Annual Report of the Judicial Codes Counselor" (May 31, 2016), 36.

almost impossible to imagine a major university like Cornell failing to notice the problem if female students were routinely being required to describe their sexual activity to rooms full of only men.

While lack of data makes statistical analysis impossible, numerous cases demonstrate the willingness of panels to attribute the active role to men and the passive or "sexually innocent" role to women despite circumstances that seem to demonstrate the opposite. In an illustrative case at Occidental College, numerous witnesses reported that two college freshmen, "John and Jane," were both drunk. Witnesses reported that "Jane was grabbing John and trying to kiss him" and that John was "not at all going for her" and that Jane got on top of John and was "kind of riding on top of John ... her hips moving." Later that night, after Jane had left with two friends, the following text exchange occurred:

JOHN: The second that you're away from them, come back
JANE: Okay
JOHN: Get the f-ck back here.
JANE: They're still with me o
JOHN: Make them leave. Tell them yoy want to sleep. I'dc. [I don't care.] Just get back here
JANE: Okay do you have a condom
JOHN: Yes.
JANE: Good give me two minutes
JOHN: Come here.
JANE: Coming
JOHN: Good girl.
JOHN: Knock when you're here

After making sure that John had a condom and letting him know that she needed a few minutes to get away from her friends, Jane texted another friend "I'm wasted" and "I'm going to have sex now." After she and John had sex, she texted a "smiley face" to another friend.[24]

Nevertheless, the college adjudicator, Marilou Mirkovic, found that Jane was too drunk to consent to sexual activity and that John was therefore responsible for sexual assault. John described the hearing room as follows:

"I was in a room full of women, and there's a crying girl with a lengthy speech about how I sexually assaulted her, and she broke down in tears," he says. "And looking around, I saw the look on all these women's faces, and they're relating. My adjudicator, hired by the school, I saw the look on her face and I'm like, *That's not good.*"[25]

---

[24] Richard Dormant, "Occidental Justice: The Disastrous Fallout When Drunk Sex Meets Academic Bureaucracy," *Esquire* (March 25, 2015), www.esquire.com/news-politics/a33751/occidental-justice-case/. According to the article: "All statements and recollections attributed to [Jane] are from the investigators' report ... [and] ... All observations attributed to witnesses in this story, as well as texts cited, are taken from that report."

[25] Id.

The investigator acknowledged that John was also very drunk at the time of the sexual encounter and, as a result, was not in a position to assess how drunk Jane was: "[John] was more intoxicated than he had ever been … this level of intoxication so impaired [John's] ability to assess [Jane's] incapacitation that he did not have actual knowledge of [her] incapacitation." However, the college found that while Jane's drunkenness meant she could not consent to sexual activity, John's drunkenness was irrelevant: "being intoxicated or impaired by drugs or alcohol is never an excuse for sexual harassment, sexual violence … and does not diminish one's responsibility to obtain consent."[26] John was expelled.

In another case, *Yu v. Vassar College*, the President of Vassar College, Catherine Hill, was concerned enough to e-mail the college dean, "It is very scary though. Two drunk kids, both out of it. Is it always the male at risk?" The dean dodged the question stating that the investigator only reported that the female complainant was drunk, not the male accused student. In fact, Yu had claimed that he was also drunk and pointed to witnesses he said would confirm that. The investigator did not include those witness statements in his report because "he did not find [them] to be important."[27] Also, the panel was specifically trained not to consider the level of the accused's intoxication. At the time of the lawsuit no female student at Vassar had ever been charged with sexual misconduct. Nonetheless, the court concluded: "Although there may well be a double standard regarding how the school regards intoxication levels by a complainant and a respondent, it is not based in gender."[28]

In her widely reviewed book, *Unwanted Advances: Sexual Paranoia Comes to Campus*, Laura Kipnis writes about the widespread acceptance of gender stereotypes in academia:

To begin with, the endangerment story produces huge blind spots, which are reproduced in every new policy and code supposedly meant to reduce unwanted sex. The policies are ineffectual because the endangerment story and the realities of sexual assault are two entirely separate things. That's blind spot number one. About those realities: the under-lying gender dynamic is blind spot number two – the dynamic between men and women. I mean men *and* women. What I'm saying is that policies and codes that bolster tradi-tional femininity – which has always favored stories about female endangerment over stories about female agency – are the *last* thing in the world that's going to reduce sexual assault, which is the argument at the heart of this book.[29]

As Kipnis also points out, the "women in peril" narrative calls for a hero to save those women, and narratives of heroism are strongly tied to narratives of vigilantism.[30] This is hardly a mind-set conducive to due process.

In sum, there are a great many red flags regarding gender discrimination. Therefore, in cases in which the accused student demonstrates that the sexual assault adjudicatory process was biased against the accused, this should be

---

[26] Id. at 3 (citing the investigator's final report to the college).
[27] Yu v. Vassar College (SDNY March 31, 2015) No. 13-cv-4373 at 11, n. 4.
[28] Yu v. Vassar College at 46–47.   [29] Kipnis, *Unwanted Advances*, 9.   [30] Id. at 10.

viewed as gender discrimination. To hold in such cases that the accused just happened to be male and that, absent a smoking gun of some sort, a demonstrably biased process is not gender discrimination flies in the face of common sense and justice.

Nonetheless, that is exactly what courts have consistently held. Unlike Title VII, which prohibits discrimination, including gender discrimination, in employment, housing, and public accommodations, Title IX does not allow "disparate impact" lawsuits.[31] Under a disparate impact theory, a plaintiff can sue if he or she can show that a policy or practice has a disproportionately negative impact on one particular race, ethnicity, or gender. Because this theory of liability is not available under Title IX, courts are not willing to make any assumptions about gender discrimination even though the accused students are virtually always male.

So, what do students have to establish to bring a gender discrimination claim if they have been found responsible for sexual assault? First, they must establish the university's decision was "erroneous" or that there is "selective enforcement" of university policies.[32] For the reasons discussed so far, there are many cases in which the student can demonstrate flawed processes that may lead to erroneous outcomes. The key barrier to such suits is the next step. The plaintiff must "allege particular circumstances that demonstrate that gender bias was a motivating factor behind the erroneous findings."[33] As disparate impact claims are not allowed, a student bringing a selective enforcement claim must also show specific facts that demonstrate that the gender imbalance is motivated by gender bias.[34]

This requirement of a smoking gun is inappropriately high. For example in *Doe v. Case Western Reserve University*, a student suspended for one year for sexual assault alleged numerous violations of due process that the court found "establish[ed] a plausible claim that Plaintiff was innocent of the charges against him and that CWRU wrongly found that Plaintiff committed the offense." However, Doe's complaint was dismissed because he could not demonstrate that "CWRU actions 'were motivated by sexual bias' ... [or show] ... that a female was in circumstance sufficiently similar to [plaintiff's] and was treated more favorably by the university."[35]

This case demonstrates the impossibly high bar for such suits. Doe could not possibly find an accused female student in similar circumstances who was treated more favorably than he was because there are virtually no female

---

[31] Doe v. Rector & Visitors of George Mason Univ., No. 1:15-CV- 209, 2015 WL 5553855, (E.D. Va. Sept. 16, 2015).

[32] Yusuf v. Vassar College, 35 F. 3d 709, 714–15 (2d Cir. 1994).   [33] Id. at 715.

[34] Emily D. Safko, *Are Campus Sexual Assault Tribunals Fair? The Need for Judicial Review and Additional Due Process Protections in Light of the New Case Law*, 84 Fordham Law Review 2289–2333, 2312 (2016).

[35] John Doe v. Case Western Reserve University (N. District Ohio 2015) Case No.1:14CV2044 at 11.

accused students. Rather than the gender imbalance putting the court on alert that gender bias might be occurring, the court instead allowed the imbalance to impose an insurmountable obstacle to bringing a suit absent some sort of overt statement such as the one made by Duke's dean of students.

Further, courts have repeatedly ruled that even if the accused student demonstrates that the procedures were biased against him, this is not enough to prevail. A bias against accused students is not the same as bias against males even though virtually all the accused students are males. For example, in *Sahm v. Miami University*, a federal judge held that:

However, these facts pleaded against [the investigator] do not suggest a gender bias against males so much as against students accused of sexual assault. Demonstrating that a university official is biased in favor of the alleged victims of sexual assault claims, and against the alleged perpetrators, is not the equivalent of demonstrating bias against male students.[36]

Similarly, a federal judge in Indiana ruled that "a bias against accused students ... says nothing about gender."[37] And in *Haley v. Va. Commonwealth University*, a federal judge ruled that "a bias against people accused of sexual harassment and in favor of victims ... indicate[s] nothing about gender discrimination."[38]

Further, even when there is some of sort of smoking gun, such as gender-biased statements by a university's top judicial officer, this *still does not demonstrate gender bias* unless the student can somehow prove that the bias affected the outcome of his hearing. In a federal appellate case, the court held: "[G]ender-biased statements made by the university's Director of Judiciaries did not taint the proceedings because the plaintiff did not show how the Director could have influenced tribunal's decision."[39]

The law here is the inverse of what it should be. Students in a system where virtually all the accused students are male should not be required to find nonexistent accused female students who were treated more fairly than they were. And courts should recognize that where all the accused students are of the same gender, bias against the accused is indeed bias on the basis of gender.

One federal appellate court has a taken an important step in the right direction. In *Doe v. Columbia*, a student was found responsible for subjecting a female student to "unreasonable pressure" to engage in sexual activity and was suspended for one and a half years. Doe alleged that the female student suggested that they have sex in the bathroom of her suite and that she left him there while she got a condom from her room. He alleged that the panel's procedures were biased against him in numerous ways and that gender bias

---

[36] Case No. 1:14-cv-698 at 7–8

[37] King v. DePauw University, CAUSE NO. 2:14-cv-70-WTL-DKL (S.D. Ind. Aug. 22, 2014) at 18.

[38] 948 F. Supp. 573, 579 (E.D. Va. 1996).

[39] Mallory v. Ohio Univ., 76 F. App'x. 634, 640 (6th Cir. 2003). Cited in Doe v. Washington and Lee (W.D. Virginia August 5, 2015) Case No. 6:14-cv-00052 at 18.

was a factor. The federal district court dismissed his suit because even if the process was biased against students accused of sexual assault:

[any bias in favor of Jane Doe] could equally have been – *and more plausibly was* – prompted by lawful, independent goals, such as a desire (enhanced, perhaps, by the fear of negative publicity or Title IX liability to the victims of sexual assault) to take allegations of rape on campus seriously and to treat complainants with a high degree of sensitivity.[40]

The district court opinion reflects the high bar for gender discrimination cases. Even if the university is biased, and even if that bias results from fear of bad publicity or Title IX liability, according to the district court, this is not gender bias under Title IX. The appellate court overturned the district court:

The Complaint alleges that, having been severely criticized in the student body and in the public press for toleration of sexual assault of female students, Columbia was motivated in this instance to accept the female's accusation of sexual assault and reject the male's claim of consent, so as to show the student body and the public that the University is serious about protecting female students from sexual assault by male students – especially varsity athletes. There is nothing implausible or unreasonable about the Complaint's suggested inference that the panel adopted a biased stance in favor of the accusing female and against the defending male varsity athlete in order to avoid further fanning the criticisms that Columbia turned a blind eye to such assaults.[41]

The appellate court added: "A defendant is not excused from liability for discrimination because the discriminatory motivation does not result from a discriminatory heart, but rather from a desire to avoid practical disadvantages that might result from unbiased action."[42] This seems like common sense. Indeed, the courts should go further. Given all the red flags discussed in the preceding text, clearly biased procedures should be considered a violation of Title IX without further proof of a "discriminatory heart."

In sum, college apparatuses set up to investigate and adjudicate sexual assault are highly gendered. As discussed, this is a system in which virtually all accused students are male despite evidence that this does not reflect reality. Universities are operating under enormous pressure to show that they are not tolerant of what the law calls "violence against women." Unfounded assertions about alcohol and male inability to sexually perform support automatic attribution of responsibility for drunken sex to male students. Gender-based stereotypes are found in training materials of major universities and colleges and a major university's dean of students can assert, without public challenge from her peers, that it is a man's job to assure the sexual consent of a woman.

While the burden should certainly remain on the accused student to demonstrate that the procedures were biased against him, once he has met that burden, it defies common sense to require him to further demonstrate

[40] Doe v. Columbia Univ., 101 F. Supp. 3d 356, 371 (S.D.N.Y. 2015) (emphasis added).
[41] 831 F. 3d 46, 57–58 (2016).   [42] 831 F. 3d at 58, n. 11.

that some sort of stereotypical, irrational hatred of men motivated the decision rather than the "practical concerns" about bad publicity or liability discussed in *Doe v. Columbia* that motivated the bias.

What would be the result? The most straightforward result would be that the courts would read Title IX to require fair process to students accused of sexual assault. Demonstrably biased process would be presumptive gender bias. It would promote clarity and uniformity for the courts to require the same standards for private and public universities. Title IX would be interpreted to apply constitutional standards of due process to private universities.

Finally, it should be clear that the inverse is true as well. If an assaulted student is denied fair process, that should also be considered a violation of Title IX. If a woman goes before a panel that hasn't reviewed the evidence, as in the William and Hobart Smith Colleges case, or doesn't let the woman see crucial testimony until the day before the hearing, as in the *Stanford* case,[43] this violates that woman's right to fair process, even though both those schools are private. If, as the Office of Civil Rights (OCR) has repeatedly stated, it is a violation of Title IX to inadequately investigate allegations of sexual assault, then how could it not be a violation to inadequately adjudicate those cases?

DUE PROCESS AND THE LAW OF CONTRACTS

"When called upon to review the disciplinary procedures of private colleges and universities, courts have struggled to find a legal theory upon which to base their reviews . . . . [but] courts most often have employed contract law principles when reviewing university disciplinary procedures."[44] However, courts are reluctant to interfere in the student/university relationship and therefore have adopted a "relaxed" contract approach, in which the court declines to treat the student/university relationship as just another commercial relationship and allows the university a great deal of discretion.

"Courts applying a relaxed or quasi-contract approach have articulated that private schools should incorporate a requirement of 'fundamental' or 'basic' fairness in disciplinary proceedings."[45] This approach provides minimum protection and few, if any, decisions applying this approach ever side with the student claiming a contract breach.[46]

Indeed, courts can interpret provisions so leniently as to deny what the court calls "rudimentary concepts of fairness." In one federal case, the student handbook stated that substantiating materials such as texts, e-mails, witness

---

[43] These cases are discussed in Chapters 1 and 2, respectively.
[44] J. Freidl, *Punishing Students for Non-Academic Misconduct*, 26, no. 4 Journal of College and University Law 710–726, 712 (2000).
[45] Id. at 722.
[46] Stephen Henrick, *A Hostile Environment for Student Defendants: Title IX and Sexual Assault on College Campuses*, 40 Northern Kentucky Law Review 49–92, 77 (2013). ("However, during

names, and so forth, "should" be provided by the accuser to the school. Although the university refused to provide the accused student with any of this information (and the fact that the university did have the information in its possession) the federal judge ruled that the word *should* makes it "by no means clear that the accuser is required to do so, or that there is any consequences for failing to do so. And there is nothing in the handbook that requires the university to share that information with the accused."[47]

Therefore, the accused had to attempt to defend himself without any of this critical information even though the court wrote that "[s]uch a refusal was unfortunate at best" and was contrary to "the most rudimentary concepts of fairness."[48]

The fundamental fairness approach does, however, at least require that the school inform the student about what he is charged with. It certainly allows universities to enforce rules that are difficult to understand. In *Fellheimer v. Middlebury College*, the court found that the charge of "disrespect for persons" was not so vague as to violate fundamental fairness. However, the university does have to at least let the student know what the charge is. Middlebury had only charged the student with sexual assault and had not found that he had committed sexual assault. The *Fellheimer* court found that it violated fundamental fairness to then punish a student for "disrespect for persons" – a violation that he had never been charged with.[49]

However, decisions such as *Fellheimer* are a rarity. Absent such a complete failure to give a student an opportunity to defend himself, courts have held that private institutions are "entitled to a very strong but rebuttable presumption that its internal administrative actions are taken in good faith."[50]

This section argues that the courts should take the opposite tack, and view student handbooks as "contracts of adhesion." While this would apply to both public and private universities, it is especially important for private university students because they are not currently protected from their universities by the Constitution. Under this interpretation, the courts should not consider student handbooks as freely negotiated contracts but rather as a situation in which "the weaker party [is] being drawn, as a moth to the flame, into a self-destructive arrangement, one that he is powerless to escape."[51] This leads to the completely opposite approach to the "relaxed" contract approach, which assumes good faith on the part of university administrators. Instead, it views the college as the stronger, more sophisticated party that imposes terms and conditions on the

his research the author was unable to find a single case of an accused student successfully pursuing a 'fundamental fairness' claim.")
[47] Doe v. Brandeis, Civ. Action No. 15-11557-FDS (3/31/16 Dist. Ct. Mass.) at 49.
[48] Id. at 594.   [49] 869 F. Supp. 238, 245 (D. Vermont 1994).
[50] Ahlum v. Adm'rs of Tulane Educ. Fund, 617 So. 2d 96, 98 (La. Ct. App. 1993).
[51] Curtis J. Berger and Vivian Berger, *Academic Discipline: A Guide to Fair Process for the University Student*, 99, no. 2 Columbia Law Review 289–364, 329 (March 1999).

weaker party: the student. Therefore, the priority of the courts in contract of adhesion situations is to protect the rights of the weaker party.

The contracts of adhesion approach is far more realistic about the power dynamics and incentives of the parties than is the relaxed contract approach. The relaxed contract approach's assumption of the benevolence and good faith of university administrators is hopelessly out of date, if, indeed, there were ever a golden era in which it were accurate. If nothing else, fear of litigation is a powerful motivation for administrators to put the university's bottom line ahead of the rights of accused students.

Also, universities are under enormous pressure to demonstrate that they do not tolerate sexual assault on campus. Just being investigated by the OCR can exact a high cost financially and in terms of bad publicity. Assuming that an administrator's highest priority will always be the fair treatment of students lacks empirical support and flies in the face of the many contradictory examples we see throughout this book. This does not mean that administrators are "bad people," just that, like all people, they are affected by concerns over liability and bad publicity. Meanwhile, student handbooks meet virtually every element of a classic contract of adhesion, in which the courts seek to protect the weaker party.

Elements of a Contract of Adhesion

It is useful to think of contractual relations as a continuum. At one end of the continuum is a bargain between two sophisticated parties of equal power. Both parties actively bargain over the terms of the contract, with each one receiving something of value for everything he or she gives up, and the parties strive to make reasonable compromises to produce an optimal result. Both parties have a clear understanding of what is in the contract and the potential consequences of what they are negotiating. Both sides have considerable expertise or are represented by someone who does.

On the other end of the continuum is a great inequality of power, knowledge, sophistication, and representation. One party, usually with the aid of counsel, drafts all of the terms of the contract. That party is in a sufficiently strong position to refuse to alter any of the terms of the proffered contract. The other party not only lacks the sophistication to understand the terms of the contract and its implications, but also is unlikely to even read the contract, due to its length, complexity, and the weaker party's lack of any life experience that would impress upon him or her the importance of wading through complicated contractual terms. This situation, at the most imbalanced end of the continuum, is called a contract of adhesion. For obvious reasons, courts are far more likely to go beyond the "four corners of the contract" to protect the weaker party in these cases.

The student handbooks at virtually all colleges meet every element of a contract of adhesion. The essential elements of such a contract are (as described in a case in which the stronger party inserted a clause into the contract in which the weaker party waived any right to sue the stronger party):

(1) the business is of a type generally thought suitable for public regulation;
(2) the party seeking exculpation is engaged in performing a service of great importance to the public, one that is often a matter of practical necessity for some members of the public;
(3) the party is willing to perform this service for any member of the public coming within certain established standards;
(4) because of the essential nature of the service and the economic setting of the transaction, the party invoking exculpation possesses a decisive advantage of bargaining strength against members of the public seeking such service; and
(5) in exercising a superior bargaining power, the party confronts the public with a standardized contract of adhesion.[52]

In terms of the first element, "the business is of a type generally thought suitable for public regulation," it is self-evident that higher education is a business of this sort.

The second element, "the party seeking exculpation is engaged in performing a service of great importance to the public, one that is often a matter of practical necessity for some members of the public," is also straightforward. Who could argue today that higher education is not a "practical necessity for some members of the public"? It is not realistic that the typical college applicant could simply decide not to attend college at all if colleges refuse to negotiate the terms of their handbooks. Nor is it realistic that the millions of students currently attending private universities could all just transfer to public universities.

The third element is also clearly met. With a few narrow exceptions for single-sex and very religious colleges, institutions of higher education are open to anyone who meets their admissions criteria. They are not private clubs.

There can also be little argument about the fourth element, which is "because of the essential nature of the service and the economic setting of the transaction, the party invoking exculpation possesses a decisive advantage of bargaining strength against members of the public seeking such service." Obviously, an incoming first-year student does not have a true opportunity to negotiate the terms of the student handbook. Can one even imagine a college individually negotiating handbook terms with hundreds or thousands of incoming students?

Worse yet, even if a student read every word of the handbooks of every college to which he or she applied and based their choice of college on what they read, the college could unilaterally change the terms of the handbook after they enrolled. In *Doe v. Brandeis*,[53] the student handbook included ample procedural rights at the time that Doe entered Brandeis. It granted accused

---

[52] Ibid., 327.   [53] Civil Action 15-11557-FDS (Dist. MA 2016).

students a hearing in which they could present and examine witnesses, present verbal arguments, bring an advisor of their choice, and remain silent if they chose. The university had to prove allegations by "clear and convincing evidence" (the "seventy-five percent" standard).

During his time at Brandeis, John Doe was accused of sexual assault, but by the time of his adjudication, most of the previously mentioned rights were gone from the handbook. In fact, there was no right to a hearing at all, and virtually all John Doe's other procedural rights were stripped away:

> The [new] process differed from [old] process significantly. It did not provide for a "hearing" in any sense of the word. Instead, the university would appoint a Special Examiner, who would investigate the claims and make a recommendation to the Dean of Student Life. The accused was given the opportunity to meet (separately) with the Special Examiner during the investigation and submit his own evidence, but was provided with little else in terms of procedural protections .... There was no requirement ... that the accused be informed of the "details of the charges" ... [or] that copies of any "substantiating materials" by the accuser, or the names of any witnesses, be shown or provided to the accused at any time ... The accused was no longer informed of his or her "rights to procedural fairness." The accused had no right to confront or cross-examine the accuser, no right to call witnesses, and no right to confront of cross-examine the accuser's witnesses. The accused had no right to review all of the evidence."[54]

Despite all this, the federal court refused to hold that these sweeping changes in the handbook rules constituted a breach of contract. The court instead held that "John and Brandeis entered into a new contractual relationship each academic year."[55]

In fact, it is currently perfectly legal for a college to draft its handbook in a manner that allows it to unilaterally change the rules at any time, not just at the beginning of a new academic year. For example, in *Millien v. Colby College*,[56] a student was cleared of charges of sexual assault by the Dean's Hearing Board. Although there was no provision in the student handbook to conduct a second hearing, the dean took the case to an appeals board, which conducted a "de novo" review (which means that it conducted a hearing as though the previous hearing had never happened) and found the student responsible for sexual assault. The student brought a lawsuit for breach of contract, but the court ruled against him, citing the handbook's "reservation clause that gives Colby the right to unilaterally alter the terms of the handbook without notice to students."[57]

In short, a student's bargaining power is virtually zero. Even in the very unlikely circumstance that a student shopped around for colleges with amenable procedures for adjudicating sexual assault, the college would be able to change the rules at its own discretion.

---

[54] Id. at 21.   [55] Id. at 54, n.23.   [56] 874 A.2d 397 (2005).   [57] 874 A.2d. at 400.

The fifth and final element of a contract of adhesion is also obviously present: "[I]n exercising a superior bargaining power, the party confronts the public with a standardized contract of adhesion." This is exactly the situation at every college. The student does not negotiate the handbook; he or she is simply presented with it.

In addition to all five of the elements of a contract of adhesion being met, there are additional factors that call for the courts to protect the rights of college students. College students are usually far more youthful and inexperienced than the college officials who draft the student handbooks. Those officials are likely advised by attorneys, while the students are not. Colleges have an indefinite time frame to think through the ramifications of every provision of the handbook, while the student has a far more compressed time frame to review all of the factors that go into his or her choice of college. And most students are likely to be far more focused on factors such as financial aid, academics, internship and athletic opportunities, living conditions, and many other issues.

In sum, college handbooks easily meet every element of a contract of adhesion and are paradigm case of where courts cannot realistically assume they represent the informed will of the parties. Surprisingly, courts have paid almost no attention to the adhesionary aspects of college/student contracts. This is especially peculiar because courts have not been shy about protecting consumers from adhesionary contracts in other areas. For example, the federal appellate court for the Ninth Circuit, which covers the entire West Coast including California, has struck down a mandatory arbitration clause foisted upon cellular customers under a contract of adhesion theory.[58] If cell phone customers cannot sign their right to fair process away in a contract of adhesion, why should the court not give students the same protection?

It is one thing to defer to campus authorities on academic matters. A judge should not be second-guessing an English professor's evaluation of a student's essay on Shakespeare, nor a math professor's evaluation of a student's theorem. That would jeopardize academic freedom and pull the judge outside or his or her area of expertise. But for student misconduct procedures, we are well away from professors' academic freedom or area of expertise. Students are closer to the position of ordinary consumers of an essential service who deserve, at a minimum, the same protection as cell phone customers.

Under the "relaxed" contract approach, courts have upheld the minimalistic protections described previously, so long as the results are not "arbitrary and capricious." In the leading article discussing contracts of adhesion in the academic disciplinary context, Columbia law professors Curtis and Vivian Berger argue that the "arbitrary and capricious" standard is far too

---

[58] Shroyer v. New Cingular Wireless Services, Inc., 498 F. 3d 976 (9th Cir. 2007). "Thus, contrary to Cingular's contention, a contract may be procedurally unconscionable under California law when the party with substantially greater bargaining power 'presents a "take-it-or-leave it" contract to a customer – even if the customer has a meaningful choice as to service providers.'"

deferential to universities. They argue such a standard is appropriate when the courts are reviewing the decision of an agency that has more expertise than the court regarding the matter at hand. This would be the case if the courts were reviewing, say, a professor's determination that a student's argument in a research paper was not original or of high quality. But for determining whether an impermissible sexual act occurred, there is no reason for such deference:

> "Arbitrary and capricious" is an administrative review standard. It is also the standard that courts have ordinarily used when testing the dismissal of a student for academic failure. This test seems appropriate where the agency's or school's decision calls for an expert judgment in the area in which the institution, not the court, has greater expertise. But where a student's career may be at stake because of an academic "crime," akin to fraud or copyright infringement, matters courts handle as fact-finders routinely, colleges should not enjoy quite the same degree of deference.[59]

What rights should students be entitled to, then, when charged with a serious crime such as sexual assault? Berger and Berger argue that where the student is charged with "the academic equivalent of criminal fraud [which is significantly less serious than being charged with sexual assault] the process should *contain most of the safeguards provided by the constitution for persons charged with an ordinary crime.*"[60]

Berger and Berger's suggestions seem to be the best approach, although perhaps, civil cases would be a better model than criminal cases. Under the contracts of adhesion approach courts should require private universities the same due process rights that public universities must grant their students. This would greatly increase certainty and uniformity of the law. All college students would receive the same procedural protections, whether they attended public or private universities.

It is important to remember that this would not interfere with the right of private universities to set their own standards for sexual conduct. Conservative religious institutions could continue to restrict sexual activity on campus if they so choose, and colleges could punish sexual acts, such as intercourse with an incapacitated person, even when those acts were not criminal in the schools' home states. But all students would receive the same level of protection against being punished for something they did not do, and all assault victims would have the same procedural protections as well.

This would be far superior to the status quo where courts have upheld grossly unfair procedures under the "relaxed contract" approach. A good example would be the case of *Schaer v. Brandeis* in which one student was found responsible for raping another student. The panel allowed extremely prejudicial testimony, such as a witness who called the accused student a "self-motivated egotistical bastard" and another witness, "a Brandeis police

---

[59] Berger and Berger, *Academic Discipline*, 334.   [60] Id. at 335 (emphasis added).

officer, [who] testified that she saw the complainant one month after the incident and that she 'looked like a rape victim.'" The Supreme Judicial Court of Massachusetts found no contractual problem with this testimony, writing:

> Although these statements would be excluded from a courtroom under the rules of evidence, a university is not required to abide by the same rules. Brandeis may choose to admit all statements by every witness or it may choose to exclude some evidence. It is not the business of lawyers and judges to tell universities what statements they may consider and what statements they must reject. We conclude that admission of these statements does not constitute a violation of the contract. The facts alleged do not show that Schaer was denied basic fairness.[61]

The court was also remarkably dismissive of Schaer's right to a record of the hearing that would allow him to appeal. Although the Brandeis handbook required the panel to produce a record summarizing the testimony and evidence at the hearing, and even though there were 13 witnesses, the panel produced a record of the proceedings that was only 12 lines in length. Under the "relaxed" approach, the court batted aside Schaer's claim that his contractual right to a record for appeal was violated, writing that the handbook does not "require the record to be any minimum length."[62] As the dissenting justices pointed out: "While it is true that the provision does not set a minimum length requirement, it does require a summary of the testimony and evidence. A claim is adequate that alleges that a twelve-line record does not summarize a hearing with thirteen witnesses."

Such shoddy protections of due process are grossly inadequate for students accused of an act as serious as sexual assault. The idea that these illusory protections are what the students contractually bargained for flies in the face of reality. Because these contracts are textbook contracts of adhesion, the courts should harmonize due process protections for public and private college students to provide uniformity and predictability of procedural requirements that would serve all parties' interests.

CONCLUSION

Private universities are currently held to an inadequate standard in investigating and adjudicating peer-to-peer sexual assault. Courts should not allow the pretense that a biased system that punishes only males does not violate Title IX's requirement of gender equality or that student handbooks are freely bargained contracts enforced by ever-benevolent administrators.

The best measurement of fair process for private universities is the constitutional standard for public universities under the *Mathews* test. As discussed in the previous chapter, that test balances three factors that are all just as relevant to private universities as they are to public universities. The test

[61] 432 Mass. 474, 481 (2000).   [62] Id. at 480.

looks first at the importance of the student's interest in not being erroneously found responsible for sexual assault (or not having the assaulting student erroneously exonerated). Then the test looks at the likelihood of an erroneous finding given the process provided and the benefit of better process in avoiding such an error. Third, the test examines the costs and administrative burden of the additional process and the interests of the university in efficient adjudication. All these factors are just as applicable to private universities as to public ones.

What about specifics? To what kind of process, exactly, are students entitled? The next two chapters delve into the specifics of due process.

PART II

WHAT PROCESS IS DUE?

4

Due Process Prior to the Hearing

In Chapter 2 we saw that all the elements of the Supreme Court's constitutional test for due process point in the direction of stronger protections for students when colleges investigate and adjudicate allegations of sexual assault. In Chapter 3 we saw that there are statutory and contractual arguments for applying the same or similar standards of due process to private universities. But what does this mean in concrete terms? In *Anderson v. Massachusetts Institute of Technology*, a Massachusetts Superior Court suggested that "fundamental fairness" means that "at the very least":

- The student should be provided written notice of the charges against him;
- A written description of the evidence upon which the charges are based;
- The names of the witnesses the school intends to call at the hearing;
- An unbiased disciplinary committee or tribunal;
- An opportunity to be heard and present witnesses in his behalf;
- And the right to confront and controvert the evidence presented by the university.[1]

These are all important elements of due process, but there are others as well. Because there are many elements to due process, this chapter will discuss only the elements that are primarily relevant to the time frame before any hearing begins. The next chapter will discuss the hearing and the appeals process. There is some overlap between the two categories, and, because the Court requires that we look at the whole process, each element is not an isolated issue. For example, the question of burden of proof depends in part upon what other protections are in place to prevent inappropriate guesswork on the part of hearing panelists.

---

[1] Lisa Tenerowicz, *Student Misconduct at Private Colleges and Universities: A Roadmap for "Fundamental Fairness" in Disciplinary Proceedings*, 42 B.C.L. Rev. 653 (2001), http://law-digitalcommons.bc.edu/bclr/vol42/iss3/4.

THE RIGHT TO A HEARING

The first issue is whether the accused student has a right to a hearing in the first place. The idea that a student accused of sexual assault is entitled to a hearing before being punished should be uncontroversial. The seminal case setting a minimum standard for college due process, *Dixon v. Alabama State Board of Education*, could not have been clearer on this point:

By its nature, a charge of misconduct, as opposed to a failure to meet the scholastic standards of the college, depends upon a collection of the facts concerning the charged misconduct, easily colored by the point of view of the witnesses. In such circumstances, a hearing which gives the Board or the administrative authorities of the college an opportunity to hear both sides in considerable detail is best suited to protect the rights of all involved.[2]

Nonetheless, many universities deny accused students the right to anything that can reasonably be called a hearing.[3] In an illustrative case involving two University of Michigan students, the accused student, Jason Sterrett was found responsible for sexual assault without a hearing.[4] As a first-year student during the 2011/2012 academic year, he had a sexual encounter with another Michigan student, "CB." As described by Emily Yoffe in *Slate*, CB first came in to contact with Heather Cowan, an Equal Opportunity Specialist at Michigan, under the following circumstances:

The events that prompted the university to take these actions against Sterrett are detailed in an affidavit sworn on Sterrett's behalf by LC, a friend of CB's and her sophomore year roommate. LC stated that in July she received a call from an "emotionally upset" CB who explained that her mother had found her diary. LC recalled that CB explained that the diary "contained descriptions of romantic and sexual experiences, drug use, and drinking." (CB confirmed the contents of the diary in her own deposition.) During the phone call, CB asked LC if she remembered the night CB had sex with Sterrett. LC didn't, because CB had never mentioned it. Now CB told her, "I said no, no, and then I gave in." Eventually, as described in CB's deposition, CB's mother called the university to report that CB would be making a complaint against Sterrett. CB's mother drove her to campus, and CB met with Heather Cowan.[5]

Over the summer of 2012, Sterrett was contacted to set up a Skype interview with Cowan and another administrator later that day but was not told anything about the subject except that it regarded an unspecified student complaint.[6] During the Skype interview he realized the seriousness of the situation and "he

[2] 294 F. 2d 150, 158–59 (5th Cir. 1961).
[3] The 2017 interim guidelines ("Q & A on Campus Sexual Misconduct") issued by the Trump administration do not require a hearing. They allow colleges to make findings of fact and conclusions of responsibility "with or without a hearing," www2.ed.gov/about/offices/list/ocr/docs/qa-title-ix-201709.pdf.
[4] Sterrett v. Cowan et al. (E.D. Michigan) Case No. 14-cv-11619 (March 9, 2015).
[5] Yoffe, "The College Rape Overcorrection."   [6] Sterrett v. Cowan at 3.

asked the administrators if he should consult a lawyer. He says they told him that if he ended the interview to seek counsel that fact would be reported to the university and the investigation would continue without his input."[7]

As a result, he agreed to continue the interview without knowing the specifics of the charges and without aid of counsel. Cowan subsequently interviewed "four unnamed witnesses" and, in September 2012, produced a one-page report "Summary of Witness Testimony and Other Evidence" that Sterrett was allowed to examine. He was allowed to respond to the report in writing but was not allowed to speak with the witnesses, hear their actual testimony, or learn their identities. Cowan then responded to his response in writing, and he, in turn, gave a written response to her. He requested an opportunity to testify under oath but was not given that chance.[8]

Based on the preceding, Cowan found Sterrett responsible for sexual misconduct in a Final Report on November 30. On December 6, Sterrett met with Vander Velde, the Associate Director for the Office of Student Conflict Resolution, and was thereafter allowed to submit a letter objecting to Cowan's findings and the school's process. Cowan agreed to reinterview Sterrett's roommate, and then issued an addendum stating her conclusions where unaltered.

Velde then provided Sterrett a "Resolution Agreement" drafted by a number of other administrators asking him to agree to a three-and-half-year suspension, plus probation when he returned, and a permanent sexual misconduct finding on his educational record. Sterrett refused and the vice president eventually imposed the sanctions anyway. He tried to transfer to another university, which initially accepted him but withdrew the acceptance when it learned of his suspension.[9]

Sterrett brought an action in federal court, claiming, among other things, that he was denied a right to a hearing. The University of Michigan moved to dismiss the suit. The judge strongly implied that the meeting with Velde satisfied the right to hearing, but the complaint would not be dismissed because Sterrett was denied the right to a hearing prior to Cowan's issuing the Final Report:

Although the allegations in the Complaint show Sterrett was able to "respond, explain and defend" the alleged misconduct against him in various writings and had the opportunity to meet in person with Vander Velde, Sterrett has stated a plausible claim that he was denied a "hearing" prior to Cowan's November 30, 2012 Final Report and Findings.[10]

The classic definition of a hearing comes from Professor Kenneth Culp Davis's 1958 *Administrative Law Treatise*: "any oral proceeding before a tribunal."[11] A contemporary definition of *hearing* from a law dictionary is:

---

[7] Yoffe, "The College Rape Overcorrection."   [8] Sterrett v. Cowan at 4–5.
[9] Yoffe, "The College Rape Overcorrection."   [10] Sterrett v. Cowan at 18.
[11] Kenneth Culp Davis, *Administrative Law Treatise* (Eagan, MI: West Publishing, 1958), Sec. 701, at 407.

a proceeding of relative formality at which evidence and arguments may be presented on the matter at issue to be decided by a person or body having decision-making authority ... NOTE: *The purpose of a hearing is to provide the opportunity for each side of a dispute, and esp. a person who may be deprived of his or her rights, to present its position. A hearing, along with notice, is a fundamental part of procedural due process. Hearings are also held, as for example by a legislature or an administrative agency, for the purpose of gathering information and hearing the testimony of witnesses.*[12]

The Michigan case stretches the understanding of a hearing beyond its reasonable limits. A meeting with an administrator is not a hearing. The administrator already had a report concluding Sterrett committed sexual assault. At the meeting, Sterrett had no genuine opportunity to examine the basis of the Final Report, present his own evidence, or present or question witnesses. He did not even know who the witnesses against him were.

Sterrett's only real opportunity to present a meaningful defense was when he brought a federal lawsuit. With a meaningful process at work, the conclusions of the Final Report quickly unraveled. For example, Sterrett said his roommate was in the bunk bed right above his and heard the entire encounter. The Final Report asserted that the reason that the roommate didn't hear CB repeatedly say "no," as she claimed she did, was that the roommate was asleep during the encounter. The Final Report also asserted that Sterrett confessed to his roommate that he assaulted CB. Neither of these claims turned out to be true:

The report said that Sterrett's roommate was asleep during the entire sexual encounter. This was contradicted by the time-stamped Facebook message complaining that he was being kept awake. The report also said that Sterrett had confessed to his roommate that he'd had a nonconsensual encounter with CB. When Cowan interviewed the roommate – who says she never told him the purpose of her investigation – he had mentioned that Sterrett said he regretted the encounter with CB. In Cowan's report, that statement is described as a confession of sexual violation. But as the roommate clarified in his affidavit, Sterrett was not expressing "that he had done anything morally or legally or ethically wrong." He was expressing regret for sleeping with someone in their group of friends.[13]

In the face of the evidence of the Final Report's flaws, Michigan quickly reversed course, "agreeing to wipe his transcript clean of any disciplinary action, and if any 'third party' asks about Sterrett, Michigan has to say that he has no violations of the Student Sexual Misconduct Policy. In exchange, Sterrett is dropping his lawsuit against the school, and has agreed not to re-apply to the University of Michigan."[14]

---

[12] http://dictionary.findlaw.com/definition/hearing.html (emphasis in original).
[13] Yoffe, "The College Rape Overcorrection."
[14] Kate Wells, "University of Michigan Drops Sexual Assault Ruling against Former Student," *Michigan Radio* (September 14, 2015), http://michiganradio.org/post/university-michigan-drops-sexual-assault-ruling-against-former-student.

Lawsuits, however, are not an adequate substitute for a fair hearing in the first place. As Johnson and Taylor point out, only the wealthiest students have the resources to bring these lawsuits. Had Sterrett been an underprivileged scholarship student, he most likely would have had to wait years to resume his education and would have had to go through life marked as a sex offender on his academic record.

The practice of denying accused students a hearing is not uncommon. According to the *Atlanta Journal Constitution*, for example, "UGA and Georgia Tech [Georgia's two largest public universities] don't even use live hearings but compile notes from separate interviews with the accuser, the accused and any witnesses. The two schools have also abandoned panels to hear cases and rely instead on a single, highly-specialized individual to investigate, decide responsibility and impose the sanction."[15] At Cornell, there is a panel, but the accused student may not appear before it or present evidence to it – only the investigator does.[16]

In fact, universities have been under government pressure to move away from hearings and instead adopt a "single investigator" approach. The White House Council on Women and Girls strongly endorsed this approach in its report on combatting college sexual assault: "The Task Force's 'Not Alone' report extolls the 'single investigator' model in school adjudications of sexual violence. The model tasks a single trained investigator or investigative team to gather evidence, interview the parties and witnesses, and render a finding or recommendation."[17] The idea is to create a quicker, less difficult process by eliminating the hearing:

Many procedures fall under the single investigator umbrella so long as a single entity investigates both the victim and the accused. Under these models, there is no hearing and therefore no cross-examination. Single investigator models eliminate the traumatic cross-examination process for the victim and cut down on lengthy, academically disruptive hearings because students need only coordinate with the investigator rather than appear in front of the board for the duration of the hearing.[18]

It is understandable why universities, even aside from government pressure, might be attracted to a single adjudicator model. Ideally, it can be less disruptive to students because they are not required to attend a hearing and can make their statements in a less formal setting. It means that the accused and accusing

---

[15] Shannon McCaffrey and Janel Davis, "Georgia Colleges Tread Where Prosecutors Won't, but Some Claim Secret Tribunals Unfair to the Accused," *The Atlanta Journal Constitution*, investigations.myajc.com/campusjudiciary/?icmp=AJC_internallink_081115_AJCtoMyAJC_college rape_special.

[16] Amanda L. Minikus, "Annual Report of the Judicial Codes Counselor" (May 31, 2016), 26.

[17] Charlotte Savino, "'Nobody's Saying We're Opposed to Complying': Barriers to University Compliance with VAWA and Title IX," Cornell Law Library Prize for Exemplary Student Research Papers. Paper 9, 12, http://scholarship.law.cornell.edu/cllsrp/9.

[18] Id. at 13 (citations omitted).

students are not in the same room at the same time. It relieves faculty and staff members from running hearings that they have little training or experience in conducting. It seems easier on everybody. Presumably this is why, as noted earlier, the interim guidance from the Trump administration does not require a hearing either.

Nonetheless, such a model deprives students of their right to a hearing and sharply limits their ability to meaningfully respond to the evidence against them. They have no right to directly present evidence to the panel that controls their fate or to make their arguments directly to them. They have no right to present evidence to the decision makers such as the timestamped Facebook message in the University of Michigan case that directly contradicted the report's statement that Sterrett's roommate was asleep during the encounter in question. And they have no right to present their own witnesses to the event, or to pose questions to witnesses against them. In cases such as Sterrett's, where the evidence comes from anonymous witnesses, it is impossible for the accused student to even understand the full case against him.

Even the most restrained model of the single investigator system, where the investigator makes a recommendation to the panel rather than deciding the case him- or herself, violates the student's right to a hearing. Even with the most fair-minded investigator in place, a single investigator is inherently incapable of fairly representing both sides. As Federal Judge Denis Saylor wrote: "The dangers of combining in a single individual the power to investigate, prosecute, and convict, with little effective power of review are obvious. No matter how well-intentioned, such a person may have preconceptions and biases, may make mistakes and may reach premature conclusions."[19]

This falls well short of the standards for due process. Courts should plainly hold that students are entitled to a hearing in which they have a meaningful opportunity to directly make their case to the people with the power to decide their fate, and they should not have all their arguments and evidence filtered through an investigator. Courts should make clear that no one person should be entrusted with this sort of power. An interview with an investigator is not a hearing.

This leaves many further questions. What are the student's rights at the hearing? What is the student entitled to know before the hearing begins? What should the burden of proof be? How can the student's right to an unbiased panel be protected? All these questions will be addressed in the following sections.

WHAT KIND OF A HEARING?

Justice Felix Frankfurter described the word *hearing* as "a verbal coat of too many colors,"[20] while Justice William Rehnquist noted, "the term 'hearing' in

---

[19] Doe v. Brandeis, Civil Action 15-11557-FDS (Dist. MA 2016) at 70.
[20] United States v. Tucker Truck Lines, 344 U.S. 39 (1959).

its legal context undoubtedly has a host of meanings."[21] This is a question that has been mired in uncertainty from its inception. Virtually all legal scholars agree that the 1970 Supreme Court case *Goldberg v. Kelly*[22] initiated the modern era of procedural due process when it required a hearing prior to the termination of welfare benefits, but that case sowed a great deal of confusion. In his classic statement on the issue, Judge Henry J. Friendly wrote, "*Goldberg v. Kelly* is the lodestar in this area, but it sheds an uncertain light. After the usual litany that the required hearing 'need not take the form of a judicial or quasi-judicial trial', Mr. Justice [William] Brennan proceeded to demand almost all the elements of one."[23]

The uncertainly is increased by the fact that it is difficult to apply the Supreme Court's case law on the constitutional requirements for hearings from other areas of law to the area of higher education. There are a number of cases in the area of public employment, but they are so contextually different from higher education that they offer little help. In many situations, a public employee has the right to a "full post-termination hearing" and, as a result, is entitled to less process prior to termination. For example, in *Cleveland v. Loudermill*, the Supreme Court held that a publicly employed security guard was entitled to "[t]he essential elements of due process [which] are notice and an opportunity to respond" but, importantly, added: "Our holding rests in part on the provisions of Ohio law for a full post-termination hearing."[24]

It should be noted though, that even with a full posttermination hearing available, the constitution still guarantees a public employee meaningful pretermination opportunity to respond to the allegations against him or her.[25]

There are some public employment cases in which the courts allowed for only minimal pretermination due process, but they involved contexts that cannot be analogized to higher education. For example, the Court upheld the summary removal of a police officer from his position after he had been arrested and charged with drug law violations.[26] This might have some application to cases in which a student was arrested for and charged with sexual assault but certainly could not be applied to students who have merely been accused. Also, in such situations, a student cannot reasonably be analogized to a position of very high public trust such as a police officer.

The Court's line of cases on procedural due process in the prison system is similarly unhelpful because prisoners inherently have limited liberty rights. In these cases, the plaintiffs are "[p]risoners held in lawful confinement [who] have their liberty curtailed by definition, so the procedural protections to which they are entitled are more limited than in cases where the right at stake is the

[21] United States v. Florida East Coast Ry., 410 U.S. 224, 239 (1973).   [22] 397 U.S. 254 (1970).
[23] Henry J. Friendly, *Some Kind of Hearing*, 123 University of Pennsylvania Law Review 1267–1317, 1299 (1975).
[24] 470 U.S. 532, 546 (1985).   [25] 470 U.S. 532, 548 (1985).   [26] 520 U.S. 924 (1997).

right to be free from confinement at all."[27] Even for prisoners though, the Supreme Court has been careful to ensure adequate process. In *Austin v. Wilkinson* the Supreme Court reviewed Ohio's procedures for sending a prisoner to a "supermax" prison. The Court upheld the procedures, approvingly noting that the process contained multiple levels of review, each of which could deny the transfer of the prisoner to a supermax prison, but none of which could overrule a decision *not* to transfer a prisoner to a supermax. As we will see in the next chapter, this is more protection than many students receive from college systems where a student found not to have committed sexual assault by the panel that heard his case can still be found responsible at a higher level.

The prison cases are a poor analogy to higher education cases for an additional reason. A full dress hearing including nonanonymous witnesses is far less practical in a prison setting because of the ever-present threat of violence to any prisoners who might testify at hearings on prison discipline:

Prison security, imperiled by the brutal reality of prison gangs, provides the backdrop of the State's interest .... Testifying against, or otherwise informing on, gang activities can invite one's own death sentence. It is worth noting in this regard that for prison gang members serving life sentences, some without the possibility of parole, the deterrent effects of ordinary criminal punishment may be substantially diminished.[28]

While the issue of witness intimidation can come up in the college context, obviously the situation is not analogous to the Hobbesian state of murder and terror described previously. Like public employment, the Court's prison due process cases shed little light on the issues discussed in this book.

Therefore, the best measure of the due process requirements for a college sexual assault hearing is to directly apply the three-part *Mathews* test discussed in Chapter 2. The three parts of the test go to the crux of the issues here. To review, the *Mathews* test balances (1) the importance of the interest at stake; (2) the risk of erroneous deprivation of the interest because of the process used and the probable value of additional safeguards; and (3) the government's interest in efficient adjudication and the burdens of any additional processes. In addition to being the constitutional standard for due process, these factors are commonsense questions to ask about process. Obviously, the importance of what is at stake, along with the likelihood of error and the benefit and costs of additional procedures, is highly relevant to the question of what procedural protections should be afforded.

As discussed in Chapter 2, all three prongs of this test point to greater protection of students' due process rights. But specifics matter. Colleges have many important interests at stake as well, especially protecting the safety and educational rights of students who allege that they were sexually assaulted.

[27] Wilkinson v. Austin, 544 U.S. 74 (2005).
[28] John W. Palmer, *Constitutional Rights of Prisoners* (New York: Routledge, 2015), 534.

And, of course, colleges are not courts. With that in mind, the next several sections look at some of the most important due process questions that arise prior to a hearing. The next chapter will examine issues regarding the hearing and thereafter.

The first issue addressed in the following text, regarding notice of charges, is arguably an easy question. After that the questions grow more difficult.

The Right to Effective Notice of Charges

There should be little dispute that students accused of serious wrongdoing are entitled to notice of the charges against them. As long ago declared in *Dixon v. Alabama State Board of Education*, "In the disciplining of college students there are no considerations of immediate danger to the public, or of peril to the national security, which should prevent the Board from exercising at least the fundamental principles of fairness *by giving the accused students notice of the charges and an opportunity to be heard in their own defense.*"[29]

The idea that an accused student should at least know the charges against him is so fundamental to due process, that it has been uncontroversially applied to private schools as well. In *Fellheimer v. Middlebury College*, a case discussed in the previous chapter, the court held that a student charged with, but found not guilty of, rape could not be found guilty of "disrespect of persons," without having been notified that he was being so charged.[30] The court found that the lack of notice was "fundamentally unfair."[31]

Courts should firmly enforce the requirement of notice of charges, defined as notice sufficient to allow the student to understand what facts, if proven, will result in his being disciplined. Applying the three *Mathews* standards, this is an easy question. As discussed in Chapter 2, the student's interest in avoiding an erroneous decision is very high. It seems self-evident that if a student does not know what facts are at issue, this makes it extremely difficult to defend against an erroneous result. Further, the college has no legitimate interest in keeping the student in the dark, nor is a clear notice of charges a drain on the resources of the university.

Clarity about the facts at issue should be the touchstone here. Universities should not be allowed to merely cite numerous sections of a handbook. Recall the case discussed in Chapter 2 of the University of Southern California student who was found responsible for encouraging two other students (from a different university) to violently slap the buttocks and otherwise exceed the consent of another student at an off-campus party and was also found responsible for endangering her by leaving her in the room with those two students. The only notice of charges the University of Southern California sent Doe was a letter informing him that he had allegedly violated 11 different sections of the

---

[29] 294 F. 2d 150, 157 (5th Cir. 1961) (emphasis added).   [30] 869 F. Supp. 238, 240 (1994).
[31] 869 F. Supp. at 246–47.

University of Southern California conduct code. As described by the appellate court:

On September 4, USC sent a letter to John stating, "A report has been received in this office that you allegedly have violated the University Student Conduct Code." It included the date of the incident, and the location as an off-campus fraternity event. The letter set out 11 different sections of the Student Conduct Code that John allegedly violated:

Section 11.32: "Conducting oneself in a manner that endangers the health or safety of oneself, other members or visitors within the university community or at university sponsored or related events."

Section 11.36A: "Causing physical harm to any person in the university community or at university-sponsored activities."

Section 11.36B: "Causing reasonable apprehension of harm to any person in the university community or at university-sponsored activities."

Section 11.38: "Behavior which disrupts or interferes with normal university or university-sponsored activities . . . ."

Section 11.40: "Unauthorized use, possession or dissemination of alcohol in the university community or at university-sponsored activities."

Section 11.44A: "Engaging in disruptive or disorderly conduct in the university community or at university-sponsored activities."

Section 11.44B: "Engaging in a [*sic*] lewd, indecent or obscene behavior in the university community or at university-sponsored activities."

Section 11.44C: "Encouraging or permitting others to engage in misconduct prohibited within the university community. Failing to confront and prevent the misconduct, notify an appropriate university official of the misconduct, or remove oneself from the situation."

Section 11.53A: "Engaging in non-consensual sexual conduct or lewd, indecent, or obscene behavior which is sexual in nature, within the university community or at university-sponsored activities."

Section 11.53B: "Non-consensual actual or attempted intercourse, sexual touching, fondling and/or groping."

Section 11.53C: "A sexual assault is classified as rape when vaginal, anal, or oral penetration takes place without the consent of the person penetrated."[32]

The court added:

The September 4 letter included no information about the incident that led to the alleged violations. The only hint that the accusation involved John's contact with Jane is that the letter instructed John to refrain from contacting or communicating with Jane. The letter also stated, "If you wish to inspect the report cited in this letter, you must make a written request to do so 24 hours in advance of the day you wish to review the report." It went on to say, "A summary of the procedures for this process is enclosed." No summary of procedures is included with the letter in the record on appeal.[33]

It is difficult to imagine how a student receiving such a lengthy and legalistic list of code violations could possibly defend himself. Throughout the process he

---

[32] Doe v. University of Southern California, 246 Cal. App. 4th 221, 229–230 (2016).
[33] Doe v. University of Southern California at 230.

believed that he was accused of sexually assaulting her by himself. While a section of the code cited did forbid "encouraging" misconduct, he had no notice that a crucial fact that would ultimately be at issue was whether his remarks about her body would be construed as encouraging a sexual assault. And even had he been a trained legal scholar, nothing in the letter could have put him on notice that his future hinged as well on the order in which he and the other two students left the room.

Colleges should not be permitted to simply write down a list of codes and leave students to guess what the facts at issue are. The standard should be a clear statement of what facts have been alleged and what facts, if proved true, would result in the student being disciplined.

Further, the notice of charges and underlying factual allegations must be *timely*. Notice is only useful if a student has an opportunity to respond to them. As Curtis and Vivian Berger note, it is certainly understandable that universities, and sometimes the students, want to move from complaint to resolution as quickly as possible:

Understandably, in most instances both the student charged with academic wrongdoing and the school bringing the charge want to resolve the complaint quickly. The student may be about to graduate, may have applications pending for post-graduate studies, may wish to register for a new semester, may be studying for exams; hence, any extended distraction or delay might seriously compromise her educational or professional future even if she is finally cleared.[34]

However, Berger and Berger caution that: "If the student decides to go to a hearing, fairness requires that she receive enough time to ready her defense." Unfortunately, many courts have been far too cavalier about allowing unrealistically short windows to respond to facts and allegation. For example, in *Yu v. Vassar College*, a student filed a complaint against a student one full year after the alleged incident. Numerous exchanges between the two students seemed to negate any inference that she felt endangered by him or that he was threatening her in any way. According to the court:

On February 19, 2013, the day after the incident, Yu sent a Facebook message to Complainant, saying "Hey, wish you didn't have a really bad hangover. I was really drunk last night and I feel maybe i was way too forward. I'd be more shy if i was more sober. I just want to make sure that you are okay." (Yu Decl. Ex. A at 4.) Complainant replied:

Peter, I was really drunk as well, don't worry I actually don't have a bad hang over today how about you? I realized I just am way too close to my previous relationship which was really serious so I can't date any one yet. I'm really sorry I led you on last night I should have known better then to let my self drink yet, I really don't want this to effect our team dynamic or friendship. I don't think any less of you at all I had a wonderful time last night I'm just too close to my previous relationship to be in one right now.[35]

---

[34] Berger and Berger, *Academic Discipline*, 345.   [35] 97 F. Supp. 3d 448, 455 (2015).

When Yu messaged her that a student had called security, she replied, "oh I'm really sorry! also did they write you up? . . . I will stand up for you because you were not[.]"

They continued to exchange cordial messages for some time. According to the court:

Approximately one month later, on March 20, 2012, Complainant sent Yu another Facebook message, saying:

Peter, I wanted to write to you to apologize for that night about two months ago, I have not been trying to avoid you since then. I am really sorry, it was very irresponsible of me to get drunk and do that with you. I really don't want it to effect our friendship or team dynamic . . . . I did not treat you very well, and it was disrespectful on my part to do what I did because I was drunk. I would really like to be your friend I think you are a really cool guy and I don't want this to get in the way! . . . [I]f you want to try to be friends I would really like that because you are also my team mate and I care about you and I never ever meant to hurt you and we were both drunk. I hope we can both put it behind us as a memory and learn from it . . . .

(*Id.* at 7.) Yu responded by saying:

[T]hanks for the concern. I am totally fine and I was honestly surprised by this extremely long message. Thanks anyway for being so considerate. I say we should just forget about it. I was so drunk I didn't know what i was doing. I am sure that's the case for you as well . . . . Just curious tho, what made you so concerned all the sudden?

(*Id.* at 8.) Complainant responded:

[H]onestly I have been feeling guilty about it for awhile and after we went on spring break and during spring break I felt worse because I hadn't said I was sorry and then when everyone was saying how much closer to the team they had gotten over spring break and stuff at the dinner last night at the team dinner, I just felt really bad.

(*Id.*) Yu and Complainant continued communicating over Facebook sporadically in May and October 2012. (*Id.* at 8–13.)[36]

At the hearing, the complaining student stated the that various messages "did not correctly reflect her feelings" because she was "in a state of 'shock and disbelief'" at the time, but nothing in the messages, from him or from her, indicated that he posed any imminent threat to her or that she perceived him as such. He thanks her for being "so considerate," and when she says that she wants to be friends, he responds politely, but doesn't suggest any specifics about getting together. There were no allegations that he engaged in any sort of threatening verbal or physical behavior toward her in the year that passed after the incident in question.

Nevertheless, once the complaint was filed, Yu was put on an extremely short time frame to review the charges and see the evidence against him. He was expelled eight days after he first saw the charges and only three days after he was first allowed to review the file. He brought legal action to contest his expulsion, but the court held that students have no right to see the charges against them or

---

[36] 97 F. Supp. 3d at 455–456.

any evidence in a timely manner. In fact, the court held that Yu was given *more* than the time that due process required:

As to the purported "rush to convict," Yu cites no authority for the proposition that eight days between the notice of charges and the verdict, or three days between the presentation of evidence and the hearing, is inherently inadequate. Indeed, courts have not disapproved of notice of charges given just one day prior to the hearing. *See Doe, 687 F.Supp.2d at 753; see also Donohue v. Baker, 976 F. Supp. 136, 145–46 (N.D.N.Y. 1997)* (telephonic notice of charges at least three days prior to the hearing and written notice one day before the hearing "would seem [to be] sufficient").[37]

In this extremely short time frame, Yu was attempting to track down witnesses, wanted to challenge the impartiality of the panel (the complaining student was the daughter of a professor at the school and at least the panel chair was aware of that fact), and had to prepare questions to ask the witnesses. Given that a full year had passed between the incident complained of and the filing of the complaint, the cordial tone of the Facebook messages, and the lack of any evidence that Yu was a danger to the complaining student, it is difficult to understand what purpose was served by giving Yu so little time to respond to the evidence against him. Further, even if the female student felt threatened, interim measures could have been taken such as initiating a no contact order.

The *Mathews* factors all point in the direction of a more reasonable opportunity to review the evidence. Yu's interest in avoiding expulsion was very strong, while there appeared to be no immediate danger to the complaining student. The ability of Yu to defend himself was quite likely diminished, and the university would not have borne any significant costs by giving him more than three days to review his file before the hearing. Yet the court's only response was that other courts had allowed even less time.

The amount of time a student needs to prepare for a hearing must surely vary with the complexity of the case. Has he been charged with a single code violation or a dozen? Are there few witnesses or many? Nevertheless, the courts should establish a minimum period to allow a student to respond to charges as serious as sexual assault. Berger and Berger suggest that:

The school can meet the fairness requirement, first, by setting reasonable intervals (in our view, about five working days to prepare for an informal discussion, about ten to prepare for a formal hearing) and second, by informing the student at the outset that, if she requires more time, the school will grant a reasonable adjournment.

Ten working days, or two weeks of notice, seem eminently reasonable before making a decision of such great importance. Of course, should there be evidence that the accused student represents an imminent danger to any student's safety, this would be a different situation. The 2017 interim guidance from the Trump administration does nothing to address this issue. It states: "The decision-maker

(s) must offer each party the same meaningful access to any information that will be used during informal and formal disciplinary meetings and hearings, including the investigation report,"[38] but does not establish any time frame for how many days prior to the hearing the information must be made available.

So far, this chapter has argued that students are entitled to a hearing and to a statement of the charges against them that is clear enough that the accused is aware of what facts are in dispute. Additionally, in the absence of exigent circumstances, students should have reasonable time to understand the charges and to prepare a response. Also, they should be informed of their rights and given an understanding of the process. This chapter argues that these should all be considered straightforward issues and should be routinely enforced by courts so that universities follow these rules as a matter of course. After that, the issues become more complicated. The next section will address the question of a student's right to access the evidence upon which the university is basing its decision as well as any exonerating evidence of which the university is aware.

Right to Evidence

The Supreme Court has been clear that, at least in a criminal case, "there is no general constitutional right to broad discovery."[39] In civil cases, broad discovery is allowed by the Federal Rules of Civil Procedure, so there has been little need for the courts to address constitutionally based due process rights to discovery of evidence.[40]

This does not mean, though, that courts should not enforce at least some discovery rights for students in sexual assault cases. As Professor Imre Stephen Szalai points out, the courts have been willing to set aside arbitration agreements that do not allow for discovery or are one-sided in terms of who benefits from discovery. Szalai argues that these decisions point to "emerging procedural norms, such as a right to discovery in certain situations."[41] For example, courts have struck down arbitration agreements where the employee had to provide a list of witnesses but the employer did not.[42] In *Fitz v. NCR Corp.*, a California appellate struck down limits on discovery in an arbitration agreement where the employer was likely to have control over most of the documents at issue and where "the burden imposed by these limits on discovery outweighed any potential benefit the employee could derive from these rights."[43] In numerous cases, state and federal courts have found

---

[38] "Q&A on Campus Sexual Misconduct," 5, www2.ed.gov/about/offices/list/ocr/docs/qa-title-ix -201709.pdf.

[39] Imre Stephen Szalai, *A Constitutional Right to Discovery? Creating and Reinforcing Due Process Norms through the Procedural Laboratory of Arbitration*, 15 Pepperdine Dispute Resolution Law Journal 337–376, 337 (2015). Citing Weatherford v. Bursey 429 U.S. 545, 559 (1977).

[40] Id. at 337.   [41] Id. at 340.   [42] Id. at 347.   [43] Id. at 352–353.

various limits on discovery to be "procedurally unfair" for limiting one or both parties' ability to ask written questions, depose witnesses, and request documents.[44]

While this claim is admittedly more adventurous than this chapter's previous arguments, this section argues that court should apply similar principles to college sexual assault tribunals. At a minimum, due process should require that universities grant the accused and accusing students *equal* access to evidence. This is especially important in sexual assault cases because outcomes often turn on the perceived credibility of the two students, which is often measured by how consistent the students are in their testimony. Lopsided access to witness statements can easily tip the scales in terms of who is able to be more consistent. In the University of Southern California case, the accusing student, Jane, was given access to all witness statements while John, the accused student, was not. The university argued that it was under no obligation to be even-handed, but the California Appellate court disagreed:

> USC argues the procedural protections required in Dixon were in place here because John had access to information submitted by the other witnesses and an opportunity to respond to that evidence – had he requested it. But requiring John to request access to the evidence against him does not comply with the requirements of a fair hearing …."[45]

The appellate court also ruled that even at a private college, the school must at least provide the accused student with the evidence upon which it is relying upon in making its decision: "Even where constitutional due process protections do not apply, common law requirements for a fair hearing under section 1094.5 do not allow an administrative board to rely on evidence that has never been revealed to the accused."[46]

It is also worth noting that, apart from constitutional issues, the OCR has taken the position in an OCR Complaint that giving the accused student more information than the accusing student violates Title IX. But confusingly, in a different context the OCR has also taken the position that an imbalance of information in favor of the accusing student does not constitute a Title IX violation.[47] This ambiguity still remains. The courts should step in here and make it crystal clear that students are entitled to equal information and that information should include all of the facts that the decision maker relied upon.

Also, courts should protect a student's right to receive exculpatory evidence in the possession of the university. There has been a constitutional obligation for prosecutors to share exculpatory evidence with the accused since the Supreme Court decided *Brady v. Maryland* in 1963.[48] One would hope that universities would, of their own accord, share exculpatory evidence because they are not prosecutors and their mission is presumably to get to the truth of

---

[44] Id. at 354–356.   [45] Doe v. University of Southern California at 29.   [46] Id. at 32.
[47] Henrick, *A Hostile Environment for Student Defendants.*
[48] Brady v. Maryland, 373 U.S. 83 (1963).

the matter. However, that does not always seem to be the case. In *Doe v. The Ohio State University* a student was contesting the school's finding that he had committed sexual assault on, among other grounds, the failure of the school to let him know that the accusing student, who was on the verge of failing out of medical school, had received substantial academic accommodations from the university as a result of the alleged assault. As will be discussed in the following text, the specifics in this case are tricky, but the university's apparent attitude about their obligations to ensure fair process and a truthful outcome are troubling indeed. As reported by Professor K. C. Johnson, the following exchange occurred between the magistrate judge and various Ohio State officials:

JUDGE KEMP: Am I stating it correctly that fair also means that you want to try to get the right result?

TITLE IX COORDINATOR KELLIE BRENNAN: We want to get the result that we can based on the information that we have.

JUDGE KEMP: [Brennan's] job is also to make sure the process is fair, right?

INVESTIGATOR JEFF MAJARIAN: *I don't know.*

JUDGE KEMP: And Ohio State has an interest in making sure the hearing panel gets it correct, don't they?

PANEL CHAIRMAN MATTHEW PAGE: I think that procedurally we want to ensure that our board members come to the decision they think is fair based on the evidence they considered.

Q: Do you have any understanding as you sit here today about whether you have an obligation to correct a false statement at a hearing panel?

SEXUAL VIOLENCE SUPPORT COORDINATOR NATALIE SPIERT: *I do not know.*

Q: [Do you have] an obligation to make sure that the hearing panel gets it right?

SPIERT: No.[49]

In fairness to Ohio State, this was a case in which reasonable people could disagree about whether the academic accommodations given to the accusing students truly cast doubt on her credibility. She was indeed in serious jeopardy of failing out of medical school and did receive a substantial reprieve and further accommodations as a result of telling a counselor that she had been sexually assaulted. However, she had already received the accommodations by the time she filed the complaint against the other student (as opposed to just telling the counselor about it). So, it is not always indisputable whether certain evidence is truly exculpatory. Therefore, an obligation to turn over exculpatory evidence no doubt would sometimes place a university in the position of having to make difficult judgment calls about whether it has exculpatory evidence in its possession and those decision that could then be second-guessed by the courts. This is not a trivial burden on the university.

---

[49] K. C. Johnson, "A Tale of Two Judges," *Academic Wonderland* (February 29, 2016), https://academicwonderland.com/2016/02/29/a-tale-of-two-judges/ (emphasis added).

Nevertheless, balancing the benefits in avoiding an erroneous decision against the burden on the university, a requirement to divulge exculpatory evidence is preferable to the status quo. The university is often in sole possession of critical information such as witness statements and police reports. A good example of the need for a rule requiring universities to reveal exculpatory evidence in their possession is *Tanyi v. Appalachian State University*. In that case, the vice chancellor of student development did not tell the accused student, Lanston Tanyi, that two other students had contacted her and offered testimony that seemingly contradicted the account of the accusing student on crucial points:

Tanyi argues that his procedural due process rights were further violated when [Vice Chancellor] Wallace failed to notify him that, in the days following Student A's rape allegation, but before Tanyi's hearing, two witnesses potentially favorable to Tanyi went to Wallace's office unprompted, and informed her that they did not believe Student A was raped. (2d Am. Compl. ¶ 53). These two students watched Student A engage Tanyi and his roommate in conversation, and lead them into the bedroom. Id. Tanyi further alleges the two students spoke to Student A in the bedroom immediately following her sexual encounter with Tanyi, and that Student A was not upset.[50]

The federal judge in that case held that Tanyi's rights were not violated because there is no duty on the part of a college to disclose exculpatory evidence to an accused student:

However, the Supreme Court "never stated that the Brady rule applies in civil cases," and this Court is aware of no Fourth Circuit case law extending the rule to civil matters, much less student disciplinary proceedings. In essence, Tanyi wishes to apply the standards of Brady disclosure, developed for federal criminal proceedings, to a university student conduct hearing. Such a standard would be wholly without precedent, and this Court declines to adopt it. As a result, Tanyi's claim will not survive Defendants' Motion to Dismiss.[51]

Courts have also held that accused students have no right to police reports, even when they result in the government declining to prosecute the accused student and where they appear to cast doubt on the accusations. In *Gomes v. University of Maine System*, for example, university officials knew about statements the accusing student made to the police that appeared to contradict her testimony at the university hearing:

The Plaintiffs argue the reports contained substantial evidence of inconsistency in the Complainant's story. They point to the fact that the Complainant made no mention of non-consensual sex with [one of the two accused students] until the third interview. Further, the police reports reveal the Complainant had consumed some alcohol during the evening leading up to the incident, and the Complainant's medical records, which

[50] Tanyi v. Appalachian State University, Memorandum and Order NO. 5:14-CV-170RLV \ (2015) at 9.
[51] Id. (citation omitted).

were before the Hearing Committee, confirmed her use of prescriptive medication, raising the question of the impact of alcohol on the medication.[52]

The accused student's lack of access to the police report allowed the accusing student's attorney to make a highly misleading claim during the closing statements of the college hearing:

The Plaintiffs argue the hearing generated the misimpression that the Complainant had been entirely consistent from the date of the incident onward. After her statement before the Hearing Committee, the Complainant called four witnesses, each of whom corroborated her version of events. This allowed the Complainant's attorney to argue in his closing statement, "You haven't heard anyone testify to any contradictory statements by [the woman] at all, other than the two Respondents .... There were no inconsistencies in her statements or her testimony or any of the things she stated throughout these proceedings.[53]

While it is certainly true that the courts have never broadly applied *Brady v. Maryland* to civil cases, this does not mean the *Mathews* factors cannot be interpreted to require disclosure of exculpatory evidence in college sexual assault hearings. In fact, the case cited by the judge in *Tanyi v. Appalachian State University* held that, in deportation and extradition cases, there *is* a right to exculpatory evidence.[54] As argued in Chapter 2, the interests of students in avoiding an erroneous finding of sexual assault is very high and, while colleges have a legitimate desire to not have to make potentially difficult decisions about what evidence is truly exculpatory, the balance here seems to clearly favor mandatory divulgence of exculpatory evidence. For a college to hold back information such as the fact that two students directly contradicted the testimony of the accused student obviously increases the chances of an erroneous decision.

Finally, it is important not to lose sight of the connections between these various issues. If a student is denied one sort of procedural protection, say adequate time to prepare a defense, logic would dictate that he should all the more be entitled to stronger protections elsewhere in the process to make up for that. However, some courts have gone in the opposite direction, using a lack of one type of protection to justify other types of lack of protection. In *Gomes*, for example, the court held that the very short time frames in which a hearing can be held just one day after a student is notified of the charges against him means that colleges do not have time to turn over evidence to students:

This chronology reflects the tight deadlines attendant to student disciplinary hearings from complaint to resolution. In *Nash*, for example, the time between the charge and the hearing was only six days, and the students received a restated notice of charges only one day before the hearing .... This tight timeframe, a timeframe not uncommon in

[52] 365 F. Supp. 2d 6, 19 (2005).   [53] Id.
[54] Demanjuk v. Petrovsky, 10 F. 3d, 338, 354 (6th Cir. 1993).

university disciplinary hearings, makes it less appropriate to impose strict legal document production requirements on the parties.[55]

In other words, the fact that a student is given so little time to review the charges and evidence against him is used to justify not giving the student crucial documents such as the police report in which his name is not mentioned the first two times the accusing student spoke to the police. The courts' reasoning should be exactly the opposite. When a student is denied certain procedural protections, such as the time opportunity to review evidence, this is a reason to *augment* other procedural protections rather than lower them.

Setting the Standard of Proof

As noted earlier, this is one of the few areas where there is a true conflict of interest between the accused and accusing students. All parties benefit from such things as a clear statement of what a student is charged with and giving both students access to the evidence upon which a tribunal relies. By contrast, a higher standard of proof increases the chance of a student getting away with sexual assault while a lower standard of proof increases the chance of an innocent student erroneously being found to have committed a sexual offense. This section argues that a low standard of proof, combined with the other procedures currently used at many colleges, violates due process. However, because the Supreme Court requires that the process be viewed holistically, a lower standard of proof, combined with stronger procedural protections, can satisfy the demands of due process.

The OCR's 2011 Dear Colleague Letter set off a storm of controversy by insisting that colleges use the "preponderance of evidence" standard, sometimes called "fifty percent plus a feather."[56] The Trump administration rescinded that directive, but it is unclear what the practical effect of that has been. In 2018 various civil rights organizations sued the Department of Education to block the change arguing that: "The department has no business creating special one-sided rights that give safe harbor to the accused."[57]

While the standard of proof issue can seem abstract, there is no question that there are cases in which the outcome will be determined by the standard of proof. For example, in *Doe v. Lhamon* a University of Virginia student, Jane Roe, alleged that she had been unable to meaningfully consent to sexual activity

[55] 365 F. Supp. 2d at 21.
[56] Rick Maese, "Minnesota Football Boycott Enters Second Day, Highlighting Complex Campus Issues," *Washington Post* (December 16, 2016), www.washingtonpost.com/sports/colleges/minnesota-football-boycott-enters-second-day-highlighting-complex-campus-issue/2016/12/16/9e386a60-c3d0-11e6-9578-0054287507db_story.html?utm_term=.dc35d17de3e6.
[57] Maria Danilova, "Civil Rights Groups Sue DeVos over Policy on Campus Sexual Assault" (January 25, 2018), www.pbs.org/newshour/nation/civil-rights-groups-sue-devos-over-policy-on-campus-sexual-assault.

with Doe due to her incapacitated state. She filed a complaint a year and half after the incident, so it was difficult to ascertain the truth. As described in *the Atlantic*:

> The adjudicator – a retired justice of the Supreme Court of Pennsylvania – called the matter a "very close" and "very difficult case." She found Mr. Doe responsible, she said, because the evidence "slightly" tipped in favor of responsibility, and she was "required" by "the Office of Civil Rights and the Department of Education" to apply "the weakest standard of proof" available – preponderance of the evidence – which is satisfied whenever the evidence is "tipped very slightly" in favor of responsibility.
>
>   The adjudicator also explained that two other commonly used evidentiary standards – the "clear and convincing" evidence standard and the "reasonable doubt" standard – would "tip the scale much more," thereby indicating that, but for UVA's mandated use of the preponderance standard, Mr. Doe would not have been found responsible.
>
>   After explaining why, in her view, the evidence before her "made it slightly more likely than not" that Mr. Doe had not properly obtained "effective consent" from Ms. Roe given her intoxication, the adjudicator again emphasized, at the end of her ruling, that the case was a close one.[58]

At the same time, a higher standard of proof might allow a possibly dangerous wrongdoer to remain unpunished and on campus. For example, a study of the impact of the "clear and convincing" evidence standard in child protection cases found that the higher standard made it 14 percent less likely that a parent would be found to be a danger to their children.[59]

As Johnson and Taylor point out, the 2011 Dear Colleague Letter's requirement of a lower standard of proof applies only to sexual assault, resulting in a counterintuitive situation in which a student accused of sexual assault has less protection against an erroneous decision than students facing far less life-altering accusations:

> Cornell University … the first elite university to fully implement the Obama administration's April 2011 marching orders, created a two-tier disciplinary system that gave students charged with the most serious offense – sexual assault – the weakest procedural protections. When facing charges of plagiarism or petty theft … there needed to be "clear and convincing evidence" (roughly a 75 or 80 percent probability) of his guilt. But when facing a sexual assault accusation … [he] might be found guilty so long as the accusation was deemed 50.001 percent true.[60]

By contrast, Lavinia Weizel argues that the seriousness of sexual assault is exactly what makes a lower standard of proof appropriate in those cases because a sexually assaulted student has a great deal at stake in making sure that her assailant is not erroneously cleared of responsibility:

[58] Conner Friedersdorf, "What Should the Standard of Proof Be in Campus Rape Cases," *Atlantic* (June 17, 2016).

[59] Nicholas Kahn et al., "The Standard of Proof in the Substantiation of Child Abuse and Neglect," *Journal of Empirical Legal Studies* 14 (June 2017), 333–369.

[60] Johnson and Taylor, *The Campus Rape Frenzy*, 153.

Additionally, the physical, mental, and emotional consequences of rape can be devastating for the victim. College-student victims struggle to maintain their grades and attendance and are likely to drop out of school. Moreover, rape victims are six times more likely to attempt suicide than are victims of other crimes. Compounding the rapes and sexual assaults many young women suffer is the equally troubling reality that many victims feel re-victimized by the responses of their schools.[61]

Weizel argues that not punishing a sexual perpetrator can send a signal that sexual assault is not taken seriously and thereby compound the already significant harm to the victim. She concedes that the accused students also have a great deal at stake but that the nearly 50–50 preponderance of the evidence standard does the best job of recognizing the accused and accusing students' equally strong interests in the process.

Applying the first prong of the Mathew test, the importance of the liberty interest at stake, Weizel says that while the accused's interests are strong, they are not quite as strong as in the type of cases in which the Supreme Court has mandated the use of the higher clear and convincing evidence standard:

Yet the Supreme Court has typically reserved the clear and convincing evidence standard for cases in which fundamental liberty interests are foreclosed. For example, the Court has described the interests at stake for parents facing permanent termination of their parental rights as a "unique kind of deprivation" in which the state seeks permanent termination of an interest "far more precious than property" – a parent's legal relationship to his or her natural children .... As compared to permanent civil commitment or the irrevocable termination of one's parental rights, the reputational interest [in a college sexual assault case] is not quite so fundamental.[62]

Weizel is certainly correct that civil commitment and termination of parental rights, for which the Supreme Court requires clear and convincing evidence, are unique kinds of deprivation. Nevertheless, a student accused of sexual assault has far more at stake than the defendant in a typical civil suit in which the standard of proof is preponderance of the evidence. In a civil suit, the goal is to make the plaintiff whole, not to punish the defendant. Many successful, well-regarded business people have lost multiple civil lawsuits without damage to their reputations. Donald Trump lost dozens of civil cases in which he or his companies were defendants[63] but was able to be elected president of the United States. By contrast, as discussed in Chapter 2, a student found responsible for sexual assault is at serious risk of being unable to graduate from college, attend

---

[61] Lavinia M. Weizel, *The Process That Is Due: Preponderance of the Evidence as the Standard of Proof for University Adjudications of Student-on-Student Sexual Assault Complaints*, 53 *Boston College Law Review* 1613–1655, 1614 (2012) (citations omitted).

[62] Id. at 1647.

[63] Nick Penzenstadler and Susan Page, "Trump's 3,500 Lawsuits Unprecedented for a Presidential Nominee," *USA Today*, www.usatoday.com/story/news/politics/elections/2016/06/01/donald-trump-lawsuits-legal-battles/84S995854/.

professional school, or get a decent job, and, if a foreign student, faces deportation.

In fact, the Supreme Court's opinion requiring clear and convincing evidence for a civil commitment hearing includes language clearly stating that the higher standard is sometimes appropriate for civil suits and should be used where the charges are "quasi-criminal":

> The intermediate standard, which usually employs some combination of the words "clear," "cogent," "unequivocal" and "convincing," is less commonly used, but nonetheless "is no stranger to the civil law." *One typical use of the standard is in civil cases involving allegations of fraud or some other quasi-criminal wrongdoing by the defendant ... .* Similarly, this Court has used the "clear, unequivocal and convincing" standard of proof to protect particularly important individual interests in various civil cases.[64]

College sexual assault cases seem to be a paradigm example of the Supreme Court is referring to: a case involving an allegation of criminal-type wrongdoing. So, requiring a clear and convincing standard of proof would be reasonable.

All of these situations – parental termination, civil commitment, run-of-the-mill civil suits, and sexual assault tribunals – are very different and we are inherently comparing apples and oranges. But if we are comparing sexual assault tribunals to civil lawsuits, it should be noted that defendants in civil lawsuits have a plethora of protections not enjoyed by students accused of sexual assault. They have the right to a lawyer, the right to broad discovery, ample time to prepare a defense, the right to directly cross-examine witnesses against them and produce their own witnesses, and, usually, to a jury of their peers. As Harvard law professor and self-described feminist advocate Nancy Gertner puts it, sexual assault tribunals are "the worst of all worlds, the lowest standard of proof, coupled with the least protective procedures."[65]

Also, it seems clear that a student's interest in not erroneously being found responsible for sexual assault is at least as great as a professor's interest in not being erroneously found guilty for sexual harassment. However, in 2011, Ann Greene, then the Chair of the Committee on Women in the Academic Profession of the American Association of University Professors, wrote the OCR to protest its endorsement of the preponderance of evidence standard where the accused person is a faculty member:

> While clear policy statements and timely responses are key for both the complainant and the accused, preserving a higher standard of proof is vital in achieving fair and just treatment for all. We urge you to reconsider "the preponderance of evidence" standard.[66]

---

[64] 441 U.S. 418, 424 (1979) (citation omitted, emphasis added).
[65] Nancy Gertner, "Sex, Lies and Justice: Can We Reconcile the Belated Attention to Rape on Campus with Due Process?," *The American Prospect* (Winter 2015).
[66] American Association of University Professors letter, August 18, 2011.

If this is true for accused professors, it is equally true for accused students.

Weizel argues that even if the accused student's interest is comparable to other cases in which the Court has required clear and convincing evidence, the second prong of the *Mathews* test, the risk of erroneous deprivation, also points toward the preponderance of evidence test. This is because the accusing student has an equally strong interest in not having her claim erroneously rejected and because sexual assault is hard to prove clearly and convincingly. Because the accusing student's interest in a correct outcome is just as strong as the accused student's, a 50–50 standard properly allocates the risk of an erroneous deprivation of those interests.

Yet this argument proves too much. Society certainly has a great deal at stake in making sure that a murderer doesn't go free, but prosecutors still must meet the highest burden of proof. And, some criminal charges are notoriously more difficult to prove than others, but no one suggests that the standard of proof should therefore be lower. Similarly, an abused child has an enormously strong interest in not being left in the control of parents who might do him or her harm. Yet the state still must meet the "clear and convincing" threshold of evidence to take that child away from the control of his or her parents. In fact, in almost every case in which a higher standard of proof is required, one can make the argument that both sides have a very strong interest in avoiding an erroneous outcome. The argument is no more compelling in cases of college sexual assault than it is for murder or child abuse.

Weizel also argues that the third prong of *Mathews* points toward the lower standard of proof:

Additionally, the clear and convincing evidence standard could impose costly administrative burdens on colleges and universities by promoting increasingly formalistic campus disciplinary proceedings ... A clear and convincing evidence requirement could burden a school's limited investigatory and adjudicatory resources by requiring a school to present evidence of significant quantity and quality in order to meet its burden.[67]

Here, Weizel's argument seems to point in the exact opposite direction than she intends. Don't we want a university "to present evidence of significant quantity and quality" before a student is expelled and labeled a sex offender? This goes to Gertner's observation that the current system is the worst of all worlds – with a low standard of proof *and* the absence of protections that defendants normally get in run-of-the-mill civil cases.

It is also important to distinguish between two confusingly similar sounding concepts: "burden of proof" and "standard of proof." Burden of proof is the question of *which* party has the burden of establishing facts. Standard of proof is the question of *how significant* that burden should be. So, when the Obama OCR said the standard of proof should be preponderance of the evidence, it was

[67] Weizel, "The Process That Is Due," 1654.

not questioning whether universities bear the burden of proof. It is saying that the universities' burden should be less than it would be under a clear and convincing evidence standard.

However, campus tribunals are not usually staffed by attorneys, and it is quite possible that they can confuse a low standard of proof with the idea that the burden of proof is not on the university (and therefore students should not be presumed innocent). For example, in *Yu v. Vassar College*, a case in which the main issue was the question of whether the accusing student was too drunk to consent to sexual activity, the investigator's report "state[d] that the information gathered '*appears* to suggest' that Complainant *may* have made a series of decisions and exhibited behaviors to *suggest* that she was incapacitated prior to, and during, the incident."[68]

If the most that the investigator can conclude is that the evidence "appears to suggest" the student "may" have behaved in a manner "to suggest" that she was too drunk to consent, it is very difficult to believe that the university truly accepted that it bore the burden of *proving*, by whatever standard, that Yu committed sexual assault.

Clear and convincing evidence might also be the most appropriate standard for these cases given the inherent ambiguity in the way that many colleges now define sexual assault and consent. For example, Georgia Southern University defines *consent* as follows: "Consent is a voluntary, sober, imaginative, enthusiastic, creative, wanted, informed, mutual, honest, and verbal agreement."[69] As will be discussed in Chapter 6, many other schools have similar definitions. If the definition of *consent* turns on so many subjective adjectives, then a low standard of proof becomes a trap for the unwary. Given the grave consequences of being declared a sex offender, a college should have to show that the lack of "enthusiasm" or "honesty" in a student's consent was "clear," as opposed to "more likely than not."

Again, it should be emphasized that questions of due process should be looked at holistically. Because it is a balancing test, a lower standard of proof can arguably satisfy the *Mathews* test if other procedural protections are in place to assure that the burden of proof does not shift to the accused student and to assure that the panel understands that even with a low standard of proof, the panel must find for the accused student rather than merely taking their best guess if both sides are equally credible. Sarah Edwards suggests that the preponderance of evidence standard satisfies due process if the panel includes at least one attorney who is trained to understand concepts such as burden of proof and if the panel must make a unanimous decision:

[68] 97 F. Supp. 3d 448, 467 (2015) (emphasis added).
[69] Jacob Gersen and Jeannie Suk, *The Sex Bureaucracy*, 104 California Law Review 881–947, 925–926 (2016).

Although the clear and convincing evidence standard sets a higher burden, the preponderance of the evidence standard is not easy to meet if the hearing panel is well trained and relies on a unanimous vote. The complaining student receives the benefit of a "more likely than not" standard instead of "highly probable or reasonably certain," while the accused student receives the benefit of the hearing panel requiring a unanimous vote in order to find the student not responsible.[70]

As noted, this is a tricky issue in which reasonable arguments can be made for either standard of proof. But this question cannot be answered with easy assertions about preponderance of evidence being the civil standard. Nor is it addressed by saying that any other standard fails to value the interests of the accusing student. The question can only be answered holistically. Given the lack of procedural protections we have seen in many cases, a clear and convincing standard would go far in protecting against erroneous decisions. If additional procedural protections are in place, such as most of those suggested in this book, then a preponderance standard could be considered sufficient under the *Mathews* test so long as the burden of proof remains on the university. But without a hearing, a requirement of timely and specific statements of charges, meaningful access to evidence, and other crucial protections, the courts should require a showing of clear and convincing evidence.

An Impartial Tribunal

The Supreme Court has clearly stated that "an impartial decisionmaker is essential" to due process.[71] The reasons for an impartial decision maker are almost too obvious to state. "The neutrality requirement helps to guarantee that life, liberty, or property will not be taken on the basis of an erroneous or distorted conception of the facts or the law.... At the same time, it preserves both the appearance and reality of fairness."[72]

While there is little debate about the essentialness of an unbiased panel, the devil is in the details. Some academics argue that the training some schools provide to their sexual assault tribunals are designed to make sure that sexual assault adjudicators are anything but impartial. Harvard Law School's Janet Halley describes the school's training materials as follows:

The take-away lesson of these pages is that a victim of sexual assault may experience trauma, which in turn causes neurological changes, which in turn can result in "tonic immobility." Tonic immobility, in turn, can cause the victim to appear incoherent and to have emotional swings, memory fragmentation, and "flat affect." Her story "may come out fragmented or 'sketchy,'" and she can be "[m]isinterpreted as being cavalier about

[70] Sarah Edwards, "The Case in Favor of OCR's Tougher Title IX Policies: Pushing Back against the Pushback," *Duke Journal of Gender Law and Policy* 23 (2015): 121–144, 133.
[71] Goldberg v. Kelly, 397 U.S. 254, 271 (1970).
[72] www.law.cornell.edu/anncon/html/amdt14dfrag14_user.html (citations omitted).

[the event] or lying." ... It is 100% aimed to convince them to believe complainants, precisely when they seem unreliable and incoherent.[73]

While Halley cites materials that she says train panelists to believe accusers even when their stories are "unreliable and incoherent," others point to materials that tell panelists that they should not believe accused students who are too coherent or are too convinced of their own innocence. The training materials for Stanford University include under the heading "Indictors of an Abuser": "An Abuser will ... Act persuasive and logical" and "Assertively claim to be a victim." The same materials state: "The great majority of allegations of abuse – though not all – are substantially accurate. And an abuser almost never 'seems like the type.'"[74]

While these materials are concerning, it is difficult to draw conclusions about whether they amount to a denial of the right to an impartial adjudicator. From some university's perspective, seemingly biased training materials serve to "rebalance" the knowledge of adjudicators who might be more familiar with concepts like proof beyond a reasonable doubt from popular media, but less aware of how trauma may affect memory.[75] The question whether this is true may not be a question that is amenable to judicial resolution except in extreme cases. The best approach may be a requirement that training materials be transparent on the theory that accountability promotes fairness.

Another concern about bias stems from possible conflict of interest. Stephen Henrick argues: "Assuming that university administrators had the necessary training and experience to competently adjudicate sexual assault claims – which most do not – four interests would still seriously impede their objectivity."[76] The first conflict of interest involves money:

The most obvious is financial. As detailed supra, acquitting an accused student carries the threat that OCR could exercise its enforcement authority and thereby cost a college over half a billion dollars in federal funding. There could also be civil litigation from the complainant, which to date has had more high-profile impact on college campuses than comparable suits from accused students ... As a pure matter of risk aversion, therefore, colleges have a very strong incentive to convict accused students in all circumstances.[77]

Henrick argues that career incentives provide another conflict of interest because an administrator is far more likely to face organized student protest for a finding in favor of student accused of sexual assault than the opposite finding.[78] The third conflict of interest involves a school's reputation: "Because

[73] Janet Halley, *Trading the Megaphone for the Gavel in Title IX Enforcement*, 128 Harvard Law Review Forum 103, 109–110 (February 18, 2015).
[74] www.thefire.org/deans-administrative-review-process-training-materials-2010–2011/.
[75] Savino, "Nobody's Saying We're Opposed to Complying," 16, n. 99, http://scholarship.law .cornell.edu/cllsrp/9 (citing interview with Mary Beth Grant, Cornell University Title IX Coordinator).
[76] Henrick, *A Hostile Environment for Student Defendants*, 80–81.   [77] Id. at 81.
[78] Id. at 82.

universities appeal to popular sentiment to attract students and receive alumni donations, they shun negative publicity." He quotes an unnamed administrator as saying:

[M]y fear – yes, it's fear – of seeing my institution's name in Inside Higher Ed or The Chronicle of Higher Education as the subject of an investigation, or, even worse, having the "letter of agreement" OCR makes public displayed for all to read – makes me tow [*sic*] the line in a way I sometimes have trouble justifying to myself.[79]

Henrick also argues that ideology can lead to a biased panel, citing some of the seemingly biased language in the training materials of various universities.[80] These are all legitimate concerns, but they are also quite speculative. Universities also face possible negative financial consequences and bad publicity for erroneously finding an innocent student guilty of sexual assault, even if the risks are not symmetrical. The point about students being more likely to protest a school's administration for being insufficiently responsive to sexual assault than for denying due process may well be accurate but does not likely amount to a constitutionally cognizable conflict of interest.

There is, though, an issue regarding impartiality that courts should take far more seriously than they currently do. Courts have been far too tolerant of the same person or people serving as both investigators and adjudicators of sexual assault allegations.

The Supreme Court has wisely said, "A genuinely impartial hearing, conducted with critical detachment, is psychologically improbable, if not impossible, when the presiding officer has at once the responsibility of appraising the strength of the case and of seeking to make it as strong as possible."[81]

However, the Court has also held that this concern must be balanced against a presumption of good faith on the part of administrators:

The contention that the combination of investigative and adjudicative functions necessarily creates an unconstitutional risk of bias in administrative adjudication has a much more difficult burden of persuasion to carry. It must overcome a presumption of honesty and integrity in those serving as adjudicators; and it must convince that, under a realistic appraisal of psychological tendencies and human weakness, conferring investigative and adjudicative powers on the same individuals poses such a risk of actual bias or prejudgment that the practice must be forbidden if the guarantee of due process is to be adequately implemented.[82]

While the presumption of honesty and integrity is important, the Court has also acknowledged that the potential for conflict between the roles of investigator and adjudicator is "substantial." Therefore, there is no "one-size-fits-all" answer to whether a person playing such a dual role violates due process:

---

[79] Id. at 82–83.   [80] Id. at 83–84.   [81] Wong Yang Sung v. McGrath, 339 U.S. 33, 44 (1950).
[82] Withrow v. Larkin, 421 U.S. 35, 47 (1975).

That is not to say that there is nothing to the argument that those who have investigated should not then adjudicate. The issue is substantial, it is not new, and legislators and others concerned with the operations of administrative agencies have given much attention to whether and to what extent distinctive administrative functions should be performed by the same persons. No single answer has been reached.[83]

This section argues that all the elements of the *Mathews* point squarely toward forbidding the same person or people to investigate and adjudicate the same claim of college sexual assault. The first element of *Mathews*, the importance of the interest, is very great, as has been discussed several times. As for the second element, the danger of an erroneous decision, it is worth remembering that few college officials are legally trained. While investigating claims of sexual assault, they are immersing themselves in highly emotional situations. The students they are investigating may be hearing about the allegations for the first time, and might well be fearful, defensive, angry, hostile, and uncooperative. It would be quite a great deal to expect of college administrators, who may be first meeting students at one of the most stressful moments of their lives, to enter a hearing with a truly open mind. And we have seen numerous examples in this book of cases where it would be reasonable to question the impartiality of some investigators.

And, finally, the third element of *Mathews* points against this sort of dual role. Having a panel of adjudicators that does not contain the investigators imposes little burden upon the college.

Courts have been far too dismissive of this concern. As discussed in Chapter 2, many courts have a tendency to selectively cite the 1975 case *Goss v. Lopez*, which stated: "At the very minimum, therefore, students facing suspension and the consequent interference with a protected property interest must be given some kind of notice and afforded *some* kind of hearing."[84] Ignoring the "at the very minimum language," and the fact that *Goss* merely involved the 10-day suspension of a high school student, some courts choose to cite the minimalist language of "some kind of hearing" rather than analyzing the merits of the claim that mixing investigation and adjudication jeopardizes the impartiality of the adjudicating panel. For example, in *Marshall v. Indiana University*, an expelled student challenged the university's process on the grounds that the person "who led the investigation into the charges against Marshall, also improperly participated in the panel's deliberation."[85]

In support of his argument, Marshall cited *Whitford v. Boglino*, in which a prisoner was given six months of disciplinary segregation by an "adjustment committee." The inmate protested that two members of the committee were involved in the investigation of his transgressions. The court wrote: "If an officer is substantially involved in the investigation of the charges against an

[83] Id. at 51.   [84] 419 U.S. 565, 579 (1975).
[85] Marshall v. Indiana University, 170 F. Supp. 3d 1201, 1207 (2016).

inmate, due process forbids that officer from serving on the adjustment committee."[86]

The *Whitford* case was decided by a federal appellate court whose decisions are binding upon the lower court hearing Marshall's claim. Yet, rather than giving Marshall's claim the benefit of any real analysis, the court simply relied upon "the only process that required was 'some kind of notice'" language from *Goss v. Lopez.*[87]

As noted earlier, it can be difficult to apply due process rules from one walk of life to another, and, admittedly, prisons are very different institutions from colleges. Nonetheless, the analogy between the *Marshall* and *Whitford* cases is certainly not trivial and the *Marshall* court owed the expelled student a much more serious analysis than it gave him.

In fact, in the area of college sexual assault, courts can be very tolerant of even decision makers who admit that they have a considerable bias heading into hearing the case. In *Doe v. Rector and Visitors of George Mason University*, "The undisputed record facts reflect that, as of the time plaintiff was allowed to present his defense before [Assistant Dean] Ericson, Ericson admits that he 'had prejudged the case and decided to find [plaintiff] responsible' for sexual assault."[88] Notably, the court stated that "the mere fact that Ericson determined based on prior involvement in the investigation that plaintiff was likely guilty is *not* a constitutionally significant inadequacy."[89] The student did win on this point but only because "the record here discloses that Ericson made up his mind so definitively that *nothing* plaintiff might have said at his meeting with Ericson could have altered Ericson's decision."[90] This is far too stingy a standard for due process. Few administrators would be candid enough to indicate that their minds were absolutely closed when they heard a case. Further, this distinction that creates a needless difficulty by asking courts to somehow distinguish between an adjudicator who believes the accused student is likely guilty (which is acceptable) or believes he is definitely guilty (which is unacceptable). And even if such distinctions are possible, a student accused of sexual assault surely deserves better than a hearing before someone who already believes that he is probably guilty.

Courts should protect against any nontrivial bias at a hearing, not just insurmountable bias, and they should eschew reliance on the minimalist language of *Goss* and apply the *Mathews* test in a serious manner. Given the importance of the interest, the obvious potential for bias, and the lack of any sort of onerous burden on the university, the best approach would be for courts to clearly hold that due process is best served by separating investigation and adjudication.

---

[86] Whitford v. Boglino 63 F. 3d 527, 534 (7th Cir. 1995).   [87] 170 F. Supp. at 1207.
[88] Case No. 1:15-cv-209 (February 25, 2016, E.D. VA.) at 20–21.
[89] Id. at 21–22 (emphasis added).   [90] Id. at 22.

CONCLUSION

Not all these issues are one sided. Some of them involve judgment calls that could be decided in several ways. But taken together, they represent a clear violation of students' due process rights. Furthermore, these only represent issues leading up to the hearing. The next chapter addresses many difficult issues regarding the hearing, such as the right to an attorney and the right to cross-examine witnesses.

5

Due Process during and after the Hearing

This chapter examines due process issues during the hearing and the appeal from that hearing. We begin with two of the most controversial issues: the right to an attorney and the right to confront witnesses. These two issues are closely related because of the expertise of attorneys in cross-examining witnesses and the undesirability of having students cross-examine one another.

THE RIGHT TO AN ATTORNEY

In *Powell v. Alabama* the Supreme Court famously stated: "The right to be heard would be, in many cases, of little avail if it did not comprehend the right to be heard by counsel."[1] However, *Powell* was a capital, criminal case. For criminal cases, the right to counsel is protected by the Sixth Amendment: "In all criminal prosecutions, the accused shall enjoy the right ... to have the assistance of counsel for his defence." For student disciplinary cases, the right to counsel would have to come from the due process clause and the *Mathews* test. This has produced a confusing hodgepodge of lower court decisions.

Prior to the Supreme Court's 1975 decision in *Goss v. Lopez*, a number of courts held that students were entitled to counsel during disciplinary hearings.[2] Recall that *Goss* involved a relatively mild infraction by a high school student. The Court held that he was entitled to "some kind of hearing" but added:

We stop short of construing the Due Process Clause to require, countrywide, that hearings in connection with short suspensions must afford the student the opportunity to secure counsel, to confront and cross-examine witnesses supporting the charge, or to call his own witnesses to verify his version of the incident.[3]

---

[1] 287 U.S. 45, 69 (1932).
[2] See Ellen L. Mossman, *Navigating a Legal Dilemma: A Student's Right to Legal Counsel in Disciplinary Hearings for Criminal Misbehavior*, 160 University of Pennsylvania Law Review 585–632, 600 (2012).
[3] 419 U.S. at 583.

As discussed extensively in Chapter 2, *Goss* is best understood as setting a floor rather than a ceiling on student's due process rights. Being suspended or expelled from college for sexual assault is a very different matter than being suspended from high school for 10 days. Additionally, *Goss* predates the *Mathews* test. However, some post-*Goss* courts have held that college students have no right to counsel during sexual assault hearings. In *Osteen v. Henley* the Seventh Circuit Court of Appeals wrote: "But when we consider all the factors bearing on the [the student's] claim to right of counsel, we conclude that the Constitution does not confer such a right on him. We doubt that it does in any student disciplinary proceeding."[4]

Most courts have not gone as far as the seventh circuit, whose decision was written by Judge Richard Posner, who is known for his pugnaciousness. The First Circuit Court of Appeals has held that a student is entitled to an attorney in his disciplinary proceeding when there is a parallel criminal investigation: "Only a lawyer is competent to cope with the demands of an adversary proceeding held against the backdrop of a pending criminal case involving the same set of facts."[5]

In *Osteen*, Judge Posner conceded that when there is also a potential criminal charge "it is at least arguable" that a student has the right to have an attorney present at the hearing to advise him on such matters as when to plead the Fifth Amendment and invoke the right to silence.[6] Without at least this limited right to counsel the accused student faces a complex quandary that would be virtually impossible to navigate without the advice of counsel. Invoking the right to silence is very tricky issue. In a college proceeding, the college is allowed to make negative inferences when a student does not answer a question. But if the student does answer the question he has waived his right against self-incrimination in a criminal investigation. However, Posner averred that the right to counsel only extends to this sort of advice and would not allow for more active participation by counsel such as addressing the panel directly or examining witnesses.[7]

So we see that in terms of right to counsel, the courts have created a number of distinctions. They differentiate between cases in which there are and are not pending criminal charges. They also differentiate between counsel being present to advise the accused student and counsel actively participating in the hearing. In *Flaim v. Medical College of Ohio* the Sixth Circuit Court of Appeals drew two more distinctions, noting that "counsel may be required by the Due Process Clause to ensure fundamental fairness when the school proceeds through counsel or the procedures are overly complex."[8]

[4] 13 F. 3d 221, 226 (7th Cir. 1993).
[5] Gabrilowtz v. Newman, 582 F. 2d 100, 106 (1st Cir. 1978).   [6] 13 F.3d 221 at 225
[7] 13 F. 3d at 225.
[8] 418 F. 3d 629, 636 (6th Cir. 2005) (citing Jaksa v. Regents of Univ. of Mich., 597 F. Supp. 1245, 1252 (E.D.Mich. 1984), aff'd, 787 F. 2d 590 (6th Cir. 1986)).

Not surprisingly, colleges, both public and private, vary widely on this issue:

Understandably, disciplinary codes vary significantly among different schools. Because public schools must comply with due process, their school codes are often more comprehensive and conclusive concerning hearing rights. On the other hand, a number of private schools also afford significant procedural protections. Many colleges and universities permit some representation in disciplinary hearings, although the extent and formality of this representation varies from school to school."[9]

The range of college policies is even wider than the range of legal opinions described in the preceding text:

A common code formulation allowing assistance during a disciplinary proceeding permits a student to consult with an advisor before and during the proceeding. Universities employing this provision vary on whether the advisors can participate or can be attorneys. Princeton University and Colgate University, both private, insist that the advisor be a member of the university community, effectively precluding participation by an attorney at Princeton and explicitly doing so at Colgate. Temple University, a publicly funded institution, allows the student to have an advisor present at the hearing, and allows the advisor to be an attorney; however, the advisor may not actively participate in the hearing. The University of Iowa, also publicly funded, does not place any limits on the representation by an advisor. The City University of New York and the University of Wisconsin system – both publicly funded – allow an advisor or legal counsel to represent the student. The publicly funded University of New Mexico gives the responsibility of presenting a case to the student alone, stating that "advisors (including attorney advisors) are therefore not permitted to present arguments or evidence or otherwise participate directly in the hearing."[10]

In 2014, Columbia University became one of the first universities "to offer free legal help to both accusers and accused."[11]

As with many of the issues discussed in this book, it would be ideal if legislators would step in to clarify the rights of students. For example, when students with disabilities attend hearings to decide if they are entitled to various accommodations, Congress has protected their right to counsel very clearly:

Notably, Congress has explicitly permitted counsel in another type of school administrative hearing where the proceeding's outcome implicates similarly significant rights. Parties in hearings involving handicapped students under the Individuals with Disabilities Education Act (IDEA) have the right to counsel. Furthermore, if parents successfully challenge in court the administrative findings about their child with disabilities and the accommodations to be made, the statute provides for attorney's fees.[12]

[9] Mossman, "Navigating a Legal Dilemma," 596–597 (citations omitted).
[10] Id. at 597–598 (citations omitted).
[11] Ariel Kaminer, "New Factor in Campus Sexual Assault Cases: Counsel for the Accused," *New York Times* (November 19, 2014), www.nytimes.com/2014/11/20/nyregion/new-factor-in-campus-sexual-assault-cases-counsel-for-the-accused.html?_r=0.
[12] Mossman, "Navigating a Legal Dilemma," 602 (citations omitted).

This confusing hodgepodge of legislation, court decisions, and university policies is a poor way to handle so fundamental a right as the right to counsel. This section argues that courts should hold that the *Mathews* test requires that schools allow full participation by attorneys in student sexual assault hearings in any case in which the possible consequences include suspension, expulsion, or a permanent notation of a sexual offense on a student's record.

The first prong of the *Mathews* test is the importance of the right at stake. This is also discussed extensively in Chapter 2. Even the Association for Student Conduct Administration (ASCA), which is generally skeptical about the role of attorneys in student disciplinary hearings,[13] recognizes that in many cases the stakes are too high for the student to proceed without an attorney:

> There are times when the participation of an attorney in a campus student conduct process would be appropriate. These situations do not include minor infractions and policy violations, (i.e. underage alcohol possession, minor vandalism, or noise violations) but rather more serious violations potentially leading to a separation from the institution. Student conduct professionals understand the importance and career altering scenarios in which the assistance of legal counsel would be appropriate but believe that the bar should be set high. Such scenarios would include situations in which separation from the institution by suspension or expulsion are potential outcomes and/or facing parallel criminal charges. In addition, when a student is enrolled in a program that involves licensing by a board or state agency, (i.e. applications to practice medicine, nursing, education, or law, or extensive employment background checks; high level governmental security clearances) the assistance of an attorney will likely be important.[14]

This seems a perfectly sensible position. A noise violation will not have a significant impact on a student's future. However, as explained in Chapter 2, cases of sexual assault inherently involve the sort of serious sanctions described previously. An analysis of claims data from 2011 to 2013 shows that suspension, and most likely expulsion, usually results from a finding of responsibility for sexual assault. According to the education risk management firm United Educators: "Expulsion was the most frequent sanction. Our data suggests that when sexual assaults are adjudicated, institutions frequently impose their severest sanction. Only 18 percent of claims involved sanctions in which the perpetrator did not receive a suspension or expulsion."[15]

---

[13] See, ASCA publication: Tamara King, JD and Benjamin White, JD, "An Attorney's Role in the Conduct Process": "When attorneys are introduced into the equation, the focus shifts from taking responsibility for one's actions to 'getting the student off.'" www.theasca.org/files/Best%20Practices/Attorney%20role%20in%20conduct%20process%20%202.pdf.

[14] Id. at 5.

[15] United Educators, *Confronting Campus Sexual Assault: An Examination of Higher Education Claims* (Bethesda, MD: EduRisk Solutions, 2015), 19, www.ncdsv.org/ERS_Confronting-Campus-Sexual-Assault_2015.pdf.

ASCA also avers that counsel is appropriate when the student is involved in programs that involve licensing such as law, medicine, nursing, and education. However, so many undergraduates end up in one of these programs eventually that a permanent mark on many undergraduate's records implicates the same concerns that it does for students attending those programs.

The second prong of the *Mathews* test is the likelihood of an erroneous decision if the student is forced to proceed without active assistance of counsel. In *Osteen*, the student at issue had already been arrested and charged for a serious assault that he committed in front of multiple witness and did not dispute that he committed the crime, so the Court considered risk of error trivial.[16] So that case is relevant, at most, to cases in which the accused student has, at a minimum, already been arrested and charged for sexual assault.

Moreover, as we have seen in many of the cases discussed so far, many college sexual assault cases often involve complicated, disputed facts; few or no witnesses; and alcohol-impaired memories. As discussed in Chapter 2, they are not always "he said/she said" cases in which the only job of the panel is to decide who is "lying." In many cases, both sides are telling the truth as they see it, but even when the facts are largely agreed upon, these involve difficult interpretations of facts and rules where the type of trained precision lawyers bring is important.

A good example of this is *John Doe v. UCLA* where the two students gave essentially the same account of the facts, but questions of interpretation were so difficult that two different panels came to two different conclusions, with the second panel finding that sexual assault did not occur.[17] In that case, Jane Doe texted John Doe "Great I'll pencil you in" and John Doe replied "Only if I can be in you."[18] The students had prior sexual experience with one another and both understood the second message to be an invitation to sexual activity. Jane Doe told her friends that she went to John's room to tell him that she thought his message was crude. Both students agreed that she did not deliver that message and that they sat down together to watch television. John began kissing Jane and removing her clothes. The two students disagreed about whether Jane helped John remove her clothes, but the investigator concluded that Jane "likely assisted [John] in taking off her pants ... [and] assisted him in removing her underwear as well." When John began to perform oral sex on Jane, she stated, "you don't have to" and he replied, "but I want to." Jane

---

[16] 13 F. 3d at 226.

[17] As will be explained later, the first panel applied an incorrect version of the student code, although that does not appear to have been the basis for the differing conclusions.

[18] All facts come from the written decision of the Rehearing Panel, Exhibit 1 to "Notice of New Findings on Remand in Favor of Petitioner and Report Re Status Conference," Case No. BS155236 (January 7, 2016).

interpreted this as her objecting to sexual contact and John interpreted this as her telling him she only wanted sex if he wanted sex.

Jane then asked John to retrieve a condom, which John interpreted as assent to intercourse. However, Jane "stated [to the investigator] that she feared that the Respondent would proceed despite her objections, so she requested that he use a condom to ensure that the sexual intercourse would be safe." The situation was complicated by the fact that John and Jane had a history of consensual sexual activity that involved rough behavior, including hair pulling and spanking. In fact, during the act of intercourse that formed the basis of her complaint, John pulled her hair sufficiently hard that she complained to him (both sides agree he then let go of her hair) and he spanked her. John described the behaviors as "playful" but Jane stated "that she had been coerced into complying with his verbal commands out of fear of physical violence from Respondent." John stated that "he had smacked the Complainant's bottom during previous sexual encounters with Complainant without objection or complaint."

This turned out to be a difficult case to adjudicate. As noted earlier, two different panels came to two different conclusions despite the fact that John and Jane agreed on most of the observable facts. In a case such as this, it can be difficult to focus on the precise issues that have to be determined. Unlike professors and administrators, lawyers are well trained to look past distracting emotions and focus on the questions at issue. For example, what was UCLA's claim? Was it that:

- Jane never effectively consented to sexual activity;
- She consented but revoked consent at some point. If so, when precisely was it revoked and how was that revocation communicated?
- She never clearly revoked consent, but he exceeded the scope of her consent;
- It was John's responsibility as the initiating party to affirmatively ensure that she was explicitly consenting to each new stage of sexual activity; or
- Was it that under university policy, a student cannot consent to this sort of sexual conduct?

Allowing a lawyer to participate plays an important role in avoiding erroneous decisions because he or she can demand clarity on questions such as these. This way everyone knows what facts and rules are in dispute. Despite the stereotype of lawyers as obfuscators, lawyers are trained to ask precise questions and are attuned to questions of contested or ambiguous definitions of crucial terms such as *effective consent*. Without a lawyer it is all too easy for panelists to filter the situation through their own reaction to the sort of sexual practices in which John and Jane had a history of engaging.

It is not just students in John's position who benefit from having an attorney actively involved in the hearing. Jane clearly would have benefited as well. An attorney would have understood that the investigator had already come to the decision that she helped John take off her clothes and that Jane needed to explain why that happened, or why, at the very least, she allowed him to take her clothes off. An attorney would have helped her explain to the panel what John was doing differently that night that intimidated her, causing a false appearance of consent. Was it John's tone? Body language? Choice of words? Degree of force? If she had an attorney, the attorney could have kept the panel's focus on the university rules that the initiating person must gain the clear consent of the other person throughout sexual activity and helped her explain how John's pulling of her hair was an act of intimidation.

Another illustrative example of the necessity of a fully participating attorney in protecting the rights of the accusing student is the Hobart and William Smith Colleges case, discussed in Chapter 1. Recall that, according to the New York Times account, a first-year student was brutally sexually assaulted by multiple football players who were exonerated by the college panel. The panelists did not seem to always correctly recall the testimony of witnesses. One witness had testified that one of the football players had wanted to go upstairs and have sex, but a panelist said the witness had testified that it was the victim who wanted to go upstairs for that reason. Expecting the victim, a first-year student, to stand up to an adult panelist distorting the details of a highly traumatic event is an absurd demand. Obviously it would have been much better if she had a lawyer to catch the error and correct the panelist. The Times also reported that panelists interrupted her answers and asked her about a campus police report she had never seen before. A lawyer could have protected her ability to finish her sentences and objected to her being asked questions about a report she had never seen. Some judges have expressed concerns about lawyers slowing down proceedings, but, as this case shows, some proceedings are better off being slowed down.

Lawyers also have extensive training in interpreting complex legal rules and many college policies have become complex indeed. Recall the Doe v. University of Southern California case, discussed in Chapters 2 and 4. In that case, Doe was accused of a long list of school rules. He was not found to have engaged in nonconsensual sexual activity with the complainant but was found to have endangered her by leaving her in a room with two other people who had forcefully struck her on her buttocks and who otherwise exceeded the scope of her consent. However, the school argued that because the two other students were engaging in misconduct, John Doe violated the University of Southern California (USC) student handbook Section 11.44C, which required him to "remove [himself] from the situation."[19]

In short, the complex interplay of school rules put John Doe in a position where he was supposed to remove himself from the room but also remain in the room to protect the complainant from the other two people (who were not USC students). To expect a college-age person with no legal training to understand the contradictory requirements, much less defend himself from such a "Catch

[19] Doe v. University of Southern California (April 5, 2016) at 34.

22" set of alleged violations, is completely unrealistic. Lawyers are trained to spot and deal with these sorts of contradictions.

In sum, sex and consent issues are inherently complex and emotional. It is not realistic to expect young, inexperienced men and women to understand what exactly the facts and rules in dispute are or to stand up to panelists who may have preconceived notions or who simply make mistakes.

In *Osteen*, Judge Posner agreed that "[t]he canonical test for how much process is due, [including the right to counsel] was laid down by the Supreme Court in *Mathews v. Eldridge*," but he averred that erroneous deprivations of liberty are unlikely because universities are so eager to keep their source of tuition dollars:

The danger that without the procedural safeguards deemed appropriate in civil and criminal litigation public universities will engage in an orgy of expulsions is slight. The relation of students to universities is, after all, essentially that of customer to seller. That is true even in the case of public universities, though they are much less dependent upon the academic marketplace than private universities are. Northern Illinois University can't have been happy to lose a student whom it had wanted so much that it had given him a football scholarship, and who had made the team to the greater glory of the institution.[20]

But despite whatever deficiencies universities have in addressing sexual assault, there is no evidence that sexual assault panels are unwilling to punish accused students. Indeed, it appears that sexual assault panels are considerably more likely to find an accused student responsible than not responsible.[21] Despite Posner's speculation that universities will be especially reluctant to expel athletes, the evidence indicates that campus are more likely to find athletes responsible for sexual assault than they are for nonathletes and are just as likely to expel them.[22] Further, Posner neglects to mention the importance of an attorney to the accusing student as well.

The third prong of the *Mathews* test is the burden on the university, which has been oft-mentioned by the courts. The Supreme Court has admonished that "[a] school is an academic institution, not a courtroom or administrative hearing room."[23] However, in that same decision, the Court acknowledged that "that there are distinct differences between decisions to suspend or dismiss a student for disciplinary purposes and similar actions taken for academic reasons which may call for hearings in connection with the former but not the latter."[24]

The sixth circuit has expressed concerns about attorneys adding "expense" and "complexity" to disciplinary panels:

[20] 13 F. 3d at 226.   [21] United Educators, *Confronting Campus Sexual Assault*, 10.
[22] Id. at 13.
[23] Board of Curators of the University of Missouri. v. Horowitz, 435 U.S. 78, 88 (1978).
[24] Id. at 87.

While the additional safeguard of professional advocacy may lessen the risk of erroneous expulsion by improving the quality of the student's case, the administrative burdens to a university, in the business of education, not judicial administration, are weighty. Full-scale adversarial hearings in school disciplinary proceedings have never been required by the Due Process Clause and conducting these types of hearings with professional counsel would entail significant expense and additional procedural complexity.[25]

But how true is this? Dissenting from a case upholding a policy limiting legal representation by attorneys of veterans seeking disability benefits, Justice John Stevens wrote:

[T]here is no reason to assume that lawyers would add confusion rather than clarity to the proceedings. As a profession, lawyers are skilled communicators dedicated to the service of their clients. Only if it is assumed that the average lawyer is incompetent or unscrupulous can one rationally conclude that the efficiency of the agency's work would be undermined by allowing counsel to participate whenever a veteran is willing to pay for his services. I categorically reject any such assumption.[26]

Finally, there is a significant possibility that attorneys will *lower* costs by limiting future litigation. As noted in the preceding text, there were two different panels in the *UCLA* case that reached two different conclusions. There reason for the second panel was that the first panel erroneously applied a version of the handbook that was not yet in effect at the time of the disputed incident. According to the male student's attorney, the differences in the two versions of the handbook applied by the two different panels were minor and probably did not affect the outcome of the case.[27] Yet the mistake resulted in litigation and the court required UCLA to hold a new hearing applying the correct version of the handbook. This meant UCLA incurred the expense of two hearings as well as the very substantial cost that litigation always entails. Had the accused student been represented by counsel at the hearing, a single objection by that attorney could have saved UCLA a great deal of money by pointing out an easily avoidable error.

The *UCLA* case is far from unique. Colleges spend many millions of dollars litigating claims from both male and female students who argue that the process for investigating and adjudicating sexual assault was not fair.[28] While allowing greater access to lawyers certainly won't eliminate all this litigation, it is likely to reduce it by eliminating easily avoidable mistakes such as applying the wrong version of the student handbook.

One might object that allowing full participation by attorneys gives wealthier students an advantage over those who cannot afford attorneys. However, as Johnson and Taylor point out, almost all of the litigation by students in these

[25] Flaim v. Medical College of Ohio, 418 F. 3d 629, 640–641 (6th Cir. 2005).
[26] Walters v. National Assn' of Radiation Survivors, 473 U.S. 305, 363 (1985).
[27] Author interview with attorney Mark Hathaway, June 30, 2017.
[28] United Educators, *Confronting Campus Assault*, 14.

cases has been brought by students from wealthy families.[29] As expensive as attorneys are, surely it is far less expensive to have an attorney involved at the college level than it is to hire an attorney for a court case and subsequent appeals. Therefore, preventing attorneys from participating in the college proceedings exacerbates the gap between the ability of rich and poor students to protect their rights.

Further, the same argument could be made about allowing legal representation in any sort of civil proceeding including hearings on disability benefits and on parental fitness, both of which allow for legal representation. The argument has no special force with regard to college assault cases that would not apply to these other kinds of cases.

THE RIGHT TO CONFRONT WITNESSES

The question of whether students or their representatives may confront, or cross-examine,[30] the witnesses against them is one of the most controversial issues of due process. Cross-examination has been famously called the "greatest legal engine ever invented for the discovery of truth."[31] The Supreme Court has said: "Cross-examination is the principal means by which the believability of a witness and the truth of his testimony are tested."[32]

The *Mathews* test is a balancing test though, so the importance of cross-examination must be weighed against the university's interest in excluding it or limiting it. The most obvious cost of cross-examination is that it might retraumatize a victim of sexual assault and that the prospect of it might even keep the victim from coming forward at all. Given the extremely high interest a university has in protecting students from sexual assault, this is a strong interest indeed.

The 2011 Dear Colleague Letter therefore strongly discourages colleges from allowing students to cross-examine or question one another personally. This certainly makes sense. The problems with victims being aggressively questioned by their alleged attackers are obvious.

Much of this discussion will focus on the difficult issue of questioning the alleged victim. However this section will begin by discussing what should be a much easier question. Why can't the alleged assailant or, preferably, his

---

[29] Johnson and Taylor, *The Campus Rape Frenzy*, 95.

[30] I use the terms *confront* and *cross-examine* interchangeably here. The Supreme Court notes that "The main and essential purpose of confrontation is *to secure for the opponent the opportunity of cross-examination.* The opponent demands confrontation not for the idle purpose of gazing upon the witness, or of being gazed upon by him, but for the purpose of cross-examination, which cannot be had except by the direct and personal putting of questions and obtaining immediate answers." Davis v. Alaska, 415 U.S. 308, 316 (1974) (emphasis in original).

[31] 5 John Henry Wigmore, *Evidence in Trials at Common Law,* § 1367, ed. James H. Chabourn (New York: Little Brown, 1974), 32.

[32] Davis v. Alaska, 415 U.S. at 316.

attorney confront witnesses *other* than the alleged victim? This section argues that under the *Mathews* balancing test, the right to confront these witnesses is clearly required by principles of due process. Nor should this right be limited to the accused students; the alleged victim should have this right as well, also preferably through their attorney. In the Hobart and William Smith Colleges case, *the New York Times* reported that "[The t]wo football players accused of sexual assault lied to the police and then changed basic parts of their accounts after witnesses contradicted them. The college panel that cleared both players failed to ask them any questions about why they had lied."[33] Justice would likely have been far better served had the young woman been represented by counsel who could have cross-examined her alleged attackers.

When the witness in question is an adult, the balance should be presumed to be in favor of allowing cross-examination. For example, in a 2018 case, there was substantial evidence that William Richey, a police detective for the University of Cincinnati was having an affair with, and had professed his love for, the alleged victim, Jennifer Schoewe.[34] Richey was the detective investigating the case: "Detective Richey conducted the only interrogation of Gischel [the accused student], he spoke multiple times with Schoewe during the course of the investigation, and he obtained statements from five witnesses about Schoewe's level of intoxication and her interactions with Gischel on the night of the incident."[35] There was ample reason to suspect that Richey was not impartial:

UC conducted an internal investigation concerning the relationship between Detective Richey and Schoewe. Schoewe posted on social media a picture of her wearing a police hat and vest with a caption that included the saying "my detective loves me." Schoewe's friends reported reading text messages in which Detective Richey stated that he loved Schoewe and indicated he had given her a massage.[36]

The panel did not allow Gischel to question the alleged victim about her relationship with the detective. While a close case, one could argue that it was best to shield her from such inquiries. What is much more difficult to understand is why Richey was not available to be questioned at the hearing. Gischel was expelled without an opportunity to ask him a single question. No reasonable balancing test should be understood to allow such a result.

Other situations might be more complicated. If the witness is a student rather than an adult professional, and there is good reason to believe that the accused or accusing student has a history of violence, there may be legitimate issues of witness intimidation. Such situations may be best dealt with by a no-contact order rather by preventing cross-examination, but it would obviously be

---

[33] Bogdanich, "Reporting Rape, and Wishing She Hadn't."
[34] Gischel v. University of Cincinnati, U.S. Dist. Western Ohio (January 23, 2018) Case: 1:17-cv -00475-SJD, Doc #: 14, https://kcjohnson.files.wordpress.com/2018/01/gischel-cincinnati-decision.pdf.
[35] Id. at p 6.   [36] Id. (citations omitted).

a closer call under a balancing test than confrontation of a professional police officer or detective.

Similarly, under the *Mathews* balancing test, it seems clear that both the accused and accusing student should have the right to cross-examine the investigator who writes a report with findings of fact and conclusions about whether the accused student is responsible for sexual assault. Recall in the *Sterrett* case, discussed in the previous chapter, that the accused student never had a chance to confront the investigator who concluded that he committed sexual assault. As we saw, in that case the investigator's report contained a number of crucial assertions for fact that were demonstrably incorrect. When this came out at trial, the University of Michigan conceded that Sterrett had not committed sexual assault, but had Sterrett lacked the resources to bring a lawsuit he would have been expelled.

An investigator is a trained professional who is hardly likely to be traumatized by cross-examination. As we have seen, an investigator's report carries great weight and the *Mathews* test seems to clearly weigh in favor of allowing a student or the student's lawyer to directly question the investigator about the basis for his or her conclusions.

Nevertheless, the courts have not consistently protected the right to confront hostile witnesses even in what this section argues should be easy cases. The Supreme Court, at the beginning of the modern due process era, stated: "In almost every setting where important decisions turn on questions of fact, due process requires an opportunity to confront and cross-examine adverse witnesses."[37] However, the Supreme Court has not pressed this point and lower courts have not seen fit to apply it to educational settings. "However, we have not expanded the *Goldberg* procedural requirements for quasi-judicial termination of welfare benefits in student disciplinary hearings. Where basic fairness is preserved, we have not required the cross-examination of witnesses and a full adversary proceeding."[38]

In *Winnick v. Manning*, a student who was suspended for refusing to leave a classroom as part of a demonstration protesting the Kent State shootings wanted to cross-examine the dean who identified him as the "ringleader" of the demonstration. The Court held that he had no due process right to do so: "The right to cross-examine witnesses generally has not been considered an essential requirement of due process in school disciplinary proceedings."[39] The *Manning* court did include an important caveat: "[I]f this case had

[37] Goldberg v. Kelly, 397 U.S. 254, 269 (1970).
[38] Nash v. Auburn University, 812 F. 2d 655, 664 (11th Cir. 1987). (Citing Boykins v. Fairfield Board of Education, 492 F. 2d 697, 701 (5th Cir. 1974), *cert. denied,* 420 U.S. 962, 95 S.Ct. 1350, 43 L.Ed. 2d 438 (1975); Dixon v. Alabama State Board of Education, 294 F. 2d at 159; accord, Blanton v. State Univ. of New York, 489 F. 2d 377, 385 (2d Cir. 1973); Jaksa v. Regents of the Univ. of Mich., 597 F. Supp. 1245, 1252-53 (E.D.Mich. 1984), *aff'd.,* 787 F. 2d 590 (6th Cir. 1986).
[39] 460 F. 2d 545, 549 (1972).

resolved itself into a problem of credibility, cross-examination of witnesses might have been essential to a fair hearing."[40]

A number of courts have held that in an educational context, cross-examination of witnesses, including the accusing student, is essential to due process when their relative credibility is at issue. In *Doe v. Ohio State*, a federal court ruled:

> The Due Process Clause generally does not guarantee the right to cross-examination in school disciplinary proceedings ... But where a disciplinary proceeding depends on "a choice between believing an accuser and an accused ... cross-examination is not only beneficial, but essential to due process."[41]

Similarly, in *Doe v. University of Cincinnati*, the court held: "In this case, the ARC Hearing Committee was given the choice of believing either Jane Roe or Plaintiff, and therefore, cross-examination was essential to due process."[42]

In sexual assault cases, the credibility of witnesses is virtually always at issue. The case inevitably comes down to whose interpretation of events is more credible. In the context of parole violations, the Supreme Court has ruled that "the minimum requirements of due process" includes "the right to confront and cross-examine adverse witnesses (unless the hearing officer specifically finds good cause for not allowing confrontation)."[43] For college sexual assault cases, the courts should find the same "minimum due process" requirement – the right to confront witnesses unless the college "specifically finds good cause for not allowing confrontation."

Yet, courts do not agree on this, and even go so far as allowing evidence from anonymous witnesses, which makes it virtually impossible for the accused student to respond effectively. In *Sterrett v. Cowan* the case relied upon the statements of anonymous witnesses. These anonymous witnesses were supposedly repeating what the accusing student had told them but their stories seemed to contradict what the accusing student later said under oath:

> On Nov. 9, 2012, Sterrett was given a one-page document titled "Summary of Witness Testimony and Review of Other Evidence." It consisted primarily of summaries of statements from anonymous witnesses. For example, it stated: "Two witnesses stated the Complainant reported to them that she tried to push the Respondent off her." (CB [the complainant] didn't know who these two witnesses were. She confirmed in her deposition that in her original statement to Cowan, she never said that she had tried to push Sterrett off her.) It also stated: "[A] witness reported that the Respondent told them that he engaged in penetration with the Complainant and 'she was saying "no," and that it was just – it was "just like a second," and then he stopped, and then the Complainant

---

[40] 460 F. 2d at 550.

[41] Doe v. Ohio State Univ., No. 2:15-CV-2830, 2016 WL 6581843 (S.D. Ohio Nov. 7, 2016) at 10.

[42] Case No. 1:16cv987, Opinion and Order (November 30, 2016) at 10. This is a different case than the one involving the alleged affair between the complainant and the detective.

[43] Morrissey v. Brewer, 408 U.S. 471, 489 (1972).

left.'" (In her deposition, CB acknowledged this was not how their sexual encounter transpired, although she maintained that at some point she said "no.")[44]

The *Sterrett* court found that this anonymous testimony, even in the absence of any stated reason that they might be afraid of Sterrett, was not a constitutional violation: "However, confronting the Complainant, let alone other witnesses, is not an absolute right and is generally not a part of the due process requirement in a school disciplinary setting."[45] The courts should rethink this. Absent a finding of potential witness intimidation or a risk to student safety, no one should be labeled a sex offender on the basis of anonymous witnesses.

The most important, and most difficult issue, is cross-examination of the accusing student. It is no easy task to balance fairness to the accused with the very strong interest in not retraumatizing a sexually assaulted student and not discouraging the reporting of sexual assault. However, colleges must do better than they currently are.

We have previously looked at a number of cases in which the accusing student's account of a sexual encounter was apparently contradicted by various texts, Facebook messages, and so forth. These do not necessarily mean that the accusing student is lying. The trauma of a sexual assault can provoke reactions that seem inappropriate or suspicious to outside observers:

Rape victims' statements almost always have inconsistencies for a variety of reasons. First, victims' memories are distorted by trauma. The flood of stress hormones dulls the frontal cortex, responsible for rational planning and memory, and turns on the more primitive part of our brain responsible for survival. Given a choice between accurately witnessing a horrific event or living through it, our bodies choose survival. Rape victims also suffer PTSD at extraordinary rates, like soldiers returning from war. They use denial as a psychological tool of survival, blocking memories they cannot afford to process. When forced to recount the rape, victims act in ways that challenge their credibility. They sometimes laugh inappropriately and at other times disassociate, seeming strangely unemotional. Their memories twist into an incoherent jumble and change over time as details slip past the walls of denial.[46]

Nevertheless, even with the understanding that trauma victims deserve great understanding of how their experiences might affect them, and that they should not be expected to be "perfect victims," sexual assault hearings cannot proceed on the presumption that the accused student is guilty. For process to be fair, an accused student must have an opportunity to attempt to demonstrate that seemingly exonerating texts are indeed exonerating. As we have seen, there are numerous cases in which a student has been found responsible for sexual assault despite text message chains that raise credibility issues far beyond being "jumbled" or "seeming strangely unemotional."

---

[44] Yoffe, "The College Rape Overcorrection."   [45] *Sterrett* at 85 F. Supp. 3d at 929.
[46] Tania Tetlow, "Inconsistencies in Rape Victims' Statements about the Trauma Are Understandable," *Nola* (December 2, 2014), www.nola.com/crime/index.ssf/2014/12/inconsistencies_in_rape_victim.html.

A good example of the importance of cross-examination is *Doe v. Western New England University*, where a student was suspended for two years as a result of a sexual encounter described by a federal judge as follows:

Doe [the accused student] and Loe [the pseudonym for the accusing student] met at a party. They consumed some alcohol, but not enough to be impaired. They went to Doe's room, ostensibly to watch a movie. They began kissing. By mutual consent, they both removed all their clothing. Loe said she did not want to have penile-vaginal intercourse, and Doe respected this. By mutual consent, they began performing oral sex on each other. At some point, Loe said she did not want to continue this, and Doe stopped. At this point, Doe's and Loe's versions of what happened appear to diverge slightly. According to Doe, he asked Loe to "finish him off" so that he would not be left with "blue balls." She then masturbated him to ejaculation. (Id. at 5.) According to Loe, Doe said, "Now you have to finish me off," placed her hand on his penis, and held it there until he ejaculated. (Id.) It is undisputed that Loe never explicitly voiced any disinclination to masturbate Doe or tried to pull her hand away.[47]

The accusation in this case came nine months after the previously mentioned incident; but shortly after the event in question, Loe had a lengthy exchange of texts with a friend that, according to the complaint,[48] included numerous emojis of "smiley faces" and "A-Ok" signs by Loe, describing the encounter as "my first kiss and hook up."[49] The texts also appeared to contradict Loe's statement that when someone walked into the room during the encounter she did not react to the door opening because she was "shocked by what was happening" and "she felt paralyzed when the door opened."[50] According to the complaint, Loe's texts said that she actively pulled the covers over herself when someone walked in:

LOE: Literally someone was knocking and we threw the covers over us and then they didn't come in and then all of a sudden some girl walks in ..."
FRIEND: Gotta learn lock your door ;)
LOE: The door was locked [frown face emoji] she used the roommates key and then asked if the roommate could come in haha
FRIEND: I would have [thrown] something at her
LOE: I just didn't look at her in the eyes [double smiling emojis].[51]

Even considering important lessons about the impact of traumatic experiences on victim behavior, these texts certainly seem to contradict her assertion that she was "paralyzed" when the room was entered. The OCR's 2011 Dear Colleague Letter strongly discourages students from directly cross-examining one

[47] Doe v. Western New England University (D.C. Mass. January 10, 2017) C.A. No. 15-30192-MAP.
[48] The Verified Complaint alleges that the plaintiff's attorney was not allowed to make any photocopies of the documents at issue in the case but that all the text messages previously mentioned were hand copied by the attorney.
[49] Verified Complaint and Jury Demand (Filed November 2, 2015) at 6.
[50] Id. at 30, quoting the "Interview Summary." [51] Id. at 8.

another but is silent on cross-examination by a student's representative. While precautions (discussed in the following text) should be taken to prevent abuse, an accused student should be entitled to ask his accuser about texts such as these.

One compromise approach taken by some universities is to allow the accused student to submit questions to the panel, which the panel, at its discretion, asks to the accusing student. However, the administrators and professors on these panels are generally not attorneys. Cross-examination is largely the art of attentive listening and carefully framed follow-up questions. Without the ability to follow up an evasive or vague answer with a clarifying question, effective cross-examination is virtually impossible and it is harder still when questions are being paraphrased. A good example is *Doe v. Washington and Lee*, where a federal judge described the questioning process as follows:

> Plaintiff was required to submit written questions to Mr. Simpson [the panel chair], who would review them for relevancy before passing them on to the members of the SFHB [the hearing panel] for further review of their relevancy. The SFHB panel would proceed to ask the questions only if they deemed them to be appropriate, and when they did so, they would often paraphrase the questions and ask them in an order different than what was requested by Plaintiff. The SFHB refused to ask Jane Doe questions when it calculated that doing so would cause her emotional distress.[52]

According to the judge, the panel's questions and lack of follow-up effectively prevented the accused student from asking the accusing student to explain any of the inconsistencies in her version of the events:

> The SFHB generally did not question Jane Doe about [the various] inconsistencies. One panelist, however, did ask Jane Doe why she could recall her statements purporting to object to sexual intercourse so clearly, while she was unable to recall other parts of the evening with the same clarity. In response, Jane Doe stated, "I know I said it because I know I said it," which ended that line of questioning.[53]

The cross-examination issue is nonetheless tricky because it is so important that sexual assault victims not be retraumatized. Even here, there are a few caveats. Sometimes the questions that might be asked of the accusing students, while highly relevant, do not involve the alleged assault and are therefore less likely to force someone to relive the experience. For example in the *USCD* case, discussed earlier, the accusing student had apparently stated that she was very inexperienced with alcohol but also apparently made a reference to "the guy who usually buys us alcohol."[54] The issue in that case involved her consumption of alcohol and her ability to give effective consent, so the veracity of her statement about being inexperienced with alcohol was crucial. The panel did not allow the accused student's attorney to question her on this seeming contradiction.

---

[52] Memorandum Opinion, Case No. 6:14-cv-00052 (W.D. Virginia, August 5, 2015).
[53] Id. at 11.   [54] Johnson and Taylor, *The Campus Rape Frenzy*, 144.

Even more importantly, it is possible to allow for cross-examination while shielding vulnerable individuals from abuse. Even in the case of the most vulnerable of all possible individuals – child victims of abuse – the courts allow cross-examination of such victims, with such limits as are necessary to protect them from abuse:

Embarrassing questions. The court may limit questions which are unduly embarrassing for the child. In the context of sexual abuse litigation, the nature of the case often makes it necessary for the crossexaminer to delve into embarrassing matters, and trial courts respect counsel's need to ask such questions. Improper limitations on questions about embarrassing topics could violate the confrontation clause.[55]

To protect the child witness from abusive cross-examination, courts allow various limitations:

Irrelevant or collateral matters. The court may disallow cross-examination on irrelevant, marginally relevant, and collateral matters.
Undue consumption of time. The court may limit examination which constitutes an undue consumption of time, or which is unduly repetitive.
Assuming facts not in evidence. Questions which assume facts not in evidence may be excluded.
Confusing, misleading, ambiguous, unintelligible, or compound questions. The court may instruct counsel to refrain from questions which are unintelligible or which confuse the witness. This authority is particularly important with children, many of whom are easily confused. When it is apparent that a child is confused, the court may require the attorney to phrase questions in a manner that is understandable to the child.
Harassment or annoyance. The court may curtail questions designed to harass or annoy the witness.[56]

Obviously, this is an imperfect analogy. The Sixth Amendment's confrontation clause does not apply to college tribunals. Nonetheless, it does show that the courts believe that even the most vulnerable victims of sexual abuse can be shielded from harassment and abuse during cross-examination. Certainly harassing, irrelevant, repetitive, and argumentative questions should be disallowed. Cross-examination can be allowed under the same guidelines that control cross-examination of child sexual abuse victims.

A possible objection to this suggestion is that it would require a certain amount of sophistication on the part of panel chairs to enforce these limitations. However, one can argue that *it is already true* that the panel chair should have a firm grasp of legal basics such as the difference between relevant and irrelevant testimony or the difference between harassing and permissible lines of questions. Indeed, that is exactly what the ASCA already recommends:

[55] John E. B. Myers, *The Child Witness: Techniques for Direct Examination, Cross-Examination, and Impeachment*, 18 Pacific Law Journal 801–942, 876 (1987).
[56] Id. at 876 (citations omitted).

Some student conduct professionals have a law school education or professional legal background, experiences that provide credibility when working with attorneys and help them understand the attorney's experience, approach, and training. Those without these valuable experiences, however, need equivalent knowledge, skills, and abilities. Therefore, ASCA should ensure that professionals working in student conduct offices who do not have such background attend the Gehring Academy or the equivalent for requisite training in this area. Such training would bridge the gap between those with legal education/ experience and those without. It would also provide a base of knowledge for professionals working with attorneys in a confident, reasonable, and non-threatening manner.[57]

While such training involves university expense, the same could be said of a multitude of training sessions, seminars, and retreats that are commonplace for various professionals across all manner of university departments including human resources, business and accounting, student life, and so forth. While the *Mathews* balancing test takes the cost to universities into account, the costs of properly training panel members hardly seem onerous given that this is what they are already being advised to do.

There are other measures that can be taken to protect accusing students from trauma during cross-examination. Rape shield laws should be extended to college proceedings. Such laws exclude evidence about the victim's past sexual behavior not directly related to the accusation at issue and also exclude evidence about the victim's "reputation." The OCR 2014 Guidance Letter prohibits questions about the accusing student's previous sexual encounters other than with the accused. This should be written into legislation.

There are other commonsense measures that can be taken. The alleged assailant can be removed from the room during the alleged victim's cross-examination with the alleged assailant by listening to the testimony using a speaker phone or Skype. The attorney questioning the accusing student can be required to remain seated and be placed a reasonable distance from the accusing student. Of course, the accusing student can have her own attorney or support person.

The Right to Present Witnesses

In his seminal 1975 law review article "Some Kind of Hearing," Judge Henry Friendly stated: "Under most conditions there does not seem to be any disposition to deny the right to call witnesses, although the tribunal must be entitled reasonably to limit their number and the scope of examination."[58]

[57] Tamara King and Benjamin White, "An Attorney's Role in the Conduct Process," *Association for Student Conduct Administration* (n.d.), www.theasca.org/files/Best%20Practices/Attorney%20role%20in%20conduct%20process%20%202.pdf.
[58] Henry J. Friendly, *Some Kind of Hearing*, 123 University of Pennsylvania Law Review 1267–1317, 1282 (1975).

Curtis and Vivian Berger, writing in the *Columbia Law Review*, call the right to present witnesses on one's own behalf a "bedrock" principle of due process:

Fact-finders generally are skeptical of self-serving statements. Witnesses with a less obvious bias than the accused may be more persuasive to the hearing board ... In a nutshell, it makes no more sense in an academic disciplinary forum than in a courtroom for fact-finders to exclude data that bears upon the disputed issues. Furthermore, to do so in a lopsided fashion disadvantaging only the student whose whole career may be at stake is worse than senseless: It is fundamentally unfair.[59]

The OCR has no objection to allowing students to call witnesses so long as both students have an equal right to do so.[60] Yet, this right has not been consistently enforced by the courts. Recall that in *Sterrett v. Michigan* the accused student never had an opportunity to offer the testimony of his roommate who was in the bunkbed directly above the two students at issue. It was only during the civil lawsuit that the roommate was able to testify that he had not told the investigator that he was asleep during the incident and even had a timed Facebook message complaining about the noise the pair were making.

Without the right to present one's own witnesses, the risk of error is far greater either because the testimony is filtered through an investigator who may have confirmation bias or the testimony might not be heard at all. In *Sahm v. Miami University*, the investigator not only refused to call one of the accused student's witnesses, a friend of the accusing students referred to as "AT," but also she *actively discouraged* her from testifying:

Tobergte [the investigator] interviewed Sahm and A.T., A.P.'s sorority sister, about the incident. Tobergte did not disclose her positions with the Police Department or on the Task Force to Sahm or A.T. Tobergte discouraged A.T. from testifying at Sahm's disciplinary hearing and she told A.T. to "Google" facts and statistics about campus sexual assaults.[61]

The Court stated that the investigator's discouragement of a witness from testifying was "troubling," but it was a *not* a violation of the accused student's rights.

A number of courts have held that refusal to let an accused student present witnesses might be evidence of gender bias, if the refusal were part of a pattern of discriminatory behavior. In *Doe v. Columbia University*, the Second Circuit Court of Appeals refused to dismiss a gender discrimination complaint based in significant part on the panel's refusal to hear testimony from various witnesses whom the accused student stated would support his case. The student was found responsible for "inflict[ing] nonconsensual sex on Jane Doe, by virtue of having coercively pressured her over a period of weeks to have sex with him."[62] Columbia claimed that the accused student's witnesses did have any relevant evidence, but the court rejected that contention:

---

[59] Berger and Berger, *Academic Discipline*, 289–364.
[60] Russlynn Ali, Dear Colleague Letter (April 4, 2011), www2.ed.gov/about/offices/list/ocr/letters/colleague-201104.html.
[61] 110 F. Supp. 3d 774, 775 (2015).   [62] 831 F. 3d 46, 50 (2d Cir. 2016).

Columbia's proffered explanation that those witnesses were not sought out because they had no relevance to whether Plaintiff had coerced Jane Doe by unreasonable pressure during the preceding weeks does not justify the dismissal of the Complaint ... it is not correct that the potential witnesses suggested by Plaintiff related exclusively to the events of the night of the sexual encounter and not to the preceding weeks. At least one was allegedly identified as a friend and potential confidante of Jane Doe's and not as a person who observed the interaction between John and Jane on the night of the encounter.[63]

However, judicial recognition that refusal to let a student present witnesses, or even to interview witnesses sought by the accused student, might bolster a claim of Title IX gender discrimination is far short of holding that due process requires that students are allowed to present witnesses. Accused students (and sometimes accusing students) are often forbidden from contacting or discussing the case with anyone, so in a single investigator model, if the investigator refuses to interview a witness or to report his or her testimony then the panel will never hear from those witnesses or even know of their existence.

Applying the *Mathews* balancing test this should be an easy issue to decide. Depriving an accused student of such a "bedrock" principle of due process obviously increases the risk of an erroneous decision. As the OCR recommends, the right should be provided to both the accused and accusing student, so that the likelihood of an erroneous decision in either direction is reduced. As for the third prong of the *Mathews* test, the burden on the university – the burden of witness testimony – can be limited in the commonsense manner described by Judge Friendly (as mentioned previously), reasonably limiting the number of witnesses and the scope of testimony to relevant facts.

THE RIGHT TO APPEAL

As of 1996, the OCR took the position that only the accused student should have the right to appeal a university's sexual assault panel's decision, reasoning that the accused student "is the one who stands to be tried twice for the same allegation."[64] However, the OCR latter reversed course, stating in the 2011 Dear Colleague Letter: "OCR also recommends that schools provide an appeals process. If a school provides for appeal of the findings or remedy, *it must do so for both parties.*"[65] The 2017 "Q & A on Campus Sexual Misconduct" from the Trump administration took the opposite tack and removed the guidance language recommending a right to appeal and allows schools to offer only the accused student a right to appeal.[66]

---

[63] 831 F. 3d at 56, n. 10.
[64] Henrick, "A Hostile Environment of Student Defendants," 49–92, 66.
[65] Dear Colleague Letter at p. 12 (emphasis added).
[66] www2.ed.gov/about/offices/list/ocr/docs/qa-title-ix-201709.pdf, 7. ("If a school chooses to allow appeals from its decisions regarding responsibility and/or disciplinary sanctions, the school may choose to allow appeal (i) solely by the responding party; or (ii) by both parties, in which case any appeal procedures must be equally available to both parties.")

Even taking a strong position on due process rights, as this book obviously does, it seems that the Trump administration's position is a step backward. Allowing schools to simply not offer an appeal at all clearly violates the *Mathews* test. Further, the OCR's 2011 position, requiring colleges to both sides to appeal did not, in and of itself, violate any person's due process rights. As rape survivor advocates often point out, Title IX is a civil law, not a criminal law, and, in civil rights cases, both sides have a right to appeal. We have seen that sexual assault panels can render seemingly unfair decisions in favor of the accused student as well as against him, and no principle of due process prevents a victimized student from challenging demonstrable defects in the initial process.

Nonetheless, colleges need to tread carefully here. Recall from Chapter 4, when the Supreme Court applied the *Mathews* test to a prison administration's decision to transfer a prisoner to a "supermax" facility, it approvingly noted that the process contained multiple levels of review, each of which could deny the transfer of the prisoner to a supermax prison, but none of which could overrule a decision *not* to transfer a prisoner to a supermax.[67]

While allowing an alleged victim to appeal does not per se mean that, as the OCR once said, an accused student "stands to be tried twice for the same allegation," various examples show how exactly that can happen and even worse. The case of *Doe v. Alger*,[68] involving James Madison University, a public university in Virginia, well illustrates how a university's appellate process can severely violate an accused student's due process rights. John Doe was found by a university panel not to have sexually assaulted Jane Roe. Roe appealed the decision. Despite the fact that the panel found Doe not responsible, and even though the appeals panel had not yet made any determinations, Doe was suspended from campus:

Roe filed her appeal on December 10, 2014, the final day for doing so. The semester ended, and all of the dorms closed two days later on December 12, 2014. Doe went home for break and was pre-registered for five new classes for the spring semester. The appeal review board (or appeal board) met while he was on break, and determined that he should be suspended, so he was not permitted to return to JMU or to take those classes.[69]

The university did not allow Doe to appear before the appeals panel. The university tried to claim that he could have so appeared if he had tried harder, a suggestion that was fairly laughed off by Federal Judge Elizabeth K. Dillon, an Obama appointee:

Defendants acknowledge that Doe was told he "would not appear," but argue that he was not told that he "could not" appear, suggesting that there is a difference between the two. In particular, they point out that he could have asked for permission to do so because the policy permits OSARP to allow an appearance in "extraordinary

[67] Austin v. Wilkinson, 544 U.S. 74 (2005).
[68] Memorandum and Opinion (December 23, 2016) Civil Action No. 5:15-cv-00035.
[69] Doe v. Alger at 8 (citations omitted).

circumstances." The court finds that argument meritless. The people tasked by JMU with advising Doe about the procedure told Doe repeatedly that he would not be present at any appeal board meeting.[70]

In addition to suspending Doe despite the "not responsible" finding of the first panel, and not allowing him to appear before the appellate panel that suspended him, the appellate panel also relied upon new evidence that had not been before the original panel and that Doe had no opportunity to respond to, or even see:

> The undisputed facts establish that there were several pieces of evidence that were presented to the appeal board. Doe describes much of it as "new evidence" to which he was not given an adequate opportunity to respond. Construing the facts in the light most favorable to defendants, some of the evidence may not have been entirely new, but some indisputably was. And while Doe was given an opportunity to respond, in writing, to some of this evidence, some was not even provided to him. The court discusses the evidence in detail, because it is important to the court's analysis.[71]

Further, even where Doe was aware of new evidence before the appeals panel, a mixture of university policies forbidding him from contacting witnesses, and a seemingly random approach of the appeals panel as to what sort of evidence they would consider, created a situation in which Roe's new evidence could not be challenged:

> Despite this [new allegation of Roe's] that a witness had lied, no member of the appeal board asked for testimony from either the suitemate or the roommate, nor could they direct a rehearing on that issue. Further, Doe was prohibited under JMU's policy from contacting the roommate or any witness. Thus, he could not obtain testimony from her that she had not lied or ask her to reaffirm her previous testimony.[72]

In addition, Roe submitted a voicemail purportedly showing that she was very drunk at the time of the alleged assault, but it turned out that the voicemail was from a date other than when the alleged assault took place. However, Doe did not receive notice of the new evidence in time to respond to it:

> Third, Roe submitted a statement and a voice-mail from a friend of hers at another college. According to both the screen shot and the statement, the voicemail was one that Roe had left her friend at "11:39 p.m. on August 21, 2014," which was approximately 24 hours before Roe alleged the assault occurred. According to the statement, the voice-mail showed that Roe had consumed alcohol ... Roe claimed that the voicemail "emphasizes that I was drunk and unable to give consent to sex." The additional Roe statement was submitted to [the hearing board] on December 17, 2014, but was not provided to Doe until after he filed a response on December 22.[73]

One of the reasons that Doe did not see much of the new evidence against him was that the university violated its own rules regarding deadlines for submitting evidence in favor of Roe. This included an expert statement about the likely effects of Roe mixing alcohol and Prozac:

---

[70] Id. at 8, n. 7.   [71] Id. at 9.   [72] Id. at 10 (citations omitted).   [73] Id. at 11.

Finally, the file given to the December 5 hearing board included a three-page statement from a licensed clinical social worker, describing the effects of alcohol consumption on a user of Prozac, and a statement from a pharmacy that showed medicines prescribed to Roe, including Prozac. Doe has testified that the statement, although dated December 5, was not added to the case file until after the December 5 hearing, and that he did not see it prior to or during the December 5 hearing, or at any point during the appeal process. Defendants admitted in their answer that it was not placed in the file until after the time permitted by its own procedures. And they have not offered any evidence to show that it was ever provided to or made available to Doe.[74]

In addition, the appeals board reviewed the case *de novo*, which means that they were not merely reviewing the first panel's decisions for specific errors, but deciding the case as if it were being decided for the first time even though they did not meet with any witnesses:

The appeal board consisted of three faculty members ... All three testified that they gave no deference to the initial hearing board's decision, but reviewed all the evidence, including the audio recording of the initial hearing, to render a decision ... . The board members did not attempt to speak with any of the witnesses, or with Doe or Roe, before rendering their decision. Instead, the members met on January 8 and reviewed the documentation in the file and discussed it.[75]

The appeals board then suspended Doe for more than five years, without explaining why it was overturning the initial finding that Doe was not responsible for sexual assault:

The appeal board then issued a written document that simply described its decision as "Sanction Increased." It imposed a "new sanction" on Doe of immediate suspension from JMU through Spring 2020 and would allow Doe's readmission only if he completed an education/counseling program and then reapplied. It also banned Doe from Greek involvement and functions. Nowhere did the statement expressly state that it found him responsible for sexual misconduct, nor did it contain any reasoning or explanation for its decision.[76]

In sum, while it is probably wise policy to allow both students to appeal procedurally deficient decisions, the James Madison case shows the importance of strongly enforcing principles of due process in these appeals. It is virtually inconceivable that the previously mentioned process could be found constitutional under the *Mathews* balancing test. Therefore, the remainder of this chapter will discuss the essential elements of due process in the appellate process.

The Appellate Decision Maker Must Be Distinct and Independent from the Initial Decision Maker

It seems too obvious for extended argument that an appellate decision maker should not be the same person as the initial decision maker. In a judicial context, a party can ask the judge to reconsider his or her decision, but that is an entirely

[74] Id. at 12–13 (citations omitted).   [75] Id. at 13 (citations omitted).   [76] Id. at 13–14.

different process than an appeal. The *Merriam-Webster Dictionary* defines *appeal* as "a legal proceeding by which a case is brought before a higher court for review of the decision of a lower court."[77]

Yet, as reported by Johnson and Taylor, at Brown University the chair of the Title IX Committee appoints all three members of the initial sexual assault panel and can serve as both the chair of the initial panel and the appellate panel.[78] A federal judge found numerous procedural errors in the initial panel's decision including the finding that the accused student "manipulated" the student into having sex with him even though there was nothing about such an offense in Brown's writing policy that time.[79] Obviously, a truly independent panel would have been far more likely to correct that mistake, saving both the university and the accused student a great amount of legal expenses.

Similarly, it seems obvious that an appellate decision maker should not be a subordinate of the person who made the initial decision. However, the courts have been unwilling to enforce this commonsense requirement. In *Henley v. Osteen*, the appellate panel at Northern Illinois University was chaired by an "assistant judicial officer" who was a subordinate of the person who made the initial determination punishing the accused student.[80] Nevertheless, the federal appellate court upheld the university's process and punishment.

Further, any appellate decision maker should not be a person or persons who have significant independent contact with or views about the accusation at issue. For example, in a case discussed earlier, a dean who had a number of "off the record and *ex parte* meetings with plaintiff's accuser [meaning the accused was neither present nor aware of the meetings] assigned the appeal to himself."[81] As the Court noted, even the "*appearance* of impartiality is one of the many facets of procedural fairness."[82]

New Facts or Charges on Appeal

In the James Madison case, discussed in the preceding text, we saw the danger of error when an appeals panel considers evidence that had not been presented previously. Similarly, in a number of cases discussed previously, one of the procedural defects was the reliance on new charges or theories that were not explicitly at issue in the initial panel. In *Doe v. University of Southern California*, the initial panel found that Jane Doe had not consented to sexual activity with multiple men, but the appeals panel upheld John Doe's punishment based upon the "endangerment" and "encouragement" theories discussed

---

[77] www.merriam-webster.com/dictionary/appeal.
[78] Johnson and Taylor, *The Campus Rape Frenzy*, 255–256.   [79] Id. at 256.
[80] 13 F. 3d at 224.
[81] Doe v. Rector and Visitors of George Mason University, Memorandum and Opinion 1:15-cv -209 (February 25, 2016, E.D. Virginia) at p. 19.
[82] Id.

earlier. The appellate court held that "John was not afforded any opportunity to address the Appeal's Panel's new theory."[83]

Similarly, in *Sterrett v. Cowan*, on appeal, the university added the theory that the accusing student was too drunk to consent. At the initial stage of adjudication, the university's theory had been that Sterrett used force.[84]

This practice of adding new theories at the appeals stage clearly increases the chance of an erroneous decision because they make it difficult if not impossible for the accused student to respond to the new allegations. For example, in *Tanyi v. Appalachian State University* one of the two accusing students was allowed, on appeal, to add an entirely new claim that the accused student sexually harassed her as well as sexually assaulted her. As a result, the accused student was unable to adequately respond to the harassment charges. He was once again cleared of the assault charges but found responsible for the harassment charge that arose only on appeal. According to the court:

> Following Tanyi's exoneration by the Student B panel, Student A posted a message on Facebook naming Tanyi and his roommates as rapists, and alleging that Appalachian State was attempting to protect them because they were football players. The post garnered statewide media attention. Student B appealed the panel's ruling, and on March 9, 2012, Defendant Gonzalez granted Student B's appeal. At the new Student B hearing, Student B also accused Tanyi of harassing her on campus, in addition to the original allegations. Tanyi alleges he was not informed of the new harassment charge until the night before the hearing, and had no time to prepare witnesses to rebut the charge. On March 29, 2012, the panel cleared Tanyi of Student B's sexual misconduct allegations, but did find Tanyi responsible for the new charge of harassment.[85]

Such practices should be clearly forbidden under the *Mathews* balancing test, unless there is some demonstrable reason that the new charges could not have brought earlier. And even then, the new charges should result in a new hearing, not new charges on appeal. Not only does this practice create unacceptable risks of erroneous decisions, but, absent some demonstrable reason otherwise, requiring the university to present its theory of the case at the initial hearing is not an onerous burden to the university.

A Record for Appeal

Obviously, a student has no effective right of appeal if there is no record of what transpired at the hearing. In today's technological environment where digital recording is widely and inexpensively available, it is not an onerous burden on a university to create a record of the hearing. In fact, such a recording also

---

[83] Doe v. University of Southern California at 24.
[84] Yoffe, "The College Rape Overcorrection."
[85] Tanyi v. Appalachian State University, Order and Memorandum NO. 5:14-CV-170RLV (July 22, 2015) (citations omitted).

protects the university's interests as well as the students and provides an incentive for the panel to follow established procedures:

> Fundamental fairness in the disciplinary process requires a hearing record that can be used by hearing board members during their deliberations and in the event of an appeal ... A complete record also protects the school on appeal: the accused student must be able to point to error or fundamental unfairness in the record in order to take meaningful advantage of the right to appeal. Finally, knowing that the proceedings are being recorded and may become "public record" if the student appeals the disciplinary decision, hearing board members may have a greater incentive to strictly conform their behavior to established procedures.[86]

CONCLUSION

In this chapter and the previous chapter, we have reviewed the most important elements of procedural due process. All the rights discussed in these chapters should be equally available to both accused and accusing students. Sexual assault is too important an issue and too serious an accusation to allow the sort of practices we have seen. Anonymous witnesses, evidence never seen by the accused, new theories added after a student is found not responsible, lack of opportunity to confront adult professionals for bias, even a love affair with the complainant, and so forth – all without either student allowed the aid of an attorney – does not meet the balance of interests required by due process.

In addition to these very important procedural issues, there are some equally important substantive issues. As a result of state government mandates and individual university policies, schools have begun to regulate how students engage in sex. The next chapter argues that the Supreme Court has held that people have a right to sexual autonomy broad enough to allow both heterosexual and homosexual sodomy as well as access to contraceptives. The next three chapters will also explore whether college regulation of student's sexual activities has become sufficiently extensive as to violate students' rights to sexual autonomy.

---

[86] Lisa Tenerowicz, *Student Misconduct at Private Colleges and Universities: A Roadmap for 'Fundamental Fairness' in Disciplinary Proceedings*, 42 B.C.L. Rev. 653, 689 (2001).

PART III

SUBSTANCE AND SOLUTIONS

6

Sexual Assault and Affirmative Consent

So far, this book has focused on procedural issues. However, there is also an important controversy over the *substantive* regulation of student sexual activity, that is, how should sexual assault be substantively defined on college campuses? Much of this debate revolves around the movement toward defining *sexual assault* by the absence of "affirmative consent."

In the fall of 2014, California Governor Jerry Brown signed the nation's first mandatory affirmative consent legislation, which applies to all schools, public or private, receiving state funds. The law states:

An affirmative consent standard in the determination of whether consent was given by both parties to sexual activity. "Affirmative consent" means affirmative, conscious, and voluntary agreement to engage in sexual activity. It is the responsibility of each person involved in the sexual activity to ensure that he or she has the affirmative consent of the other or others to engage in the sexual activity. Lack of protest or resistance does not mean consent, nor does silence mean consent. Affirmative consent must be ongoing throughout a sexual activity and can be revoked at any time. The existence of a dating relationship between the persons involved, or the fact of past sexual relations between them, should never by itself be assumed to be an indicator of consent.[1]

New York State has adopted similar legislation and more than 1,400 colleges and universities have also adopted affirmative consent policies defining *sexual assault*.[2] Several other states are considering legislation that would mandate affirmative consent as the standard for sexual assault on college campuses. Perhaps surprisingly, the OCR has not expressed an opinion on affirmative consent. The trend in this direction has been the result of state legislation and decisions made on individual campuses.

Just from reading the California statute, one might wonder why this policy is so controversial. After all, sexually touching someone without their consent

---

[1] http://leginfo.legislature.ca.gov/faces/billNavClient.xhtml?bill_id=201320140SB967.
[2] Deborah Tuekheimer, *Affirmative Consent*, 13, no. 2 Ohio State Journal of Criminal Law 441–468, 442 (2016).

seems to be an obvious act of sexual assault. The University of California system had an affirmative consent policy in place even before the California legislature passed the law.[3]

The idea behind affirmative consent is that the alleged victim no longer needs to show that she or he resisted or said no to any sexual touching or act. A sexual touching that the recipient did not visibly and clearly consent to ahead of time is sexual assault. However, much of the criticism of affirmative consent stems from the breadth of the laws and policies enacting it. Kimberly Kessler Ferzan, the Harrison Robertson Professor of Law at the University of Virginia, writes:

> Moreover, there are reasons to be skeptical of whether affirmative consent standards can be successful even on campus. First, these provisions are absurdly sweeping. They bar not only sex but sexual contacts. They cover not only students but also [sometimes] faculty. They include not just first encounters but also married couples.[4]

Advocates for affirmative consent laws argue that they are vital to protecting victims. Affirmative consent is often referred to as a "yes means yes" rule and is contrasted with the rule that "no means no." Affirmative consent advocates argue that "no means no" leaves too many gaps in protection for victims of sexual assault:

> The problem with a "no means no" model is that a statutory scheme that prohibited sex by force, threat, or in the face of a "no" would still be woefully under-inclusive in capturing some culpable actors. Imagine that a man gropes a women on a subway. He does not use force, threat, or get a "no," but his conduct is most certainly a crime.[5]

Indeed, a small but not insignificant percentage of men in college admit to the tactic of engaging in sexual penetration before the woman can object: "Specifically, when asked how they would indicate consent to vaginal–penile intercourse, a small percentage of men wrote that they would insert their penis into a woman's vagina and pretend as though it occurred by mistake."[6]

Advocates of affirmative consent also argue that the standard prevents fact finders from improperly impugning the motives or character of the person alleging sexual assault:

> Affirmative consent standards are not simply victim-protecting because they offer clear rules for the morally obtuse. They are purportedly victim-protecting because they prevent a searching inquiry into the victim's state of mind. To the extent that the search for victim consent has been an avenue for unfair exploration and exposure of a victim's

---

[3] Napolitano, "Only Yes Means Yes," 387–402.

[4] Kimberly Kessler Ferzan, *Consent, Culpability, and the Law of Rape*, 13, no. 2 Ohio State Journal of Criminal Law 397–439, 437–438 (2016).

[5] Ibid., 397–439, 429.

[6] Kristen N. Jozkowski and Zoë D. Peterson, "College Students and Sexual Consent: Unique Insights," *The Journal of Sex Research* 50 (2012): 517–523, 520. This should be interpreted with caution though. Due to a small sample size, only 11 college men admitted to this sort of behavior.

sexual past, it is easy to see the benevolent desire to spare a victim from this inquiry. If the only question is what she said and not what she meant, then say the reformers, we need not delve into the hidden recesses of her mind, but merely look superficially at her actions.[7]

Advocates also believe that affirmative consent shields women in particular because they have been socialized to accept a passive view of their role in a sexual encounter, whereas men are taught to be aggressive:

The current societal script on sex assumes that passivity and silence – essentially, the "lack of a no" – means it's okay to proceed. That's on top of the fact that male sexuality has been socially defined as aggressive, something that can result in men feeling entitled to sex, while women have been taught that sex is something that simply happens to them rather than something they're an active participant in. It's not hard to imagine how couples end up in ambiguous situations where one partner is not exactly comfortable with going forward, but also not exactly comfortable saying no.[8]

All this seems sensible. Nonetheless, affirmative consent has had just as many detractors as defenders. The next several sections of this chapter will examine these criticisms, including the charge that affirmative consent puts the burden of proof on the accused; is both under- and overinclusive; is too vague; and is subject to arbitrary and racially biased enforcement. The next chapters will look at constitutional issues and at the major empirical debates regarding sexual assault on campus.

CRITICISMS OF AFFIRMATIVE CONSENT LAWS AND POLICIES

Do Affirmative Consent Laws and Policies Reverse the Burden of Proof?

Nadine Strossen, the former president of the American Civil Liberties Union, argues that:

These affirmative-consent rules violate rights of due process and privacy. They reverse the usual presumption of innocence. Unless the guy can prove that his sexual partner affirmatively consented to every single contact, he is presumed guilty of sexual misconduct.[9]

Critics of affirmative consent fear that if any sexual touching without prior consent is sexual assault the natural result will be that accused students will be punished if they cannot demonstrate that they had such consent. Instead of being presumed innocent, they will be presumed guilty unless they can prove otherwise.

---

[7] Id at 430. (To be clear, Ferzan is describing these arguments, not endorsing them.)

[8] Tara Culp-Ressler, "What 'Affirmative Consent' Actually Means," *Think Progress* (June 25, 2014), https://thinkprogress.org/what-affirmative-consent-actually-means-ea665b32b388/.

[9] Quoted in Paul H. Robinson, "The Legal Limits of 'Yes Means Yes," *The Chronicle* (January 10, 2016), www.chronicle.com/article/The-Legal-Limits-of-Yes/234860.

Defenders of affirmative consent dispute this, arguing that the burden remains on the accusing student. Only the questions will change, not the burden of proof:

> At Stanford University, an affirmative-consent standard simply changes the elements that have to be proved, says Michele Landis Dauber, a professor of law who helped design the university's disciplinary process for sexual-misconduct cases. Instead of having to prove that she resisted, or said no, the accuser has to persuade investigators that she did not give consent, or that she withdrew it at some point. The accused would then have the opportunity to explain how he concluded, through words, body language, or other clues, that she was, in fact, a willing participant. The burden of proving that she did not consent stays on the accuser throughout the proceeding, Ms. Dauber says.[10]

At least in theory, under affirmative consent, the burden is on the accusing student to demonstrate that she was sexually touched without her consent. The big change is that the accused cannot simply say "she never objected."

So, who is right – do affirmative consent laws shift the burden of proof? In an ideal world, defenders of affirmative consent are correct. Defining sexual assault as sexual contact without clear consent does not inherently shift the burden of proof. However, affirmative consent can make it very difficult for fact finders to presume innocence as they should.

An excellent illustration of both points is *Mock v. University of Tennessee at Chattanooga*.[11] In that case, the accusing student stated that she had so much to drink during the night in question that her memory was "like a fog" and that Corey Mock had sex with her without her consent. The Administrative Law Judge (the ALJ) found that the accusing student's claim that she was too intoxicated to consent was not credible. The ALJ found in favor of Mock. The school petitioned for reconsideration and the ALJ, without changing any of her findings of fact, nonetheless concluded that Mock had committed sexual assault. Mock then appealed to the chancellor, who decided to expel him.

Mock brought a legal action, claiming, among other things, that the chancellor improperly shifted the burden of proof to require that Mock demonstrate that he had received consent. The school's Student Code of Conduct (SOC 7) had an affirmative consent provision. The judge rejected the argument that the school's affirmative consent rule inherently shifted the burden of proof. "The language in SOC 7 states that 'It is the responsibility of the person initiating sexual activity to ensure the other person is capable of consenting to that activity.' However this does not shift the burden of proof to Mr. Mock to disprove the charges against him."[12]

---

[10] Katherine Mangan, "What 'Yes Means Yes' Means for Colleges' Sex-Assault Investigations," *The Chronicle of Higher Education* (September 3, 2015), www.chronicle.com/article/What-Yes-Means-Yes-Means/232839.

[11] Chancery Court of Davidson County No. 14–1687-II (August 4, 2016), https://kcjohnson.files .wordpress.com/2013/08/memorandum-mock.pdf.

[12] Id. at 11.

So according to the court, affirmative consent rules do not necessarily shift the burden of proof. The accusing student must still prove that she did not consent. However, the court also held that the chancellor *applied* SOC 7 in a way that shifted the burden of proof. Mock claimed that the accusing student took off her bra and helped position him for sexual intercourse. The accusing student did not testify otherwise and the ALJ had rejected her claim that she was too drunk to consent or to recall having done so. The court ruled that the chancellor's "interpretation of SOC 7 and implementation of that rule erroneously shifted the burden of proof to Mr. Mock, when the ultimate burden of proving a sexual assault remained on the charging party."[13]

In short, affirmative consent laws do not inherently shift the burden of proof. However, they are likely to lead to a good deal of confusion about burden of proof in practice. If the violation is defined as sexual contact without clear consent, and there was undisputedly sexual contact, it is natural to ask whether the accused student can show that he ensured that there was consent. This is especially true in states like California where the law mandates the relatively low preponderance of the evidence standard. As discussed in the previous chapter, the preponderance of the evidence standard already invites guesswork, even without the affirmative consent standard.

Indeed, even one of the California law's cosponsors, Assemblywoman Bonnie Lowenthal, appeared to be confused as to whether the law shifted the burden of proof to the accused. "When the *San Gabriel Valley Tribune* asked Lowenthal how an innocent person could prove consent under such a standard, her reply was, 'Your guess is as good as mine.'"[14]

This is likely to lead to a good deal of litigation. Of course, affirmative consent might be worth the litigation if it makes it more likely for fact finders to hold sexual wrongdoers accountable. We will see in Chapter 9, though, that there are arguably clearer standards than affirmative consent that are more protective against sexual assault.

Why Does Affirmative Consent Only Apply to College Students?

Another criticism of affirmative consent is that it is limited to college students. It is always dangerous for societies to allow legislators to pass laws that do not apply to the legislators or to most of the voters. As the Court long ago observed in a case striking down a law selectively restricting access to contraceptives:

The framers of the Constitution knew, and we should not forget today, that there is no more effective practical guaranty against arbitrary and unreasonable government than to require that the principles of law which officials would impose upon a minority must be imposed generally. Conversely, nothing opens the door to arbitrary action so effectively

[13] Id. at 13.
[14] Cathy Young, "Campus Rape: The Problem with 'Yes Means Yes,'" *Time* (August 29, 2014), http://time.com/3222176/campus-rape-the-problem-with-yes-means-yes/.

as to allow those officials to pick and choose only a few to whom they will apply legislation, and thus to escape the political retribution that might be visited upon them if larger numbers were affected. Courts can take no better measure to assure that laws will be just than to require that laws be equal in operation.[15]

If sexual touching without affirmative consent is sexual assault, why do we allow everybody who is not a college student to get away with it? Yale law professor Jeb Rubenfeld argues that: "Moreover, sexual assault on campus should mean what it means in the outside world and in courts of law."[16]

Writing in the *Washington Post*, law professor David Bernstein argues that applying affirmative consent to students, but not professors, college administrators, or state legislators is a product of panic, not logic:

Two obvious questions arise: (1) Why just on campus? If this is a good idea, why not make it part the tort system? If that's too drastic, let's start, with say, members of the California legislature. For internal disciplinary purposes, their sexual activity should be governed by the same standard they want to impose on students. What plausible grounds could they have for rejecting application of a standard they would impose on students to themselves? (2) If we're limiting things to campus, why just students? Why should students be judged under this standard, but not faculty and administrators? It's hardly unheard of for professors, administrators, and even law school deans to engage in sexual relationships of dubious morality. The answer is that it's not a good idea, and it's a product of the current moral panic over the hookup culture.[17]

One justification offered for limiting affirmative consent to college students is that students are more youthful and inexperienced than the general population and therefore need more protection and regulation. Vanessa Grigoriadis – a contributing editor to the *New York Times Magazine* and *Vanity Fair* and the author of *Blurred Lines: Rethinking Sex, Power, and Consent on Campus* – avers:

Again, these are 19 or 20 year olds. These are not adults who have had a ton of sex and feel like it's not hot to have to ask somebody what they want. There's definitely a lot of adults who feel that way, right? Like, "That just takes the fun out of everything." If you think about a promiscuous woman who wants to have sex and be in the mile-high club, versus a 19-year-old girl who's had sex once, these are like apples and oranges. I feel like that argument is just . . . you can kind of brush that aside. Let's not compare it with what a 50-year-old might want to do it on an airplane.[18]

---

[15] Eisenstadt v. Baird, 405 U.S. 438, 454 (1972) (quoting Justice Jackson, concurring in Railway Express Agency v. New York, 336 U. S. 106, 336 U. S. 112-113 [1949]).

[16] www.nytimes.com/2014/11/16/opinion/sunday/mishandling-rape.html?mcubz=3&_r=0.

[17] David Bernstein, "You Are a Rapist; Yes You!," *Washington Post* (June 23, 2014), www .washingtonpost.com/news/volokh-conspiracy/wp/2014/06/23/you-are-a-rapist-yes-you/? utm_term=.2937202ec03a.

[18] Quoted in Isaac Chotiner, "A New Standard for Sexual Assault," *Slate* (September 5, 2017), www.slate.com/articles/news_and_politics/interrogation/2017/09/in_search_of_a_new_stan-dard_for_sexual_consent_on_campus.html.

Yet this justification of special rules for college students is decades out of date. "The typical college student is also not fresh out of high school. A quarter of undergraduates are older than 25, and about the same number are single parents."[19] Therefore affirmative consent standards largely apply to adults (even assuming that persons under 25 are not fully adult), many of them parents. Yet they do not apply to any of the other adults in or out of university settings.

Further, the idea that even traditionally aged college students are likely to have had little sexual experience is well off the mark. According to the CDC, in 2016, 30 percent of high school students were "currently sexually active."[20] That figure applies to all high school students, so the percentage of sexually active seniors about to enter college is likely much higher.

Another justification offered for limiting affirmative consent laws to students is that college students are more likely to be sexually assaulted than their peers who are not in college. Nancy Chi Cantalupo, a leading scholar on sexual assault and a prominent antirape advocate, makes this claim: "[C]ollege women are more at risk for rape and other forms of sexual assault than women the same age but not in college."[21]

Cantalupo is a fine and generally careful scholar, but this assertion lacks any real evidence and is most likely wrong. She bases her claim on a 2003 Justice Department document used for police training,[22] which, in turn, cites a 2000 study, *The Sexual Victimization of College Women*, which is based on a 1997 survey.[23] However, as its title indicates, that study surveyed only college women, which means that it cannot be used to make any reliable comparisons between college women and other women. Importantly, the Department of Justice commissioned another study, published in 2014, that does compare women in college with college-aged women not in college, using the same methodology and definitions across all subjects. It concluded that women outside of college face significantly *greater* risk of sexual assault than their cohorts enrolled in college.[24]

[19] Gail O. Mellow, "The Biggest Misconception About Today's College," *New York Times* (August 28, 2017), www.nytimes.com/2017/08/28/opinion/community-college-misconception.html?mcubz=3.

[20] www.cdc.gov/features/yrbs/index.html.

[21] Nancy Chi Cantalupo, *Burying Our Heads in the Sand: Lack of Knowledge, Knowledge Avoidance and the Persistent Problem of Campus Peer Sexual Violence*, 43 Loyola University Law Journal 205, 210 (2011) (quoting Rana Sampson, "Acquaintance Rape of College Students" 3, US Department of Justice, Problem-Oriented Guides for Police Series No. 17 [2003]), www.cops.usdoj.gov/pdf/e03021472.pdf, 8.

[22] Sampson, "Acquaintance Rape of College Students," 3.

[23] B. Fisher, F. Cullen, and M. Turner, *The Sexual Victimization of College Women* (Washington, DC: US Department of Justice, National Institute of Justice and Bureau of Justice Statistics, 2000).

[24] Sofi Sinozich and Lynn Langton, "Rape and Sexual Assault Victimization among College-Age Females, 1995–2013" (December 2014), 4, www.bjs.gov/content/pub/pdf/rsavcaf9513.pdf.

This should not be surprising given that noncollege students as a whole are much less economically privileged group than college students.[25] Consequently, young women who do not attend college are more likely to be victims of all sorts of violent crimes, not just sexual assault.[26] We should treat laws that grant extra protection to a more economically privileged group of people with great skepticism, especially when it appears that they are in less, rather than in more, danger of being victimized.

Further, the 2014 Department of Justice study also concluded that college-age women living in rural areas who do not attend college are at the greatest risk of sexual assault – they are sexually assaulted at nearly twice the rate of college students.[27] Given that we live in a time when many rural voters believe their legitimate concerns are beneath the notice of educated elites, we should question why the current trend is to focus on college students rather than on the rural population most at risk of sexual assault.

To be fair, Cantalupo acknowledges in her footnotes that some studies contradict the claim that college students are disproportionately likely to be sexually assaulted. She attributes the conflict to the different wording of different surveys. As will be discussed in Chapter 8, it is certainly true that survey wording has a very significant impact on resulting estimates of sexual assault. And reasonable people can differ on how broadly such surveys should define *sexual assault*. Nonetheless, if we are comparing the rate of sexual assault between two groups, the most basic principles of social science research require that a survey applies the same methodology and definitions to both populations. That is what the survey finding that noncollege students are at greater risk does. There do not appear to be any surveys that follow these essential rules of social science that come to the opposite conclusion. Thus, there is no reason to believe that the population covered by affirmative consent laws is more at risk of sexual assault than their cohorts, and there is good reason to believe the opposite.

In sum, there does not seem to be any legitimate reason to punish college students for sexual conduct that is legally permissible everywhere else. It feeds the age-old narrative that "kids these days" lack the moral fiber of their parents and promotes the myth of sexually out-of-control college students. In fact, college students today are no more likely to "hook up" than their parents did.[28] It allows grossly disproportionate protection among groups, in the opposite way that justice would demand. A particularly egregious example is New York State. It was the second state to adopt statewide affirmative consent laws, yet it has a narrow definition of *rape* for everyone else: "the victim [must

[25] Sam Fulwood, "Why Economic Disadvantage Becomes Educational Disadvantage," *American Progress* (September 23, 2014), www.americanprogress.org/issues/race/news/2013/09/24/75320/why-economic-disadvantage-becomes-educational-disadvantage/.
[26] Sinozich and Langton, "Rape and Sexual Assault Victimization," 5.   [27] Id. at 10.
[28] Erin Brodwin, "Students Today 'Hook up' No More Than Their Parents Did in College," *Scientific American* (August 16, 2013), www.scientificamerican.com/article/students-today-hook-up-no-more-than-parents-college/.

have] clearly expressed that he or she did not consent."[29] That law is the opposite of affirmative consent in that it clearly puts the onus on the victim. New York State has a large rural population and, as noted, those women are at nearly twice the risk of being sexually assaulted as New York's college students. Yet, many of the very same acts that would get a student expelled from a New York State college would be perfectly legal for nonstudents. Thus, there are good reasons to question a two-tier definition of *sexual assault*.

Are Affirmative Consent Laws and Rules Overly Broad and Arbitrary?

A common criticism of affirmative consent laws is that they define too much consensual sexual contact as sexual assault, and therefore turn too many sexually active students into sex offenders. John F. Banzhaf III, a professor at George Washington University Law School, says, "The standard is not logical – nobody really works that way."[30] Michelle Goldberg, writing in the left-leaning magazine *The Nation* worries: "I'm sure we can rely on the vast majority of college students, and particularly college women, to interpret the new rules in good faith. I'm less sure if that's a good enough argument for a law so vague that, technically, it might turn most of them into rapists, victims or both."[31]

There is a good deal of empirical evidence to support the assertion that affirmative consent rules do not comport with how most students engage in sexual contact. Numerous studies indicate that "consent is often communicated and interpreted using ambiguous, nonverbal cues."[32] For both heterosexual and LGB students, the most common way of communicating consent is passive – not resisting or not saying no:

Similar to studies of heterosexual encounters, nonverbal behaviors were used more than verbal behaviors to ask for and to show consent. The behaviors used most frequently to communicate consent were behaviors loading on the No Resistance factor: not stopping their partner from kissing or touching them, not resisting their partner's advances, and not saying no.[33]

Similarly, J. Guillermo Villalobos, Deborah Davis, and Richard Leo report in their Oxford-published research:

[29] Aya Gruber, *Consent Confusion*, 38 Cardozo L. Rev. 415–458, 439 (2016).
[30] Jennifer Medina, "Sex Ed Lesson: 'Yes Means Yes, but It's Tricky," *New York Times* (October 14, 2015), www.nytimes.com/2015/10/15/us/california-high-schools-sexual-consent-classes .html?mcubz=3&_r=0.
[31] Michelle Goldberg, "Questions about California's New Campus Rape Law," *The Nation* (September 29, 2014), www.thenation.com/article/questions-about-californias-new-campus-rape-law/.
[32] Jozkowski and Peterson, "College Students and Sexual Consent," 517–523, 520 (citing several studies).
[33] Charlene L. Muehlenhard, Terry P. Humphreys, Kristen N. Jozkowski, and Zoë D. Peterson, "The Complexities of Sexual Consent among College Students: A Conceptual and Empirical Review," *The Journal of Sex Research* 53 (2016): 4–5, 457–487, 468.

Despite the obvious risks of misunderstandings, initial communication of sexual desire often occurs through nonverbal cues such as eye contact, escalating physical proximity, suggestive movements, or nonsexual touching, which then may progress to more explicitly sexual touch, passionate kissing, undressing and so on. Explicit verbal requests to engage in sexual activity are much less common, as are verbal requests for clarification or refusal of sexual advances.[34]

Perhaps surprisingly, there appears to be little difference between the genders in this regard:

Women and men showed similar patterns; the few gender differences that emerged were small (Hickman & Muehlenhard, 1999). Interestingly, both women and men reported that they most frequently showed their consent by not resisting their partners' advances. They reported using direct verbal and direct nonverbal expressions of consent least frequently.[35]

The reality of how people express sexual consent starkly contrasts with how consent is defined by many university codes of conduct. In the Connecticut State University system, the "Basic Definition of Consent" includes the requirement of "[e]qual approval given to each participant to desired sexual involvement."[36] It would be difficult for even an attorney to definitively interpret this definition, but it appears to require that all sexual partners consent to sex to an equal degree. Does this mean that if one partner consents more reluctantly than the other, this is sexual assault?

Further, the "initiator must obtain clear and affirmative responses at each stage of sexual involvement."[37] Also, "past consent to sexual activity does not imply future consent." Thus, if two students who sleep together every night, even if married, are lying naked in bed together kissing, and have developed a clear understanding of how they expect sex to progress, they must elicit unambiguous specific consent each time that they touch an intimate body part of the other. It is difficult to imagine that the great majority of sexually active couples will not run afoul of these rules at least sometimes.

Crucially, affirmative consent policies are generally not limited to requiring affirmative consent to sexual intercourse but apply to all sexual acts. California at least gives a reasonably clear definition of what is covered: "touching an intimate body part (genitals, anus, groin, breast, or buttocks) (i) unclothed or (ii) clothed." While this definition covers couples who may not want to get each

---

[34] J. Guillermo Villalobos, Deborah Davis, and Richard Leo, "His Story, Her Story: Sexual Miscommunication, Motivated Remembering, and Intoxication as Pathways to Honest False Testimony Regarding Sexual Consent," in R. Burnett, ed., *Vilified: Wrongful Allegations of Sexual and Child Abuse* (Oxford: Oxford University Press, 2015). Republished as University of San Francisco Law Research Paper 2014-33 at 4.

[35] Muehlenhard et al., "The Complexities of Sexual Consent among College Students," 468.

[36] Marybeth Sullivan and Alex Reger, "Higher Education Institutions Definitions of Sexual Assault," *OLR Research Report*, www.cga.ct.gov/2016/rpt/2016-R-0006.htm.

[37] Id.

other's specific permission each time to touch one another's fully clothed bodies, it is at least limited to contact with clearly defined areas of the body. There are other universities where the definition of sexual contact, including sexual violence, is far broader and can include kissing even in the context of a long-term relationship.

Doe v. Brandeis[38] illustrates just how broadly sexual violence can be interpreted and what consequences can follow from such a broad definition. The case involved two male students who for 21 months were "in a romantic and sexual relationship."[39] Approximately six months after the end of the relationship, one student, J.C., accused the other, John, of sexual misconduct. The university found John responsible for various forms of sexual misconduct, including "sexual violence" by waking J.C. with kisses when they were in bed together. The federal judge found that Brandeis had stretched the meaning of sexual violence too far:

The Special Examiner's findings concerning the "kissing" incidents are particularly noteworthy. The Special Examiner concluded that John had occasionally awakened J. C. with kisses, and had sometimes continued to try to kiss him after J.C. said he wanted to go back to sleep. She further concluded that those actions were acts of "violence." To reach that result, she essentially stitched together a series of broad generalizations – kissing is sexual activity; a sleeping person is physically incapacitated and therefore cannot give consent; the existence of a relationship is not relevant to consent; sexual activity without consent is sexual misconduct; sexual misconduct is a form of violence – to reach a conclusion that seems at odds with common sense and the ordinary meanings and definitions of words.[40]

The problem with what Brandeis did is not necessarily its conclusion that kissing can be a form of sexual violence. If someone goes around pinning other people to a wall and forcefully kissing them, that is obviously sexual assault. The problem, as the judge repeatedly pointed out, is that Brandeis ignored the context. If you wake up next to your boyfriend or girlfriend (or spouse) after a night of consensual sexual activity and wake them with kisses, this is simply not the same thing as pinning a stranger to a wall and forcing a kiss on that person.

College affirmative consent codes almost never recognize this distinction. The sexual misconduct policy of the University of Michigan is typical:

Consent is not to be inferred from an existing or previous dating or sexual relationship. Even in the context of a relationship, there must be mutual consent to engage in any sexual activity each time it occurs.

Consent to engage in one sexual activity at one time is not consent to engage in a different sexual activity or to engage in the same sexual activity on a later occasion.[41]

[38] Memorandum and Order 15-11557-FDS (Dist. Mass March 31, 2016). [39] Id. at 6.
[40] Id. at 76–77.
[41] https://studentsexualmisconductpolicy.umich.edu/content/prohibited-conduct.

The University of Michigan further warns that "non-verbal communication alone may not be sufficient to ascertain consent."[42]

This refusal to distinguish between assaulting a stranger and sexually touching a person you are in a sexual relationship with, and with whom you have developed understandings of appropriateness, is no doubt well intentioned. Nobody wants to go back to the days when marriage was a license to rape. And a sexual relationship is not an excuse for sexual assault. Nonetheless there needs to be a path in between these extremes. As the federal judge wrote in the *Brandeis* case:

> In short, the existence of a relationship was unquestionably a central issue in assessing John's behavior and resolving the issue of consent. The existence of a relationship did not immunize John from the consequences of any improper behavior. But neither should it have been dismissed out of hand simply on the basis of a broad generalization that sexual misconduct can, and sometimes does, occur in the context of a relationship.[43]

Of course, not all sexual acts in college occur in the context of relationships. There is a much-documented culture of casual sexual "hookups" in college.[44] While this picture of college life is often exaggerated and is no more prevalent than it was a generation ago,[45] it certainly exists. This in turn leads to another problem with affirmative consent laws. While advocates argue that it leads to clear rules, virtually all college codes state that even an express "yes" is negated by too much alcohol. Therefore, an unclear policy on how much alcohol it takes to negate consent can result in someone accidently becoming a sex offender. Many universities have been making their alcohol policies clearer in recent years. The University of Michigan, which used to have a confusing policy that defined *incapacitation* differently in different places, now has a reasonably clear policy that can be understood by students:

> One is not expected to be a medical expert in assessing incapacitation. One must look for the common and obvious warning signs that show that a person may be incapacitated or approaching incapacitation. Although every individual may manifest signs of incapacitation differently, typical signs often include slurred or incomprehensible speech, unsteady manner of walking, combativeness, emotional volatility, vomiting, or incontinence. A person who is incapacitated may not be able to understand some or all of the following questions: Do you know where you are? Do you know how you got here? Do you know what is happening? Do you know whom you are with?[46]

Other universities have much more ambiguous policies. As described in Chapter 1, there is a difference between *incapacitation*, which is described in the University of Michigan policy, and mere *intoxication*. *Intoxication* means "stimulation,

---

[42] Id.   [43] *Brandeis* at 77.

[44] See, e.g., Lisa Wade, *American Hookup: The New Culture of Sex on Campus* (New York: W. W. Norton, 2017).

[45] www.scientificamerican.com/article/students-today-hook-up-no-more-than-parents-college/.

[46] https://studentsexualmisconductpolicy.umich.edu/content/prohibited-conduct.

excitement, or impaired judgment caused by a chemical substance, or as if by one."[47] The idea that an "incapacitated" person cannot consent to sexual activity is common sense, but it hardly makes sense to say that people who express clear consent to sexual activity were assaulted because they have been "stimulated" or "excited" by alcohol. But some universities blur these distinctions or explicitly reject incapacitation as the standard for negating consent. At the University of North Carolina–Chapel Hill, the policy states reasonably: "Where alcohol or drug use is involved, Incapacitation is a state beyond intoxication, impairment in judgment, or 'drunkenness.'" However, it continues: "Where an individual's level of impairment does not rise to Incapacitation, it is still necessary to evaluate the impact of intoxication on Consent." It further states that "A person's level of intoxication is not always demonstrated by objective signs."[48]

How is all of this to be interpreted by college students? Is sexual contact with an intoxicated but not incapacitated student considered sexual assault? The passive voice statement that "Where an individual's level of impairment does not rise to Incapacitation, it is still necessary to evaluate the impact of intoxication on Consent" provides virtually no guidance and even less so when it warns that intoxication might not be demonstrated by objective signs. Yet a student might find himself suspended or even expelled from college on this basis. Further, the University of North Carolina definition of *sexual assault* includes kissing someone on the mouth, so kissing your dance partner at a party can be determined to be sexual assault if they have had a few drinks, even if they are not incapacitated and did not show objective signs of intoxication.

The University of Illinois is even more sweeping, explicitly stating that sexual contact with an "intoxicated" person is a violation.[49] As noted in the preceding text, almost any consumption of alcohol can result in "intoxication" and turn a seemingly consensual encounter into sexual assault.

Other major universities go even further. At the Massachusetts Institute of Technology, "only a sober 'Yes' means yes."[50] This is a standard that is far broader than "intoxication." The first definition of *sober* in the *Oxford English Dictionary* is "not affected by alcohol."[51] Surely a very large percentage of students have committed sexual assault under this definition.

Alcohol is not the only way that apparent consent can be negated under some college policies. At Brown University, consent can be negated by a finding of "manipulation," even though that term is nowhere defined in the student code.[52] In the absence of some defining language, it is obviously extremely unclear what sort of conduct this covers. A student who was disciplined under

---

[47] http://medical-dictionary.thefreedictionary.com/intoxication.
[48] http://policies.unc.edu/files/2013/04/PPDHRM.pdf.
[49] http://studentcode.illinois.edu/Pocket_Code_web2012.pdf.
[50] http://studentlife.mit.edu/vpr/all-about-consent.
[51] https://en.oxforddictionaries.com/definition/sober.
[52] www.brown.edu/about/administration/title-ix/policy#policy7B.

this provision brought a lawsuit in federal court. The judge pointed out that the term could include giving flowers to someone to persuade that person to engage in sex.[53] However, the judge never had to ultimately rule on the meaning of "manipulate" because he held that Brown improperly applied a 2015 code provision to an incident that occurred in 2014.[54]

Finally, many universities, both public and private, have added additional adjectives to their definitions of consent, requiring that effective consent must be "enthusiastic," "honest," "wanted," and so forth:

Georgia Southern University explains in its 2015 Annual Security Report definition of consent, which goes significantly further than even affirmative consent: "Consent is a voluntary, sober, imaginative, enthusiastic, creative, wanted, informed, mutual, honest, and verbal agreement." Many schools have recognized the same definition. According to these schools, consent is not just an affirmative agreement. It is an agreement that is, [among other things] "imaginative," "enthusiastic," and "creative." Because consent is "verbal," a nod or smile cannot be consent. The inclusion of the term sober in the consent definition also seems to indicate that consent is invalid when a person is tipsy or drunk – not just when they are incapacitated. This school's federally reported definition of consent is in effect not consent, but rather something far more. The school is instructing students to be imaginative and creative in their sexual encounters, to be explicit, and to do more than nod or smile during sex to indicate the required enthusiasm.[55]

The interpretive problems with requiring "enthusiasm" for sexual consent are presumably self-evident. However, even requiring that consensual sex be "wanted" is more problematic than some might think. We all consent to do things we do not necessarily want to do, including sexual acts: "Studies find that college students, female and male, widely agree to 'unwanted sex,' meaning sex that is not physically desired. They engage in this unwanted sex for a variety of reasons, including status and relationship intimacy."[56]

It is one thing for a college to teach their students that all sex should be wanted, enthusiastic, and so forth, but to define all sexual acts short of this ideal as sexual assault is a distortion of that term and produces a dangerously sweeping policy of sexual regulation.[57]

---

[53] K. C. Johnson and Stuart Taylor Jr., "Students Accused of Sexual Assault Now Guilty until Proven Innocent," *LA Times* (March 3, 2017), www.latimes.com/opinion/op-ed/la-oe-johnson-taylor-campus-sexual-assault-20170303-story.html.

[54] Naomi Shatz, "Doe v. Brown University: In Narrow Decision, Federal Court, Finds Brown Failed to Follow Its Policy on Sexual Misconduct Adjudications," *Boston Lawyer Blog* (October 11, 2016), www.bostonlawyerblog.com/2016/10/11/doe-v-brown-university-narrow-decision-federal-court-finds-brown-failed-follow-policy-sexual-misconduct-adjudications/.

[55] Jacob Gersen and Jeannie Suk, *The Sex Bureaucracy*, 104 *California Law Review* 881–948, 925 (2016).

[56] Gruber, *Consent Confusion*, 426.

[57] To be clear, many of these definitions are coming from campus security authorities rather than student conduct codes. How these documents interact is not clear.

RESPONSES TO CRITICISMS

The next sections address two specific arguments. The first is that the preceding concerns are exaggerated because the only sexual contact covered by affirmative consent laws are those where someone felt sufficiently violated to file a complaint. The second is that the point of affirmative consent laws is to change how students have sex, not to accommodate it.

Affirmative Consent Laws Only Matter When a Student Files a Complaint

Defenders of affirmative consent laws argue that concerns are greatly exaggerated because the great majority of sexual encounters do not result in anyone filing a complaint: "The law has no bearing on the vast majority of sexual encounters. It only applies when a student files a sexual assault complaint."[58]

Of course, the same defense could be made of almost any regulation of sexual conduct because such conduct normally occurs in a private setting. As will be discussed in the next chapter, antisodomy laws were defended on this basis. After all, those laws were rarely enforced.

Further, making vast swaths of sexual behavior punishable, puts a Sword of Damocles over the heads of hundreds of thousands of students. Should a relationship sour or end badly, an angry student could later report the other student for sexual assault. It is important to note, this is not the same thing as saying that there would be false rape accusations (a topic covered in Chapter 2). The argument here is that many or most sexually active students would know that their partners had the option of someday reporting them for acts that are *defined as sexual assault* by their universities.

Affirmative consent laws do not ask whether the student consented, only whether consent was affirmatively and overtly manifested. Therefore, a complaining student would not have to claim that they were forced to engage in nonconsensual sex. They could accurately report that their partner once touched them intimately without receiving their clear, unambiguous prior consent. This could result in their partner being expelled from college. Thus, sweeping regulation of sexual behavior is not made less intrusive because it is sporadically enforced. Perhaps most importantly, there is no requirement that violations of campus sexual assault rules have to be reported by the students involved rather than by a third party. For example, in *Neal v. Colorado State-Pueblo*, the complaint was filed without the alleged victim even being informed of that fact and despite the alleged victim's consistent protestations that she was not raped or sexually assaulted:

[58] Amanda Marcotte, "Do Not Fear California's New Affirmative Consent Law," *The Slate* (September 29, 2014), www.slate.com/blogs/xx_factor/2014/09/29/affirmative_consent_in_california_gov_jerry_brown_signs_the_yes_means_yes.html.

A female student in the CSU-Pueblo athletic training program (referred to anonymously as "Complainant") alleged to the director of athletic training (Dr. Roger Clark) that on Saturday, October 25, 2015, Plaintiff had raped another female student in the athletic training program, referred to anonymously as Jane Doe. Plaintiff alleges that his sexual conduct with Ms. Doe was consensual and that Ms. Doe stated and acknowledged several times that their sexual conduct was consensual .... Complainant made the allegations without informing Ms. Doe or Plaintiff. Her allegations were based upon a conversation she had with Ms. Doe on October 26, occasioned by Complainant noticing a "hickey" on Ms. Doe's neck.[59]

Federal law imposes broad mandatory reporting requirements on colleges and universities, meaning that if a student tells a college employee or resident advisor about something that could reasonably be considered sexual assault under college rules, it must be reported:

Title IX uses the concept of notice, and imposes obligations for a "prompt and effective remedy" on colleges and universities when notice of sex/gender discrimination or harassment is given to a "responsible employee." A school has notice if a responsible employee knew, or in the exercise of reasonable care should have known, about the harassment. A responsible employee includes any employee who has the authority to take action to redress the harassment, who has the duty to report sexual harassment to appropriate school officials, or an individual who a student could reasonably believe has this authority or responsibility. Your college or university will define for you if you are a "responsible employee." Some faculty members will be, and some will not.[60]

In fact, many colleges are adopting mandatory reporting policies that go even further than federal law requires. "A growing number of [colleges and universities] are ... adopting policies requiring all faculty members and other professional employees – not just those obligated by law to do so – to report sexual misconduct to designated administrators, who may then initiate investigations and alert authorities."[61] This means that if a student says anything to a professor, coach, or university staff member that the listener interprets as possibly violating the student sexual conduct code, they *must* report it.

There are some good reasons for mandatory reporting laws. Although most university employees are surely well intentioned, faculty and resident advisors are generally not experts on counseling or sexual assault. Mandatory reporting laws can help ensure that a victimized student is referred to someone with the proper training to effectively help her or him. Also, if a student is serially

[59] Neal v. Colorado State University–Pueblo, Civil Action No. 16-cv-873-RM-CBS (Dist. Colorado February 16, 2017) (citations omitted).
[60] https://atixa.org/wordpress/wp-content/uploads/2012/01/WHO-IS-A-MANDATED-REPORTER-OF-WHAT-GETTING-SOME-CLARITY.pdf.
[61] Colleen Flaherty, "Endangering a Trust," *Inside Higher Education* (February 4, 2015), www.insidehighered.com/news/2015/02/04/faculty-members-object-new-policies-making-all-professors-mandatory-reporters-sexual.

assaulting other students, mandatory reporting increases the chance that the university will become aware of this pattern.

However, it also means that students are not really in control of whether the university investigates or punishes their sexual partner. There are very few statistics on what percentage of sexual assault complaints are filed by third parties, but it is possible that it is a substantial number:

There are no national data that let us know the prevalence of third-party reports, but they appear to be a significant source of allegations. The University of Michigan's most recent "Student Sexual Misconduct Annual Report" says that the school's Office for Institutional Equity "often receives complaints about incidents from third parties." Yale releases a semiannual report of all possible sexual-assault and harassment complaints. Its report for the latter half of 2015 included a new category: third-party reports in which the alleged victim, after being contacted by the Title IX office, refused to cooperate. These cases made up more than 30 percent of all undergraduate assault allegations.[62]

Further, in such third-party complaint cases, the investigation can be even more intrusive into students' intimate details because the victim may be considered a witness not a complainant. Emily Yoffe reported in *The Atlantic* a case that illustrates this problem. A female student's roommate thought that she was too drunk to consent to sex and reported this to a residential advisor, who was, in turn, required as a mandatory reporter, to contact a Title IX officer. Not only was her boyfriend suspended over her objection, but she was compelled to testify about the sexual encounter, including intimate details:

Because the school considered her a witness, the [allegedly victimized student] was compelled to answer questions; had she refused to cooperate, she could have been disciplined. (If she had been the complainant, she would have had the right to decline.) [Her boyfriend's attorney] told me she "was in tears because she was required to explain to total strangers intimate sexual details." The school concluded, despite her statements to the contrary, that she couldn't have consented to the sexual encounter, and suspended her boyfriend for a semester. He was also required to attend eight sessions with a therapist on the topic of alcohol and sexual relationships.[63]

In short, rules prohibiting sexual activity that is commonly engaged in on campus cannot be justified by assuming that those rules will only be applied when there is a complaint. It is no small thing for students to know that their private sexual conduct could result in expulsion or other serious punishment should it be found out. And, although information on third-party complaints is hard to come by, we cannot simply assume that they are the rare exceptions.

---

[62] Emily Yoffe, "The Uncomfortable Truth about Campus Rape Policies," *The Atlantic* (September 6, 2017), www.theatlantic.com/education/archive/2017/09/the-uncomfortable-truth-about-campus-rape-policy/538974/.
[63] Id.

Affirmative Consent Laws and Rules Are Norm Changing

While the defense of affirmative consent discussed in the preceding text emphasizes the supposedly limited impact of such laws and policies, this defense takes the opposite attack. It assumes that such rules will change the norms of how all students engage in sex. Students will no longer proceed when signals are mixed. They will have to slow down and make certain they have consent rather than keep going until they are rebuffed:

> Brett Sokolow, a higher education risk management consultant who supports affirmative consent policies and the bill in California, uses a traffic metaphor to describe the kind of behavior these policies are designed to prevent. "You go forward on a green light. You stop on a red light. But most people tend to run the yellows. They tend to increase their speed rather than slowing down to look both ways. Affirmative consent is telling you to slow down at the yellow light. You've been able to fondle, pet, kiss, if you assume those lead you to the next behavior without permission, then you are running a yellow light. You are putting your needs to get through the intersection above the needs for others' safety." Sokolow said the affirmative consent policy is preventative – it won't stop predators, but it will coax some male students towards a healthier norm.[64]

There are, however, great dangers in using punitive measures to change norms regarding widespread behaviors. Because not all violations of "yes means yes" can be punished as a practical matter, changing norms will require some people to made examples of. *Philadelphia Magazine* reported this story under the headline "Rape Happens Here":

> Sendrow is a 23-year-old brunette from Princeton, New Jersey. Her mother is from Mexico; her dad is a Jewish guy from the Bronx. She graduated last spring and works in health care in Washington, D.C. If 3,000 smiling Facebook photos are a good barometer, her four years at Swarthmore seem to have passed by untroubled. But in the midwinter of 2013, Sendrow says, she was in her room with a guy with whom she'd been hooking up for three months. They'd now decided – mutually, she thought – just to be friends. When he ended up falling asleep on her bed, she changed into pajamas and climbed in next to him. Soon, he was putting his arm around her and taking off her clothes. "I basically said, 'No, I don't want to have sex with you.' And then he said, 'Okay, that's fine' and stopped," Sendrow told me. "And then he started again a few minutes later, taking off my panties, taking off his boxers. I just kind of laid there and didn't do anything – I had already said no. I was just tired and wanted to go to bed. I let him finish. I pulled my panties back on and went to sleep."[65]

It is certainly true that under affirmative consent, the male student in this situation committed sexual assault. Nonetheless, this is a case about which reasonable people can disagree. She was not frightened, asleep, frozen, or

---

[64] Eliza Gray, "California Passes First-Ever Bill to Define Sexual Consent on College Campuses," *Time* (August 28, 2014), http://time.com/3211938/campus-sexual-assault-consent-california/.

[65] Simon Van Zuylen-Wood, "Rape Happens Here," *Philadelphia Magazine* (April 24, 2014), www.phillymag.com/articles/rape-happens-here-swarthmore-college-sexual-assaults/#VooLs2QTR8kAET7L.99.

incapacitated in any way. A person in the man's position might have interpreted her getting into bed with him as sign of sexual interest, especially given their previous sexual experiences together.

Of course, a reasonable person could argue that she had already said no once and that he knew he was proceeding without her consent. Many people would agree that it would be good to live in a world where the norm was that he would not try again without her clear, even enthusiastic, consent. But would expelling the student as a sex offender be the right way to change norms? Changing norms through education is very different than changing norms through punishment, especially if the punishment will necessarily be inflicted on a small subset of those violating the norms.

Also, there is no guarantee that those who are made examples of will be chosen for the noblest of reasons. Sex and its social aftermath often does not bring out the best in people. In a case that is unusual in that the expelled student was female, a male student reported her for initiating sex with him after they had participated in a drinking game. She believes that he filed the claim because she is overweight, and he was socially stigmatized for sleeping with her.[66]

There is also a real possibility that under a broad definition of *sexual assault* some students will be singled out for the worst of all reasons: racial bias. There is a disturbing history in this country of sexual paranoia regarding minorities, especially African American men. For example, as of our nation's bicentennial, "[O]ut of 455 men executed for rape since 1930, 405 were black ... Almost all of the complainants were white."[67] While the Supreme Court has since ruled that the capital punishment for rape is unconstitutional, there are ample contemporary statistics demonstrating that race and allegations of sexual misconduct are often a toxic mix of racism and, at best, an innocent mistake:

- Judging from exonerations, a black prisoner serving time for sexual assault is three-and-a-half times more likely to be innocent than a white sexual assault convict. The major cause for this huge racial disparity appears to be the high danger of mistaken eyewitness identification by white victims in violent crimes with black assailants.
- Assaults on white women by African American men are a small minority of all sexual assaults in the United States, but they constitute half of sexual assaults with eyewitness misidentifications that led to exoneration. (The unreliability of cross-racial eyewitness identification also appears to have contributed to racial disparities in false convictions for other crimes, but to a lesser extent.)
- Eyewitness misidentifications do not completely explain the racial disparity in sexual assault exonerations. Some misidentifications themselves are in part

[66] www.buzzfeed.com/emaoconnor/alleged-assault-at-wsu?utm_term=.wrPE82DL7n#.tlG8oPlozJ.
[67] Vivian Berger, *Man's Trial, Woman's Tribulation: Rape Cases in the Courtroom*, 77, no. 1 Columbia Law Review 1–103, 4 (January 1977).

the products of racial bias, and other convictions that led to sexual assault exonerations were marred by implicit biases, racially tainted official misconduct and, in some cases, explicit racism.

• African American sexual assault exonerees received much longer prison sentences than white sexual assault exonerees, and they spent on average almost four-and-a-half years longer in prison before exoneration. It appears that innocent black sexual assault defendants receive harsher sentences than whites if they are convicted, and then face greater resistance to exoneration even in cases in which they are ultimately released.[68]

Black males are disproportionately punished throughout their entire time in the educational system. "Black boys represent 19% of male preschool enrollment, but 45% of male preschool children receiving one or more out-of-school suspensions."[69] Further, "While 6% of all K-12 students received one or more out-of-school suspensions, the percentage is 18% for black boys."[70] Importantly, these disparities cannot be accounted for by behavioral differences between black boys and white boys.[71]

Therefore, the possibility of discriminatory enforcement of broad sexual assault rules, including discriminatory reporting, should be on the forefront of people's minds:

Far more troubling is the concern that a consent requirement would be unevenly enforced, with greatest impact on defendants of color and LGBT communities, while under-protecting minority victims. America's history of abusive rape prosecutions against Black men suspected of intimacy with white women makes worries about discriminatory enforcement readily understandable. Charging and adjudication, even in the case of lower-level offenses, could well be influenced by racial stereotypes and lack of empathy for individuals who are seen as cultural or socioeconomic outsiders.[72]

Is there a racial disparity in college sexual assault cases, as there apparently is in criminal sexual assault cases? It is difficult to tell because federal law does not require colleges to keep records on the race of accused students. "While the Office for Civil Rights ... collects a lot of data on race, it does not require

---

[68] Samuel R. Gross, Maurice Possley, and Klara Stephens, "Race and Wrongful Convictions in the United States," National Registry of Exonerations Newkirk Center for Science and Society, University of California Irvine (March 7, 2017), www.law.umich.edu/special/exoneration/Documents/Race_and_Wrongful_Convictions.pdf.

[69] www2.ed.gov/about/offices/list/ocr/docs/2013-14-first-look.pdf, 3.   [70] Id.

[71] Russell J. Skiba, Robert S. Michael, Abra Carroll Nardo, and Reece L. Peterson, "The Color of Discipline: Sources of Racial and Gender Disproportionality in School Punishment," *The Urban Review* 34, no. 4 (December 2002), 317–342.

[72] Stephen J. Schulhofer, *Consent: What It Means and Why It's Time to Require It*, 47 University of the Pacific Law Review 665, 680 (2017). To be clear, Schulhofer nonetheless favors affirmative consent laws because: "The danger of unequal enforcement, however, cannot be allowed to exert an all-purpose veto over efforts to fill gaps in the criminal law."

colleges and universities to document the race of the accused and accuser in sexual-assault complaints."[73]

Given the history of persecution of African American men for imagined sexual assaults, it is deeply disturbing that no government body is tracking racial statistics at a time that sexual regulations have become more encompassing. One of the few sources of information are accounts of people who have firsthand experience with significant numbers of cases and can form, admittedly impressionistic, estimates of racial bias. One such account comes from Harvard law professor Janet Halley:

[T]he Harvard Title IX Office, dedicated exclusively to enforcing the University's new rules on sexual and gender-based harassment, has no mandate to ensure racial equality. Case after Harvard case that has come to my attention, including several in which I have played some advocacy or adjudication role, has involved black male respondents, but the institution cannot "know" this because it has not been thought important enough to monitor for racial bias.[74]

Another possible source of information is an OCR investigation of Colgate University for racial disparities in sexual assault investigations. While the absolute numbers were too small for statistically significant conclusions, there was clearly a racial disparity:

Colgate University was recently investigated by the Office for Civil Rights for potential race discrimination, a Title VI violation, in its sexual-assault adjudication process. The university was cleared in April, on the grounds that the numbers did not allow OCR to conclude that race was a statistically significant factor in Colgate's adjudications – in any given year the number of men of any race referred for formal hearings was in the single digits. (The investigation does not appear to have examined any individual cases or otherwise reach beyond this statistical analysis.) But the report did bring those statistics to light, a rarity. In the 2013–14 academic year, 4.2 percent of Colgate's students were black. According to the university's records, in that year black male students were accused of 50 percent of the sexual violations reported to the university, and they made up 40 percent of the students formally adjudicated.

During the three academic years from 2012–13 to 2014–15, black students were accused of 25 percent of the sexual misconduct reported to the university, and made up 21 percent of the students referred for formal hearings. Fifteen percent of the students found responsible for assault in those years were black. During that same three-year period, Asian students, who constituted a little more than 3 percent of Colgate's student body in 2013, were more than 13 percent of the accused, 21 percent of those referred for hearings, and 23 percent of those found responsible. (The rest were white; no Hispanic students were accused.)[75]

[73] Emily Yoffe, "The Question of Race in Campus Sexual Assault Cases," *The Atlantic* (September 11, 2017), www.theatlantic.com/education/archive/2017/09/the-question-of-race-in-campus-sexual-assault-cases/539361/.

[74] Janet Halley, *Trading the Megaphone for the Gavel in Title IX Enforcement*, 128 Harv. L. Rev. F. 103 (February 18, 2015).

[75] Yoffe, "The Question of Race in Campus Sexual Assault Cases."

While none of this decisively demonstrates that college sexual assault investigations are racially biased, it certainly should give us pause about implementing broad definitions of *sexual assault* that cover much of the sexual activity on a college campus and assume that only the guilty will be punished and that norms will change in accordance with the rules. Punishment is a blunt instrument. People are not angels. They become angry when relationships end badly. They become embarrassed and regretful about drunken sex. They jump to conclusions about other people. And racism has not gone away. Again, this is not a question of false rape accusations. This is a question about the effect of rules that make so much current sexual activity on college campuses an actual sex offense.

CONCLUSION

For all these reasons, affirmative consent laws and policies are likely to have serious negative consequences. The next chapter will look at the question of whether affirmative consent policies at public universities, as well as state-mandated affirmative consent policies at private schools, violate the substantive constitutional rights of students.

7

Affirmative Consent and the Constitution

As discussed in the previous chapter, affirmative consent laws intrusively regulate private, adult sexual behavior. This chapter argues that when such regulations are imposed by public universities or by state laws they violate the constitutional rights of students. In a string of cases striking down restrictions on birth control and sodomy, the Supreme Court found that the due process clause of the Constitution protects a right to what has been called, alternatively, sexual "privacy" or "autonomy."[1] By regulating how students *express* their consent, rather than merely *requiring* consent, affirmative consent regimes violate this right.

This chapter will begin by briefly tracing the development of this constitutional right and its contours. It will argue that affirmative consent requirements violate this right by controlling adult, intimate relationships conducted in private settings. It will then address several possible objections to this argument, including:

- The Supreme Court has never specifically held that sexual autonomy is a "fundamental" right;
- The Court's decisions are about reproductive freedom and protecting vulnerable groups such as gays and lesbians;
- Only truly "intimate" relationships are protected, not "hook up" sex.
- The right does not extend to situations where there is an increased risk of coerced sex;
- The Court's protection of sexual autonomy only extends to criminal prohibitions.

After concluding that, despite these objections, affirmative consent policies and law violate students' rights, the next chapter will examine whether the government's interest in imposing affirmative consent is strong enough to outweigh these rights.

[1] For the sake of brevity, this chapter will refer to the right as "sexual autonomy."

SUBSTANTIVE DUE PROCESS AND SEXUAL AUTONOMY

The first several chapters of this book focus on the due process clause of the Fourteenth Amendment and its protections of procedural rights such as the right to a hearing and the right to confront witnesses. The Court has also held that the due process clause protects various *substantive* rights that cannot be abridged by the state even with proper process. These include most of the rights contained in the Bill of Rights, which is why, for example, the First Amendment applies to state laws as well as federal, even though the First Amendment, by its terms, applies only to "Congress." This very important idea is called "incorporation" because it incorporates the rights in the Bill of Rights into the Fourteenth Amendment and therefore protects these rights against state and federal interference.[2]

The Court has also held that the due process clause protects numerous "fundamental" rights that are not explicitly mentioned in the Constitution. Sometimes these are called "unenumerated" rights. These rights have been elevated to be on par with those rights enumerated in the Bill of Rights. Fundamental rights include the right to abortion and the right to vote. These rights also include such lesser-known rights as the right to travel from state to state and the right of genetically related people to live together in a neighborhood zoned for single-family housing, even if the people living in the house do not meet the law's definition of a single family. In addition, the Court has implied, if not firmly held, that fundamental rights might include access to public education (although not to an equal public education).[3]

This is a somewhat frustrating area of constitutional law. The Court has not been as clear as it should be on the relationship between the due process clause and the equal protection clause in deriving and defining these rights.[4] And, as we will see in the following text, the Court is often opaque about whether it is defining certain rights as "fundamental" rather than "liberty interests" or how much that matters, and it can be unclear about what constitutional standard it is applying to laws that interfere with these rights. The next section will explain the idea that the Court has protected a right to sexual autonomy. The question of whether this right is "fundamental" (and what the implications of that question are) will be reserved for a later section.

---

[2] Duncan v. Louisiana, 391 U.S. 145 (1968).

[3] See, respectively, Roe v. Wade, 410 U.S. 113 (1973), Griswold v. Connecticut, 381 U.S. 479 (1965), Shapiro v. Thompson, 394 U.S. 618 (1969), Harper v. Virginia Bd. of Election, 383 U.S. 663 (1966), Moore v. East Cleveland, 431 U.S. 494 (1977), Plyler v. Doe, 457 U.S. 202 (1982), and San Antonio Independent School District v. Rodriguez, 411 U.S. 1 (1973).

[4] Gerstmann, *Same-Sex Marriage and the Constitution*, ch. 4.

Contraception, Sodomy, and Sexual Autonomy

The sexual autonomy line of cases began with *Griswold v. Connecticut* in 1965.[5] Considering a statute that prohibited the use of "any drug, medicinal article or instrument for the purpose of preventing conception,"[6] the Court struck down the law, emphasizing that it "operate[d] directly on the intimate relation of husband and wife."[7] Given that the law banned birth control, there can be no doubt that the term "intimate relation" in that sentence refers to sexual relations, as opposed to emotional intimacy, which was in no way regulated by the law.

Seven years later, in *Eisenstadt v. Baird*, the Supreme Court held that unmarried couples have an equal right to use contraception: "[W]hatever the rights of the individual to access to contraceptives may be, the rights must be the same for unmarried and the married alike."[8] As a result of these two cases, there is no dispute that there is a fundamental right to access to contraceptives. There are, however, two different ways to interpret this. One way, as is argued in this chapter, is that *Griswold* and *Eisenstadt* protect the right to sexual intimacy between people. Another way to interpret these cases is that they form a line of cases along with the abortion cases that protect reproductive freedom. Without contraceptives people might become pregnant or father a child against their will, so contraceptives protect reproductive freedom. This was the position the Supreme Court majority took in the now-overruled case *Bowers v. Hardwick*: "*Griswold v. Connecticut* and *Eisenstadt v. Baird*, with contraception; and *Roe v. Wade*, with abortion ... were interpreted as construing the Due Process Clause of the Fourteenth Amendment to confer a fundamental individual right to decide whether or not to beget or bear a child."[9] Using this logic, the *Bowers* court notoriously held that same-sex sodomy laws did not violate the Constitution because they had nothing to do with reproduction.

But that argument never really made sense. After all, the most certain way to avoid pregnancy or fathering a child is to abstain from sexual intercourse. To hold that couples need contraceptives to avoid unwanted pregnancy necessarily *assumes* that there is an underlying right to engage in sexual intercourse in the first place. Imagine if a resident of California, where marijuana is mostly legal, argued that Nevada's continued criminalization of that drug violated her constitutionally protected right to travel from state to state. This would be seen as a preposterous argument because she does not have an underlying constitutional right to possess or use marijuana in the first place. By the same logic, holding that people have a constitutional right to contraceptives to maintain their reproductive control presumes that people

---

[5] 381 U.S. 479 (1965). One could argue that the line of cases begins earlier with Skinner v. Oklahoma in 1942, but the Court did not begin considering the issue in earnest until the 1960s.
[6] Connecticut General Statutes Sec. 53-32 (1958 Rev.). [7] 381 U.S. at 482.
[8] 405 U.S. 438, 453 (1972). [9] 478 U.S. 186, 190 (1986) (citations omitted).

have a constitutional right to engage in what the *Griswold* Court called "intimate relation[s]."

In addition, the opinion of the Court in *Griswold* does not even mention the word *reproduction* nor any variation or synonym of that word. It does, however, use variations of the word *intimate* eight separate times, each time clearly referencing sexual intimacy. The Court was particularly clear that it was discussing sexual intimacy, as opposed to other forms of intimacy, in the following paragraph:

Adultery, homosexuality and the like are sexual intimacies which the State forbids . . . . but the intimacy of husband and wife is necessarily an essential and accepted feature of the institution of marriage, an institution which the State not only must allow, but which, always and in every age, it has fostered and protected. It is one thing when the State exerts its power either to forbid extramarital sexuality . . . or to say who may marry, but it is quite another when, having acknowledged a marriage and the intimacies inherent in it, it undertakes to regulate by means of the criminal law the details of that intimacy.[10]

Further, the case cited in the preceding text, *Bowers v. Hardwick*, has been overruled by the Supreme Court. *Bowers* upheld the antisodomy laws of Georgia holding that there is no right to sexual autonomy. *Lawrence v. Texas* overruled *Bowers*, unequivocally stating "that liberty gives substantial protection to adult persons in deciding how to conduct their private lives in matters pertaining to sex."[11] In short, the idea that the Constitution protects only reproductive choices but not sexual intimacy was temporarily embraced by the Court in *Bowers* but was always a weak argument and has since been overruled.

Affirmative Consent Violates Students' Right to Sexual Autonomy

As explained in the previous chapter, affirmative consent regimes seek to control how adults engage in sexual conduct in private settings. This violates the rights that were established in *Griswold, Eisenstadt,* and *Lawrence*. In the words of the *Lawrence* Court: "Their right to liberty under the Due Process Clause gives them the full right to engage in their conduct without intervention of the government."[12] Under an affirmative consent regime students cannot signal their consent by simply allowing their partner to continue doing what they are doing, which, as explained in the previous chapter, is how many, if not most, people behave. They cannot effectively tell their partner that they do not have to ask permission every time they want to kiss them or to progress to the next level of a sexual encounter. This is no small thing. A regime that seeks to impose a government-approved method of sexual intimacy and tells so many

[10] 381 U.S. at 499. While this quotation references marriage, as noted previously, the Court later held that unmarried people enjoy the same rights.
[11] 539 U.S. 558, 572 (2003).　[12] 539 U.S. at 578.

people that the way that they make love is against government-imposed rules is very serious violation of people's liberty.

The *Lawrence* decision in particular focuses on protection of intimacy. The Court uses the words *intimacy* or *intimate* 13 times in its decision. Affirmative consent regimes inherently run afoul of the Court's decision because they negate the power of intimacy. Even the closest of couples must behave as if they are complete strangers to one another, as the federal judge in the *Brandeis* case noted. Affirmative consent laws, even the more restrained ones that do not require "enthusiastic" or "equal consent,"[13] require *overt* manifestation of consent and clarify that simply allowing your partner to progress is a violation of university rules or state laws. Under affirmative consent laws, waking a boyfriend or girlfriend up with kisses would be illegal, as it is literally impossible for a sleeping person to consent to such an act before it happens. But, the right to sexual intimacy would allow partners to set guidelines ahead of time that would allow this sort of unsolicited affection. Like most affirmative consent policies, Ohio State University's states that "[p]revious relationships or prior consent cannot imply consent to future sexual acts." As a point of clarification it adds: "this includes 'blanket' consent (i.e. permission in advance for any/all actions at a later time/place.)"[14] This renders impossible entire categories of sexual interactions. One significant example is bondage, discipline, dominance, and submission (BDSM), which is inherently incompatible with affirmative consent. BDSM is based upon the "relinquishing of control,"[15] while the whole point of affirmative consent is to keep people in continuous control of how, when, and where they are touched sexually. The idea behind "safe words" is that the dominant partner has presumed permission to continue and progress to further sexual acts absent use of that safe word.[16] This is the exact opposite of affirmative consent, which requires overt consent for each new stage of sexual progression.

Whether or not the government approves of BDSM, it is widely practiced by consenting adults. According to a 2017 study published in the *Journal of Sexual Medicine*:

By use of a cross-sectional survey questionnaire, the level of interest in several BDSM-related activities was investigated in a sample representative of the general Belgian population (N = 1,027) .... A high interest in BDSM-related activities in the general population was found because 46.8% of the total sample had ever performed at least one BDSM-related activity and an additional 22% indicated having (had) fantasies about it.

---

[13] See Chapter 6.   [14] https://hr.osu.edu/public/documents/policy/policy115.pdf, 3.

[15] The Merriam-Webster online dictionary defines *BDSM* as "sexual activity involving such practices as the use of physical restraints, the granting and relinquishing of control, and the infliction of pain." www.merriam-webster.com/dictionary/BDSM.

[16] Doe v. Rector and Visitors of George Mason University, 179 F. Supp. 3d 583 (2016).

Interestingly, 12.5% of the total population indicated performing at least one BDSM-related activity on a regular basis.[17]

The study concluded that "[t]here is a high level of interest in BDSM in the general population, which strongly argues against stigmatization and pathologic characterization of these interests."[18]

This is a study of Belgians, not Americans, and the authors concede in their "Strengths and Limitations" section that: "Although our findings tend to argue against it, we cannot completely rule out participation bias introduced by non-interest in the non-completers." Nonetheless, it seems unlikely that Americans are uniquely uninterested in this practice. According to National Public Radio, of the 100 million copies of the heavily BDSM-themed series *50 Shades of Gray* sold worldwide, 45 million were sold in the United States.[19]

Thus, whether college couples want to wake each other with kisses, play BDSM sex games, or simply allow themselves to be sexually touched based upon understandings come to over the course of a relationship, rather than overtly consent to every sexual interaction, affirmative consent regulates and proscribes an extraordinary range of adult, private, consensual, and intimate behavior. Advocates of affirmative consent may reasonably ask what is so difficult about always asking before touching, but the Constitution allows people to answer: "[T]hat is simply not our desire."

It is important to acknowledge that not all college sexual interactions involve gentle kisses, playful fantasy games, or welcome, if not explicitly invited, sexual touching by a long-term partner. There are far darker encounters, and these are what most advocates of affirmative consent are trying to eliminate. Yet affirmative consent policies are both far too overinclusive and far too underinclusive to accomplish that goal. They are overinclusive because they regulate all the behaviors described previously, not just sexual assault. They are underinclusive because they do not apply outside of college, including in situations of extreme power imbalances where sexual predation is a particular risk. It is worth noting that both Donald Trump and Harvey Weinstein, whom dozens of women have accused of abusing their powerful positions to sexually assault women, are from New York. As noted in Chapter 6, New York State was one of the first to pass a mandatory affirmative consent law for colleges but also has comparatively lax rape laws that give less protection to the women who have accused men such as Trump and Weinstein of sexual assault.

[17] L. Holvoet, W. Huys, V. Coppens, J. Seeuws, K. Goethals, and M. Morrens, "Fifty Shades of Belgian Gray: The Prevalence of BDSM-Related Fantasies and Activities in the General Population," *J Sex Med.* 14, no. 9 (September 2017): 1152–1159.

[18] Id. at 3.

[19] Annalisa Quinn, "Book News, 'Fifty Shades of Grey Sales,'" National Public Radio, Inc. (February 24, 2017), www.npr.org/sections/thetwo-way/2014/02/27/283342810/book-news-fifty-shades-of-grey-sales-top-100-million.

To be clear, it certainly possible that some affirmative consent laws, if interpreted or applied in a less restrictive way, might not violate students' right to sexual autonomy. California, in particular, attempted to draft its law carefully. The legislature removed language from an early draft that had warned "relying solely on nonverbal communication can lead to misunderstanding."[20] This leaves open the possibility that the government will not necessarily micromanage each stage of a couple's progression of sexual activity. However, Democratic Assemblywoman Bonnie Lowenthal, who co-authored the bill, has publicly stated a verbal yes is required.[21] So it is difficult to know exactly what the law requires. Indeed, it appears that the very people who are supposed to be educating students about what affirmative consent laws mean are confused. The *New York Times* published this account of a training session on "Yes Means Yes" at a San Francisco high school:

> "What does that mean – you have to say 'yes' every 10 minutes?" asked Aidan Ryan, 16, who sat near the front of the room.
> "Pretty much," Ms. Zaloom [the educator] answered. "It's not a timing thing, but whoever initiates things to another level has to ask."

If that is a correct answer, the government is requiring students to ask prior permission at every stage of sexual progression. As noted earlier, this is very different from the way most people conduct themselves sexually and represents a vast new government encroachment into the most personal of human activities. Aya Gruber, a law professor at the University of Colorado, has carefully reviewed the arguments on both sides and concludes that "[d]espite its somewhat ambiguous nature, the California law does appear to require some stop-and-ask ritual."[22] There is similar confusion in New York State where Governor Cuomo has publicly asserted that the affirmative consent law requires people "to say yes. It's yes on both sides."[23]

Some defenders of affirmative consent argue that concerns over the bills are "idiotic" and that the laws merely require consent in the ordinary use of the word.[24] Yet it is clearly true that affirmative consent laws change the ordinary meaning of consent. As we will see in the following text, in both civil and criminal law consent is a mental state, not a particular way of expressing a mental state. In other words, if someone borrows your cell phone, the law asks if that person had your consent, not whether or how that person "ensured" that he or she had your consent.

It is possible that, if colleges and courts interpret affirmative consent in a consistently permissive manner, it might not result in the sort of

---

[20] Cathy Young, "Campus Rape: The Problem with 'Yes Means Yes,'" http://time.com/3222176/campus-rape the-problem-with-yes-means-yes/.
[21] Id.   [22] Gruber, *Consent Confusion.*   [23] Ibid., 433 n. 74.
[24] Callie Beusman, "'Yes Means Yes' Laws Will Not Ruin Sex Forever, Despite Idiotic Fears," *Jezebel* (September 4, 2014), http://jezebel.com/yes-means-yes-laws-will-not-ruinsex-forever-despite-i-1630704944.

micromanagement of private sexual activity that would violate the Constitution. There is some "wiggle room" in how a few of these laws and policies are interpreted. However, based upon statements by various public officials who drafted and signed these laws, the way the laws are being explained by some educators, the reasonable interpretation of the language of various statutes and college policies, affirmative consent poses a serious danger of violating constitutionally protected sexual autonomy. The next several sections of this chapter look at a different issue: Whether there might be reason to believe that there really is not a right to sexual autonomy in the first place.

The following section involves a detailed examination of constitutional principles and how they apply to affirmative consent regimes. The next chapter looks at the empirical assumptions most frequently used to justify affirmative consent, such as the claims that one in five college women are sexually assaulted and that the majority of these assaults are perpetrated by serial "predators."

THE ARGUMENTS AGAINST THE EXISTENCE OF A RIGHT TO SEXUAL AUTONOMY

Not everyone agrees that there is a constitutional right to sexual autonomy. Indeed, several counterarguments have been made by various judges and scholars. These will be addressed in the following text.

The Lawrence Court Never Explicitly Stated That Sexual Autonomy Is a Fundamental Right

There is a major split among the federal circuit courts (those courts just below the Supreme Court whose various jurisdictions are divided over 12 different geographic areas of the country) about whether there is a fundamental right to sexual autonomy. The First, Fifth, and Ninth Circuit Courts have held that there is. The Seventh and Eleventh Circuits have held otherwise. There is a similar split among state courts.[25] It is highly unusual to have such a deep split among federal and state courts on a constitutional fundamental rights issue that the Supreme Court does not address.

As noted earlier, a fundamental right is a substantive right, not explicitly mentioned in the Constitution, which is protected by "strict scrutiny" – courts will strike down laws that violate fundamental rights unless such laws are "narrowly tailored to further a compelling government interest."[26] The Seventh

[25] See Hannah Hicks, *To the Right to Intimacy and Beyond: A Constitutional Argument for the Right to Sex in Mental Health Facilities*, 40 NYU Review of Law and Social Change 621–673 (2016), and cases cited at pp. 632–642.
[26] Evan Gerstmann, *The Constitutional Underclass: Gays Lesbians and the Failure of Class-Based Equal Protection* (Chicago:University of Chicago Press, 1999), 22.

and Eleventh Circuit Courts based their rejection of the claim that *Lawrence* (the case striking down antisodomy laws) in particular, recognized a fundamental right to sexual autonomy on three related arguments: (1) the *Lawrence* Court never used the term *fundamental right*; (2) the *Lawrence* Court never explicitly stated that it was applying strict scrutiny; and (3) the *Lawrence* Court did not inquire whether there is a "history and tradition" of sexual autonomy in this county.

In *Muth v. Frank*, the Seventh Circuit quotes Justice Antonin Scalia's dissent in *Lawrence*: "[N]owhere does the Court's opinion declare that homosexual sodomy is a 'fundamental right' under the Due Process Clause."[27] The *Muth* Court added: "The Supreme Court in *Lawrence* also did not apply strict scrutiny in reviewing the sodomy statute at issue."[28]

In addition, the Eleventh Circuit reasoned that:

[T]he *Lawrence* opinion contains virtually no inquiry into the question of whether the petitioners' asserted right is one of "those fundamental rights and liberties which are, objectively, deeply rooted in this Nation's history and tradition and implicit in the concept of ordered liberty, such that neither liberty nor justice would exist if they were sacrificed." [T]he opinion [also] notably never provides the "'careful description' of the asserted fundamental liberty interest" that is to accompany fundamental-rights analysis.[29]

In this view, *Lawrence* merely subjected Texas's sodomy laws to "rational basis" review – the Court's lowest form of scrutiny. The sodomy laws were struck down because "the fact that the governing majority in a State has traditionally viewed a particular practice as immoral is not a sufficient reason for upholding a law prohibiting the practice."[30]

This chapter argues that none of this reasoning can withstand any sort of serious analysis. Each of these arguments contains serious flaws. While it is true that the *Lawrence* Court did not use the term *fundamental rights*, it relied on cases that are fundamental rights cases, which indicates that it was applying fundamental rights doctrine. As the Ninth Circuit wrote in the 2008 case *Witt v. Department of the Air Force*: "[I]n Lawrence, the Supreme Court relied on Griswold, Roe v. Wade, and Carey v. Population Services International [an abortion rights case], all of which are fundamental rights cases."[31]

---

[27] Muth v. Frank, 412 F. 3d 808, 818 (7th Cir. 2005) (Quoting *Lawrence*, 539 U.S. at 586, 123 S. Ct. 2472 [Scalia, J., dissenting]).

[28] Id. at 818.

[29] Lofton v. Sec'y of the Dep't of Children & Family Servs., 358 F. 3d 804, 816 (11th Cir. 2004).

[30] *Lawrence* at 577–578 (quoting Bowers, 478 U.S. at 216 [Stevens, J., dissenting]).

[31] Witt v. Department of the Air Force, 527 F. 3d 806, 823 (9th Cir. 2008) Roe v. Wade held that there is a fundamental right to an abortion. Carey v. Population Services International 431 U.S. 678 (1977) was a US Supreme Court case in which the Court held that it was unconstitutional to prohibit anyone other than a licensed pharmacist to distribute nonprescription contraceptives to persons 16 years of age or over, to prohibit the distribution of nonprescription contraceptives by any adult to minors under 16 years of age, and to prohibit anyone, including licensed pharmacists, to advertise or display contraceptives.

Not only did *Lawrence* rely on these cases, but it repeatedly pointed out they were fundamental rights cases. In the following passage, the *Lawrence* Court uses the term *fundamental* five separate times in describing the cases:

After *Griswold* it was established that the right to make certain decisions regarding sexual conduct extends beyond the marital relationship. In *Eisenstadt v. Baird*, 405 U.S. 438 (1972), the Court invalidated a law prohibiting the distribution of contraceptives to unmarried persons. The case was decided under the Equal Protection Clause, *id.*, at 454; but with respect to unmarried persons, the Court went on to state the *fundamental* proposition that the law impaired the exercise of their personal rights, *ibid.* It quoted from the statement of the Court of Appeals finding the law to be in conflict with *fundamental* human rights, and it followed with this statement of its own:

"It is true that in *Griswold* the right of privacy in question inhered in the marital relationship . . .. If the right of privacy means anything, it is the right of the *individual*, married or single, to be free from unwarranted governmental intrusion into matters so *fundamentally* affecting a person as the decision whether to bear or beget a child." *Id.*, at 453.

The opinions in *Griswold* and *Eisenstadt* were part of the background for the decision in *Roe v. Wade*, 410 U.S. 113 (1973). As is well known, the case involved a challenge to the Texas law prohibiting abortions, but the laws of other States were affected as well. Although the Court held the woman's rights were not absolute, her right to elect an abortion did have real and substantial protection as an exercise of her liberty under the Due Process Clause. The Court cited cases that protect spatial freedom and cases that go well beyond it. *Roe* recognized the right of a woman to make certain *fundamental* decisions affecting her destiny and confirmed once more that the protection of liberty under the Due Process Clause has a substantive dimension of *fundamental* significance in defining the rights of the person.[32]

Not only did the *Lawrence* Court rely upon a string of fundamental rights cases, but it also *eschewed* reliance on *Evans v. Romer*, which is the only Supreme Court case to strike down a law targeting gays and lesbians on rational basis grounds:

The second post-*Bowers* case of principal relevance is *Romer v. Evans*, 517 U.S. 620 (1996). There the Court struck down class-based legislation directed at homosexuals as a violation of the Equal Protection Clause. . . . As an alternative argument in this case, counsel for the petitioners and some *amici* contend that *Romer* provides the basis for declaring the Texas statute invalid under the Equal Protection Clause. That is a tenable argument, but we conclude the instant case requires us to address whether *Bowers* itself has continuing validity. Were we to hold the statute invalid under the Equal Protection Clause some might question whether a prohibition would be valid if drawn differently, say, to prohibit the conduct both between same-sex and different-sex participants.

In short, the *Lawrence* Court repeatedly made clear it was applying fundamental rights cases, emphasizing that those cases protected fundamental

[32] *Lawrence* at 565 (italics added).

rights, while specifically eschewing reliance on the only rational basis case in history in which the Supreme Court struck down an anti–same sex equality law. To call *Lawrence* a rational basis case rather than a fundamental rights case is truly the tail wagging the dog.

The *Lawrence* Court did make a reference to the antisodomy law lacking a "legitimate" state interest, which is language associated with the rational basis test. However, the Court required not only a legitimate interest, but one that must be strong to justify the antisodomy law's intrusion on liberty: "The Texas statute furthers no legitimate state interest which can justify its intrusion into the personal and private life of the individual."[33] The rational basis test is not a balancing test that weighs the state interest against intrusions on liberty. Once a legitimate interest is identified, the law will be upheld as long as there is some conceivable connection between the law and that interest. As the Ninth Circuit pointed out: "Were the [Lawrence] Court applying rational basis review, it would not identify a legitimate state interest to 'justify' the particular intrusion of liberty at issue in Lawrence; regardless of the liberty involved, any hypothetical rationale for the law would do."[34]

Furthermore, the *Lawrence* Court used other language that demonstrates that it was applying heightened scrutiny to the Texas law. As the *Witt* Court noted:

[T]he language of Lawrence emphasizes the importance of the right at issue and refers to "substantial protections" afforded "adult persons in deciding how to conduct their private lives in matters pertaining to sex." "Substantial protections" are not afforded under rational basis review.[35]

"Rational basis" scrutiny is the minimum level of judicial scrutiny. As the *Witt* Court notes, the *Lawrence* Court would not be talking about "substantial protections" for sexual conduct under rational basis analysis.

The *Witt* Court also pointed out that, in *Lawrence*, the Supreme Court stated that the decision in *Bowers v. Hardwick* "failed to appreciate the extent of the liberty involved."[36] The *Witt* Court continued:

The criticism that the Court in Bowers had misapprehended "the extent of the liberty at stake" does not sound in rational basis review. Under rational basis review, the Court determines whether governmental action is so arbitrary that a rational basis for the action cannot even be conceived post hoc.[37]

Even apart from the various word choices of the *Lawrence* Court, it is clear from the substance of its holding that the Court was applying a high level of scrutiny to the sodomy law. Outside of sexual liberty, moral disapproval of practice is well within the scope of rational basis review for barring or regulating the practice. Under rational basis review, the government is free to

---

[33] *Lawrence* at 578.   [34] Witt v. Department of the Air Force, at 817.   [35] Id. at 814.
[36] 539 U.S. at 567.   [37] Witt v. Department of the Air Force, at 813.

ban gambling, "nude" dancing, and obscene movies, even if children are not exposed.[38] Therefore if the antisodomy laws were struck down because moral disapproval is not a sufficient basis for the law, this demonstrates that sexual autonomy is more protected than other activities.

Although the preceding arguments indicate that the Supreme Court has treated sexual autonomy as a fundamental right, the Eleventh Circuit's ruling disagrees, claiming that the Court did not find that such autonomy is among "those fundamental rights and liberties which are, objectively, deeply rooted in this Nation's history and tradition and implicit in the concept of ordered liberty, such that neither liberty nor justice would exist if they were sacrificed."[39] This language comes from the Supreme Court case *Washington v. Glucksberg*,[40] which held that there is no constitutional right to physician-assisted suicide.

These differing conclusions spring from the Supreme Court's inconsistent derivation of its definition of *fundamental rights*. The Court has vacillated among at least four separate tests. Justices have asked whether the right is "deeply rooted in this Nation's history and tradition," but they have also asked whether the right is "explicitly or implicitly protected by the Constitution" and whether the right is "implicit in the concept of ordered liberty."[41] Finally, the Court has said the delineation of fundamental rights is a matter of "reasoned judgment."[42] There is no consistently applied reasoning for recognizing fundamental rights.

If this was not entirely clear when the Eleventh Circuit was writing in 2004, it was made crystal clear by the Supreme Court in 2015 when it decided *Obergefell v. Hodges*:

The identification and protection of fundamental rights is an enduring part of the judicial duty to interpret the Constitution. That responsibility, however, "has not been reduced to any formula." *Poe v. Ullman*, 367 U. S. 497, 542 (1961) (Harlan, J., dissenting). Rather, it requires courts to exercise reasoned judgment in identifying interests of the person so fundamental that the State must accord them its respect. See *ibid*. That process is guided by many of the same considerations relevant to analysis of other constitutional provisions that set forth broad principles rather than specific requirements. History and tradition guide and discipline this inquiry but do not set its outer boundaries. See *Lawrence, supra*, at 572. That method respects our history and learns from it without allowing the past alone to rule the present.[43]

Indeed, the *Obergefell* majority decision went even further and explicitly listed intimacy as a fundamental right:

---

[38] Respectively, Champion v. Ames, 188 U.S. 321 (1903), Barnes v. Glen Theatre, 501 U.S. 560 (1991), and Paris Adult Theatre I v. Slaton, 413 U.S. 49 (1973).

[39] Lofton v. Sec'y (quoting Washington v. Glucksberg, 521 U.S. 702, 720-721 [1997]).

[40] 521 U.S. 702 (1997).

[41] See, respectively, San Antonio Independent School District v. Rodriguez and Palko v. Connecticut, 302 U.S. 319, 325 (1937).

[42] Planned Parenthood v. Casey, 505 U.S. 833, 849 (1992).   [43] 576 U.S. at 10.

Glucksberg did insist that liberty under the Due Process Clause must be defined in a most circumscribed manner, with central reference to specific historical practices. Yet while that approach may have been appropriate for the asserted right there involved (physician-assisted suicide), it is inconsistent with the approach this Court has used in discussing *other fundamental rights, including marriage and intimacy.*[44]

The entire argument that the string of cases protecting contraception and sodomy do not protect sexual autonomy is based upon an unrealistically mechanical view of the Court's jurisprudence. The Court often declines to expressly use terms such as *strict scrutiny* or *fundamental right* even when it is discussing fundamental rights. Abortion is a fundamental right, but the Court does not use that term in its abortion cases. Further, not only does it eschew the term *strict scrutiny* in abortion cases but also it applies a heightened level of scrutiny called the "undue burden" test.[45] The *Obergefell* Court recognized that marriage is a fundamental right but did not explicitly apply strict scrutiny. In *Troxel v. Granville*, the Supreme Court held that there is a fundamental right to control who has custody of one's children, but it also failed to apply strict scrutiny. As Justice Clarence Thomas wrote in his concurring opinion:

Consequently, I agree with the plurality that this Court's recognition of a fundamental right of parents to direct the upbringing of their children resolves this case … The opinions of the plurality recognize such a right, but curiously none of them articulates the appropriate standard of review. I would apply strict scrutiny to infringements of fundamental rights.[46]

Finally, even if we put aside all this technical legal argument, a simple, commonsense thought experiment demonstrates that *Lawrence* could not have merely been applying the rational basis test when it held that moral disapproval is not a rational basis for antisodomy laws. According to the CDC, "Anal sex is the riskiest sexual behavior for getting and transmitting HIV for men and women." Also: "Anal sex may also expose individuals to other sexually transmitted diseases or other infections."[47] While use of condoms lowers the risk of transmission, it is nonetheless true that "[t]he vast majority of men who get HIV get it through anal sex."[48] Obviously, reducing the risk of spreading infectious disease is a legitimate government interest. So, if *Lawrence* is just a rational basis decision, then if any state wants to reinstate its antisodomy laws, all it must do is say that its government purpose is preventing the spread of disease. Because women can also get HIV through anal sex (but at a lower rate than men),[49] states would have a rational for banning either all sodomy or just same-sex sodomy. Rather than being a major constitutional precedent widely taught in law schools, a rational basis

---

[44] Id. at 18 (emphasis added).
[45] Whole Woman's Health v. Hellerstadt, 136 S.Ct. 2292, 2309 (2016).
[46] 530 U.S. 57, 80 (2000) (Thomas, J., concurring).   [47] www.cdc.gov/hiv/risk/analsex.html.
[48] Id.   [49] Id.

interpretation of *Lawrence* renders it nothing more than a minor technical case that required the State of Texas to adjust its pleadings. That surely is not right.

In sum, it is clear that the Court has held, in both the contraception and sodomy cases, that the Constitution gives real protection to sexual autonomy. The Court has sometimes called this right "privacy" and other times "autonomy." It has called people's interest in this right "substantial" and has said the state must have an interest important enough to justify its infringement. It has discussed this right in the context of other strongly supported rights such as the right to an abortion. It does not matter that, as with other such rights, the Court has not explicitly used the terms *fundamental* or *strict scrutiny*.

Why the skittishness of some courts to acknowledge this? It may be similar to the courts' reluctance to acknowledge a broad right to marry prior to the Supreme Court's landmark decision in *Obergefell v. Hodges*.[50] As I have discussed extensively elsewhere, many courts were fearful that recognizing a fundamental right to marry, which is broad enough to cover same-sex marriage, would lead down a slippery slope to all manner of undesirable marriages such as incestuous and polygamous marriages. This led them to accept very weak arguments to guard against this result, all of which were eventually swept aside by the Supreme Court in *Obergefell*.[51]

Perhaps the same phenomenon is at work with the right to sexual autonomy; courts might fear that recognizing such a fundamental right would protect a parade of "horribles" ranging from bestiality to necrophilia to sex with minors. Such analogies were often applied to gays and lesbians as well.[52] This should not happen if the courts apply *Lawrence* correctly. The *Lawrence* Court's invocation of intimacy provides sufficient traction against a slippery slope. Sex with animals, corpses, and children hardly involve the type of adult, human intimacy that *Lawrence* protects. As will be discussed in the following text, *Lawrence*'s protection does not require a demonstration that each individual sexual encounter is an intimate one, but there is nothing in *Lawrence* that requires courts to extend its protections to sex with animals, corpses, or children.

As this book was being written, the Ninth Circuit demonstrated the dangers of misunderstanding *Lawrence* when it allowed, after a hearing, a challenge to California's antiprostitution lawsuit to go forward. The district court judge had ruled against the law's challengers, saying the high court ruling protected only intimate personal relationships, not commercial sex.[53] This certainly seems like the correct result given that *Lawrence* specifically pointed out that the case did

---

[50] 135 S.Ct. 2584 (2015).   [51] Gerstmann, *Same-Sex Marriage and the Constitution*, 108–125.
[52] Id. at 139.
[53] Bob Egelko, "Appeals Court in SF May Allow Challenge to State Law Banning Prostitution," *SFGate* (October 25, 2017), www.sfgate.com/news/article/Appeals-court-in-SF-allows-challenge-to-state-law-12292093.php.

not involve prostitution.[54] The Ninth Circuit, at the hearing, sidestepped the question of intimacy asking, "Why should it be illegal to sell something that it's legal to give away?"[55] This seems like an odd question. The district court judge, Jeffrey White, had ruled that "the state had adequately justified the current law as a deterrent to violence against women, sexually transmitted diseases and human trafficking."

This chapter argues that the district court judge had it exactly right when he ruled that commercial sex lacks the intimacy requirement of *Lawrence* and was also right that the state's interest in avoiding evils such as sex trafficking is more than adequate to distinguish prostitution from noncommercial sex. There is no need to deny, as the Seventh and Eleventh Circuits have done, that there is not a fundamental right to sexual intimacy at all. Nonetheless, this sort of decision may well be why some courts fear the slippery slope and have stayed with an overly cramped interpretation of *Lawrence*.

The (Misconception That the) Right to Sexual Autonomy Is Limited to Historically Unpopular or Vulnerable Minorities

In *Doe v. Rector and Visitors of George Mason University*, a student challenged his expulsion for engaging in BDSM sexual acts. Although he won his procedural due process case, the federal judge declined to hold that his substantive constitutional rights were violated. The judge held that *Lawrence*'s protection of sexual autonomy did not protect him because he was not part of a vulnerable minority group. The judge reasoned that the Supreme Court has created two different methods of deriving fundamental rights. The first way is by balancing "private interests against social needs." The second way is the method used in *Glucksberg*, the assisted-suicide case discussed in the previous section. Under that precedent, fundamental rights are defined as narrowly and specifically as possible, and they are only considered fundamental if they are part of America's history and tradition:

The Supreme Court's cases recognizing judicially-enforceable fundamental liberty interests disclose two equal but distinct lines of precedent with respect to the appropriate methodology to be used when considering whether a liberty is fundamental and therefore protected as judicially enforceable under the Fourteenth Amendment. One approach is a common law methodology articulated by Justice Harlan in dissent in *Poe v. Ullman*. This methodology balances private interests against social needs by reference to, but not bound by, historical practice. In contrast, a more restrictive and historical-focused approach was articulated in *Washington v. Glucksberg* in which the Supreme Court held that a judicially enforceable implied fundamental liberty interest must be (i) deeply rooted in the nation's history and traditions and (ii) implicit in the concept of ordered liberty.[56]

---

[54] 539 U. S. at 578. [55] Egelko, "Appeals Court in SF," 1.
[56] 149 F. Supp. 3d 602, 632 (2016) (citations omitted).

Under this analysis, the question of whether Doe's rights had been violated should be decided according to the more restrictive, tradition-based rules of *Glucksberg*:

Under the *Glucksberg* mode of analysis, plaintiff's asserted fundamental liberty interest in engaging in BDSM sexual activity is clearly not protected as judicially enforceable under the Fourteenth Amendment. Defined with specificity and cast as a negative liberty, as *Glucksberg* counsels, plaintiff's asserted liberty is a freedom from state regulation of consensual BDSM sexual activity. There is no basis to conclude that tying up a willing submissive sex partner and subjecting him or her to whipping, choking, or other forms of domination is deeply rooted in the nation's history and traditions or implicit in the concept of ordered liberty.[57]

Why were Doe's sexual practices less protected than those who engage in sodomy? Because, according to the judge in that case, T. S. Ellis III, *Lawrence* is based on equality issues as much as it is on liberty issues. If equality issues are not at play, Ellis argues the courts should apply *Glucksberg*'s approach of defining rights narrowly and only protecting those rights that are traditionally protected. Therefore, the court would not ask a question about broad rights such as sexual autonomy; the question should be whether BDSM in particular is a historically protected practice. Judge Ellis based his conclusion largely on his reading of *Obergefell v. Hodges*, the Supreme Court case holding there is a right to same-sex marriage. Ellis wrote:

Importantly, *Obergefell* explicitly establishes that the Due Process and Equal Protection Clauses are "interlocking" and each "leads to a stronger understanding of the other." In other words, *Obergefell* highlights that the decision to recognize an implied fundamental liberty interest as judicially enforceable turns, in part, on whether the liberty interest at issue has historically been denied on the basis of impermissible animus or, alternatively, on a legitimate basis aimed at protecting a vulnerable group. *Lawrence* is not to the contrary. There, the Supreme Court reasoned that a statute criminalizing homosexual sodomy violated a judicially enforceable implied fundamental liberty interest in sexual intimacy because of the history of animus towards homosexuals.[58]

So, Ellis is arguing that same-sex marriage was protected because gays and lesbians are a historically disliked, vulnerable group. But this has it exactly backward. What *Obergefell* held is that same-sex couples *cannot be denied the same rights as everyone else* just because they are historically unpopular and vulnerable. The *Obergefell* Court was very clear that it was deciding whether gays and lesbians could be excluded from *an already existing* right:

Objecting that this does not reflect an appropriate framing of the issue, the respondents refer to *Washington v. Glucksberg*, which called for a "careful description" of fundamental rights. They assert the petitioners do not seek to exercise the right to marry but rather a new and nonexistent "right to same-sex marriage." *Glucksberg* did insist that liberty under the Due Process Clause must be defined in a most circumscribed manner, with central reference to specific historical practices. Yet while that approach may have

---

[57] Id. at 632.   [58] Id. at 633 (citations omitted).

been appropriate for the asserted right there involved (physician-assisted suicide), it is inconsistent with the approach this Court has used in discussing other fundamental rights, including marriage and intimacy. *Loving* did not ask about a "right to interracial marriage"; *Turner* did not ask about a "right of inmates to marry"; and *Zablocki* did not ask about a "right of fathers with unpaid child support duties to marry." Rather, each case inquired about the right to marry in its comprehensive sense, asking if there was a sufficient justification for excluding the relevant class from the right.[59]

The same is true for the right to sexual autonomy in *Lawrence*. Gays and lesbians are not being treated as a special class. The Court merely held that they are entitled to the same rights as heterosexuals:

In explaining the respect the Constitution demands for the autonomy of the person in making these choices, we stated as follows: "These matters, involving the most intimate and personal choices a person may make in a lifetime, choices central to personal dignity and autonomy, are central to the liberty protected by the Fourteenth Amendment. At the heart of liberty is the right to define one's own concept of existence, of meaning, of the universe, and of the mystery of human life. Beliefs about these matters could not define the attributes of personhood were they formed under compulsion of the State." Ibid. *Persons in a homosexual relationship may seek autonomy for these purposes, just as heterosexual persons do.*[60]

It is true that the *Lawrence* does discuss the issue of animus toward gays and lesbians. However, the Court never implies that gays and lesbians are receiving any special rights that others do not have. Rather the Court simply holds that such animosity is not a rational basis for depriving them of the same protections that everyone else enjoys:

The second post-Bowers case of principal relevance is Romer v. Evans. There the Court struck down class-based legislation directed at homosexuals as a violation of the Equal Protection Clause. Romer invalidated an amendment to Colorado's constitution which named as a solitary class persons who were homosexuals, lesbians, or bisexual either by orientation, conduct, practices or relationships and deprived them of protection under state antidiscrimination laws. We concluded that the provision was born of animosity toward the class of persons affected and further that it had no rational relation to a legitimate governmental purpose.[61]

Furthermore, Judge Ellis's cramped interpretation of *Lawrence* ignores all the cases upon which *Lawrence* relies. As noted in the previous section, *Lawrence* derives the right of sexual autonomy from a serious of cases protecting the right of contraception and abortion. The *Lawrence* Court wrote:

Both Eisenstadt and Carey, as well as the holding and rationale in Roe, confirmed that the reasoning of Griswold could not be confined to the protection of rights of married adults. This was the state of the law with respect to some of the most relevant cases when the Court considered Bowers v. Hardwick.[62]

---

[59] 576 U.S. at 208 (citations omitted).   [60] 539 U.S. at 574 (emphasis added).   [61] Id.
[62] Id. at 566.

Recall that the dissenters in *Bowers* (the now-overruled case upholding antisodomy laws) believed that the contraception cases did not protect sexual autonomy – they were purely reproductive freedom cases. Judge Ellis held that *Lawrence* did not protect sexual autonomy but only protected unpopular minorities from discrimination in sexual regulation. To accept all of this, you would have to believe that *Lawrence* has nothing to do with these other cases – *Lawrence* and *Obergefell* protect minorities and all the other cases protect reproductive rights. The problem is that, as we have now seen, *Lawrence* and *Obergefell* repeatedly cite the contraception and abortion cases as the precedent for their autonomy holdings. Further, if Judge Ellis is right, we would have to conclude that *Eisenstadt* was wrongly decided because it protected contraceptive use by unmarried couples, and there is no tradition of protecting fornication (unmarried sex) in this nation.

Ellis's opinion ignores the overall structure of the *Lawrence* opinion, which is surely concerned about prejudice and equality but is first and foremost a defense of liberty and freedom. As Nan Hunter points out, the first word of the opinion is "liberty" and the last word is "freedom":

"Liberty" is the Court's major chord. Lawrence begins with "liberty" and ends with "freedom," and those word choices are not a fluke. The opening paragraph defines Lawrence as a case about realms where government should not go. The first four sentences of the opinion declare: Liberty protects the person from unwarranted government intrusions into a dwelling or other private places. In our tradition the State is not omnipresent in the home. And there are other spheres of our lives and existence, outside the home, where the State should not be a dominant presence. Freedom extends beyond spatial bounds.[63]

Finally, the *Lawrence* repeats in full the reasons that the American Legal Institute recommends against criminalizing sodomy. It is striking how much the reasoning applies with equal force to affirmative consent regimes:

It justified its decision on three grounds: (1) The prohibitions undermined respect for the law by penalizing conduct many people engaged in; (2) the statutes regulated private conduct not harmful to others; and (3) the laws were arbitrarily enforced and thus invited the danger of blackmail.[64]

In sum, the Supreme Court's decisions protect a right to sexual autonomy that is not confined to contraception or to unpopular minorities or to sexual practices that have been historically approved. The government could not require every person to have sex only using the missionary position or only for reproductive means. This right is broad enough to cover sexual practices ranging from morning kisses to BDSM sex play, to consensual love making based on a couple's unspoken intimate understandings with one another rather than

---

[63] Nan Hunter, *Living with Lawrence*, 88 Minnesota Law Review 1103–1139, 1104 (2004).
[64] 539 U.S. at 572.

the same sort of overt, step-by-step consent that might be appropriate for complete strangers.

The next section looks at another possible issue with this argument. Is it possible that college "hookup" sex is not constitutionally protected because it lacks the intimacy for such protection?

The Question of Intimacy

Obviously not all sexual activity takes place among people in intimate relationships. Popular culture is awash with stories about the prevalence of "hookup sex" on college campuses.[65] While the difference between the sexual behavior of today's college students and that of their parents' generation is greatly exaggerated, it is nonetheless true that a significant amount of college sexual activity takes place outside of long-term relationships.[66]

Is it possible that the right to sexual autonomy does not apply to these sexual encounters? There is an argument to be made that *Lawrence* only protects sexual activity within intimate relationships:

The most recent Supreme Court case ostensibly protecting sexual activity, *Lawrence v. Texas*, also can be narrowly construed to protect sexual conduct only when such activity promotes emotional intimacy. In holding that same sex couples possess a liberty right to engage in sodomy, the Court emphasized that sexual acts, including anal sex between two men, "can be but one element in a personal bond that is more enduring." The Court therefore did not declare that consenting adults enjoy the freedom to engage in all forms of sex. Instead, the Court suggested that sex deserves constitutional protection only when potentially in the service of emotional intimacy.[67]

One scholar goes even further, arguing that *Lawrence* is limited to protecting sex that is *transcendental* in nature: "[Lawrence] leaves little or no justification for protecting less-than-transcendental sex that is not part of an ongoing relationship."[68] This section argues that, while the *Lawrence* Court certainly discussed intimacy, it would be a mistake to assume that it was directing courts to make case-by-case findings on the degree of intimacy of each individual sexual relationship. This would be a job for which they are spectacularly unsuited. As Judge Richard Posner has pointed out: "[J]udges know next to nothing about [sex] beyond their own personal experience, which is limited,

---

[65] See Wade, *American Hook up.*

[66] Martin A. Monto and Anna G. Carey, "A New Standard of Sexual Behavior? Are Claims Associated with the 'Hookup Culture' Supported by General Social Survey Data?," *The Journal of Sex Research* 51, no. 6 (2014): 605–615.

[67] Laura A. Rosenbury and Jennifer E. Rothman, *Sex in and out of Intimacy*, 59 Emory Law Journal 809–868, 809–810 (2010).

[68] Teemu Ruskola, "Gay Rights versus Queer Theory: What Is Left of Sodomy after *Lawrence v. Texas*?," *Soc. Text* 23 (2005), 235, 239, 238–245.

perhaps more so than average, because people with irregular sex lives are pretty much ... screened out of the judiciary."[69]

The *Lawrence* Court tacitly recognized how unsuited the courts are for this by declining to examine the level of intimacy of the couple whose sexual encounter was at the center of that case. In fact, the pair in *Lawrence* were not an established couple at all and were not intimate in any sense beyond the way that any pair of individuals engaging in sexual activity would be considered intimate. Indeed, one of them was cheating on the long-term boyfriend he had, who called the police, which is how the police ended up in the bedroom in the first place:

> The defendants in Lawrence – two men discovered engaging in anal sex in a private home – did not hold themselves out as a couple nor is there any evidence that they intended to pursue an ongoing relationship comparable to dating or marriage. In fact, one of the men was "romantically involved" with another man at the time of the arrest, and it was that romantic partner who called the police.[70]

In short, the two men in *Lawrence* were engaged in exactly the sort of hookup sex in which so many college students are assumed to be engaging. If the Court protects the *Lawrence* couples' right to sexual autonomy, there is no reason to assume it does not protect sexual activity that falls well short of the romantic ideal of an intimate relationship.

What then was the point of discussing intimacy at all in *Lawrence*? The most reasonable interpretation is that the majority opinion was distinguishing the type of sex at issue in that case from the sorts of sexual encounters that, *as a class*, are unlikely to be intimate. In his dissent, Justice Antonin Scalia argued the *Lawrence* decision opened the door to sexual anarchy:

> State laws against bigamy, same-sex marriage, adult incest, prostitution, masturbation, adultery, fornication, bestiality, and obscenity are likewise sustainable only in light of *Bowers'* validation of laws based on moral choices. Every single one of these laws is called into question by today's decision.[71]

Many of the practices listed by Scalia, such masturbation and bestiality, are distinguishable from the sexual acts protected in *Lawrence* because they inherently do not involve intimacy with another human being. Indeed, numerous courts have limited *Lawrence*'s reach on this basis, holding that it does not protect sex with minors, sex toys sold for masturbatory purposes, sex in public, or nonconsensual sex.[72] The specification of intimacy also excludes

---

[69] Richard A. Posner, Sex and Reason (1992), 1 (quoted in Rosenbury and Rothman, *Sex in and out of Intimacy*, 835, n. 153).

[70] Rosenbury and Rothman, *Sex in and out of Intimacy*, 824–825.   [71] 539 U.S. at 590.

[72] Singson v. Commonwealth, 621 S.E. 2d 682, 685–686 (Va. Ct. App. 2005) (holding that offer of oral sex in a men's restroom was not protected by *Lawrence* because of the public location); *In re R.L.C.*, 635 S.E.2d 1, 3–4 (N.C. Ct. App. 2006), aff'd, 643 S.E.2d 920 (N.C. 2007); State v. Acosta, No. 08-04-00312-CR, 2005 WL 2095290, at 3 (Tex. App. August 31, 2005).

prostitution from protection because it is a commercial rather than personal activity.[73]

So, the invocation of intimacy is better understood as distinguishing between categories of sexual activity – commercial versus noncommercial, adult humans versus minors and animals, public versus private – than as inviting case-by-case determinations of adult couples' level of intimacy. As the eminent constitutional scholar Lawrence Tribe writes:

[T]he Court evidently recognized an obligation to extend constitutional protection to some brief interactions that might not ripen into meaningful connections over time – even to some that might be chosen precisely for their fleeting and superficial character and their lack of emotional involvement. Had the Court done otherwise, it would have ceded to the state the power to determine what count as meaningful relationships and to decide when and how individuals might enter into such relationships. Doing so would have drained those relationships of their unique significance as expressions of self-government.[74]

The Question of Consent and Coercion

There is no question that the constitutional protections of *Lawrence* do not apply to coerced sexual activity. The Court clearly stated: "The present case does not involve minors. It does not involve persons who might be injured or coerced or who are situated in relationships where consent might not easily be refused."[75] And, of course, the whole point of affirmative consent regimes is to avoid nonconsensual sexual contact.

So, can one argue that affirmative consent is constitutional because it does not punish truly consensual activity? Probably not. As the *Lawrence* Court points out, sodomy laws were rarely prosecuted and usually enforced only in cases of assault or where vulnerable or powerless parties were involved:

Laws prohibiting sodomy do not seem to have been enforced against consenting adults acting in private. A substantial number of sodomy prosecutions and convictions for which there are surviving records were for predatory acts against those who could not or did not consent, as in the case of a minor or the victim of an assault. As to these, one purpose for the prohibitions was to ensure there would be no lack of coverage if a predator committed a sexual assault that did not constitute rape as defined by the

---

[73] As noted previously, at the time of this writing the Ninth Circuit had allowed a challenge to California's prostitution laws to go forward, but all other courts that have ruled on this have gone the other way. E.g., State v. Freitag, 130 P. 3d 544, 546 (Ariz. Ct. App. 2006); State v. Romano, 155 P. 3d 1102, 1109–1115 (Haw. 2007); People v. Williams, 811 N.E. 2d 1197, 1199 (Ill. App. Ct. 2004); State v. Pope, 608 S.E. 2d 114, 115–116 (N.C. Ct. App. 2005). (All cited in Rosenbury and Rothman, *Sex in and out of Intimacy*, 830, n. 122.)
[74] Lawrence Tribe, Lawrence v. Texas: *The "Fundamental Right" That Dare Not Speak Its Name*, 117, no. 6 Harvard Law Review 1893–1955, 1905(April 2004).
[75] 539 U.S. at 578.

criminal law. Thus the model sodomy indictments presented in a 19th-century treatise addressed the predatory acts of an adult man against a minor girl or minor boy. Instead of targeting relations between consenting adults in private, 19th-century sodomy prosecutions typically involved relations between men and minor girls or minor boys, relations between adults involving force, relations between adults implicating disparity in status, or relations between men and animals.[76]

So, limiting sodomy prosecutions to cases of assault or situations involving vulnerable individuals did not make those laws constitutional. Further, as discussed previously, affirmative consent regimes go well beyond requiring consent. They require a particular way of engaging in sexual relations, one that is at odds with how many, if not most, people engage in sex.

Further, the state cannot evade constitutional rights by simply narrowing the definition of *consent*. For example, it could not bring back sodomy prohibitions by arguing that because sodomy is medically dangerous and without reproductive value, no person could truly voluntarily consent to it.

Nor can the state define away the ways that so many people consent to sexual activity. The law is quite clear on what actual consent means – it is a mental state and does not require any specified expression of that mental state. This is true today and it was true at the time that *Lawrence* was decided. According to the most recent draft of the *Restatement (Third) of Torts*, *consent* is defined as follows:

§ 112. Actual Consent A person actually consents to an actor's otherwise tortious conduct if the person is subjectively willing for that conduct to occur. *Actual consent need not be communicated to the actor to be effective.* It can be express or can be inferred from the facts.[77]

The authors of the Model Penal Code considered adopting a definition of *consent* that requires overt expression, but ultimately decided against doing so.[78] So consent as measure of a mental state rather than as a specific expression of that mental state is the accepted understanding in both civil and criminal law, and this was certainly the case when the Court decided *Lawrence*. Therefore, when the Court stated that its holding involved consensual sex, the obvious understanding of what they meant by *consent* would be the widely accepted definitions of that word at the time *Lawrence* was written.

Furthermore, it is important to remember that we are discussing a right to sexual *autonomy*. Restricting how a person may consent to sexual activity lessens rather than enhances their autonomy. As Kimberly Kessler Ferzan writes:

[76] 539 U.S. at 569.
[77] Restatement (Third) of Torts: Intentional Torts to Persons § 112 (Am. Law Inst., Tentative Draft No. 1, 2015) (emphasis added). (Cited in Ferzan, "Consent, Culpability, and the Law of Rape," 397–439, 407.)
[78] www.the-american-interest.com/2016/05/18/yes-means-yes-falters/.

If we think that what we are protecting is autonomy, then that autonomy is best respected by recognizing that the consenter has it within his or her power to allow the boundary crossing simply by so choosing. No expression is needed. So, if I see my neighbor walking across my lawn to get to the street, and I think "that is okay with me," then the neighbor does not wrong me even if I never communicate that to him.

In sum, it is certainly true that *Lawrence* only applies to consensual sexual activity. Nonetheless, the state cannot lessen constitutional protections by defining *consent* more narrowly than the Court did. Sexual autonomy includes the autonomy to express one's consent to intimate conduct in whatever manner one wishes including passive acceptance.

Progressives and feminists who would grant the government broad latitude to define *consent* should heed the lessons of today's legal battles over abortion and "informed consent." Pro-life legislatures have shown great interest in narrowly defining how a woman may consent to an abortion. Restrictions range from waiting periods to mandatory preabortion ultrasounds to requiring doctors to use highly emotive language about a fetus's qualities in counseling women before obtaining their consent.

"Affirmative consent" sounds a great deal like "informed consent" and for good reason: Both restrict the exercise of rights protected under the due process clause in the name of protecting women from harm and coercion. Many pro-life legislators sincerely believe that women are being coerced by their sexual partners into abortions and are quick to talk about male/female power imbalances and subtle forms of coercion. They argue that they are merely making sure that the woman's consent is genuine and considered. If the government can narrow the definition for *consent* in one area, this likely has implications for the other area.

Is *Lawrence* Limited to Criminal Laws?

The *Lawrence* Court acknowledges that many people have negative views of homosexuality and then writes: "The issue is whether the majority may use the power of the State to enforce these views on the whole society through operation of the criminal law." Because being suspended or expelled from college is not a criminal punishment, can it be argued that such sanctions are not covered by the *Lawrence* decision?

This proposition is doubtful and has been rejected in other contexts. Most famously, in *New York Times v. Sullivan*, a case granting broad First Amendment protection to those sued for libeling public officials, the Supreme Court stated: "What a state may not constitutionally bring about by means of a criminal statute is likewise beyond the reach of its civil law of libel."[79] Similarly,

---

[79] New York Times v. Sullivan, 376 U.S. 254, 257 (1964).

the Seventh Circuit Court of Appeals applied the same constitutional standards to a civil antipornography law that would apply to criminal obscenity laws.[80]

Once again, a simple thought experiment demonstrates why this argument fails. Could state legislatures require colleges to suspend or expel students for having an abortion? For possessing contraception? For homosexuality? In fact, the argument is even more compelling than usual in this case because, as discussed in Chapter 2, there are often parallel criminal proceedings in college sexual assault cases, in which the two investigations share information.

CONCLUSION

There is a clear and powerful line of cases that protects sexual autonomy, including the sexual autonomy of college students. Affirmative consent regimes violate this right by regulating how students engage in private sexual activity and by limiting how they may express their consent.

Of course, no right is unlimited. The government may limit rights if it is truly necessary to do so to protect students from sexual assault. The next chapter will critically examine whether this is in fact the case, and whether the state should place legal limits on students' sexual autonomy. Most significantly, it will critically examine the empirical assumptions that are used to justify affirmative consent regimes.

[80] American Bookseller Association v. Hudnut, 771 F. 2d 323 (1985).

8

The Empirical Claims for Affirmative Consent

The previous two chapters discussed several major criticisms of affirmative consent regimes.

- They risk shifting the burden of proof to the accused in practice, if not in theory;
- There is no valid reason for defining *sexual assault* differently, and far more broadly, for college students than for everyone else;
- They define a great deal of consensual sexual activity as sexual assault;
- They are likely to result in arbitrary enforcement;
- They may encourage racist enforcement patterns;
- They often confuse key terms such as *intoxication* and *incapacitation*;
- They are often enforced by third-party complainants rather than by the person affected; and
- They violate students' constitutional rights to sexual autonomy.

Advocates of affirmative consent primarily rely upon three empirical claims in defending these laws and rules. Their arguments are well summarized by the joint authors of the California affirmative consent bill, Kevin De Leon and Hannah-Beth Jackson. They wrote a *Washington Post* editorial entitled "Why We Made 'Yes Means Yes' California Law."

The first claim is that extremely high percentages of female college students have been sexually assaulted:

Based on one of the largest surveys of college students ever conducted – more than 150,000 students from 27 Universities participated – the report found that that nearly one in four female students said they had experienced unwanted sexual contact. The assaults were carried out by force, threat of force, or while the victim was intoxicated.[1]

---

[1] Kevin de León and Hannah Beth Jackson, "Why We Made 'Yes Means Yes' California Law," *Washington Post* (October 13 2015), www.washingtonpost.com/news/in-theory/wp/2015/10/13/why-we-made-yes-means-yes-california-law/?utm_term=.8371d94a69af.

This claim will be discussed in detail in the next section, but two things are worth noting as a preliminary matter. First, De Leon and Jackson conflate "unwanted" sexual contact with sexual "assault." This is clearly erroneous. As noted in Chapter 6, there is a difference between unwanted activity and unconsensual activity. People may consent to unwanted sexual activity for many reasons, including the hope for intimacy and making their partner happy.[2] Absent additional factors such as coercion, this is not sexual assault, and survey questions that ask students if they have ever engaged in unwanted sexual activity should not be read as measuring sexual assault.

Also, the authors of the article describe sexual activity while "intoxicated" as sexual assault. As discussed at several points elsewhere in this book, *intoxication* is a broad term that covers anyone "stimulated" or "affected" by alcohol and is not the same thing as being incapacitated. Many, many people engage in sexual activity while intoxicated, and counting such encounters as assault greatly inflates their numbers.

Some antirape activists (although certainly not all) have become disturbingly casual about defining *sexual assault* in a purely subjective manner. Referring to the oft-made claim that one in five college women are sexually assaulted, Vanessa Grigoriadis – a contributing editor to the *New York Times Magazine and Vanity Fair*, and the author of *Blurred Lines: Rethinking Sex, Power, and Consent on Campus* – said in a published interview:

Oh, yeah. I mean, I'm 100 percent on the side that 1 out of 5 is not a bogus number. Even if you want to go down the road of looking at the surveys and picking out the words that make you think that a girl could say she was raped when she wasn't, there's no question that we're having an upsurge in our culture of women saying, "I feel violated by the way that I had sex in college."[3]

If large numbers of college women subjectively feel violated by the way they and their partners engaged in sexual activity, that is a serious issue, but that is very different from saying that all these women are victims of sexual assault. However well-meaning advocates like Grigoriadis may be, we cannot effectively address broad social problems by conflating things that are so different. A feeling of violation is not the same thing as sexual assault. Wanting something and consenting to something is not the same thing. Incapacitation and intoxication are not the same thing. Accuracy is important in the realm of law, sexual regulation, and punishment.

A second oft-made empirical claim of affirmative consent advocates is that most sexual assault on college campuses is perpetrated by repeat offenders or "predators." De Leon and Jackson write:

---

[2] Charlene L. Muehlenhard and Zoë D. Peterson, "Wanting and Not Wanting Sex: The Missing Discourse of Ambivalence," *Feminism and Psychology* 15, no. 1(2005): 15–20.

[3] Isaac Chotiner, "A New Standard for Sexual Consent," *The Slate* (September 5, 2017), www .slate.com/articles/news_and_politics/interrogation/2017/09/in_search_of_a_new_standard_- for_sexual_consent_on_campus.html.

In a court of law, due process is necessary to protect the accused's liberty. With a high burden of proof, district attorneys are all too often unable to gather enough evidence to prosecute offenders. Because perpetrators are most often repeat offenders, it's important for campuses to have a way to hold aggressors accountable.[4]

This argument will be addressed in "Are Most Sexual Assaults of College Students Committed by Sexual Predators?" We will see that there is very little empirical support for this assertion. It is also worth noting that there is an important commonsense problem with it. If it is true that most sexual assaults are committed by predators, it is not at all clear that affirmative consent regimes will be better at catching and punishing them. Serial rapists are not likely to be honest people, and there will rarely be witnesses other than the two people involved. Affirmative consent regimes tell predators exactly what lie to tell – "the other person unequivocally said 'yes' and then changed their mind later." Affirmative consent is more likely to ensnare the student who genuinely believes the other student's actions constituted consent – the previous chapters are filled with examples of such students – who therefore testify truthfully about what happened.

The third empirical assertion is that a "no means no" rule is ineffective at punishing sexual assault because it puts the burden of proving resistance on the woman and, therefore, "yes means yes" will make it easier for fact finders to determine that a sexual assault occurred:

While "no means no" has become a well-known slogan, it places the burden on victims, making it their responsibility to show resistance .... Since "no means no" has proved ineffective, last year California enacted SB 967, legislation to make "yes means yes" the consent standard on college campuses and to take a major step toward preventing sexual violence.[5]

One can understand why some might think that "yes means yes" will make it easier to hold perpetrators of sexual assault accountable. The fact finder will be directed to look for overt signs of consent and to find against the accused student if those signs are absent. The question is whether there is any actual evidence for this idea. As we will see in "Is Affirmative Consent the Most Effective Standard for Punishing Sexual Assault?" there has not been much research on this question, and the one study that sheds light on it points in the opposite direction. Telling the fact finder (be it a criminal jury or a college sexual assault panel) that "no means no" is *more* likely to result in holding sexual assaulters accountable than giving a "yes means yes" instruction. In fact, "no means no" is not the legal standard in any state. The real problem in most states is the force requirement described in Chapter 1. It is simply untrue that the choice is between "yes means yes" and "no means no."

---

[4] de León and Jackson, "Why We Made 'Yes Means Yes.'"   [5] Id.

SURVEY RESEARCH AND THE RATE OF SEXUAL ASSAULT ON COLLEGE
CAMPUSES

The reported statistic that one in five women in college have been sexually
assaulted has had an enormous political impact. Speaking at the White
House, President Obama repeated the number twice for emphasis: "It is
estimated that 1 in 5 women on college campuses has been sexually assaulted
during their time there – 1 in 5."[6] Vice President Joe Biden has remarked that:
"We know the numbers: one in five of every one of those young women who is
dropped off for that first day of school, before they finish school, will be
assaulted, will be assaulted in her college years."[7]

Both Obama and Biden were citing "The Campus Sexual Assault Study"[8]
(CSA), which was conducted in 2007 for the Justice Department's National
Institute of Justice. Their reliance on this study was remarkable, because, as
discussed in the following text, its lead author has explicitly stated that the study
is not meant to be nationally representative and that the study was being used in
ways for which it was not intended and could not support.

Nonetheless, the one-in-five statistic has been widely cited by politicians,
journalists, and academics. Obama, Biden, and former Secretary of Education
Arne Duncan have all claimed that there is an "epidemic" of sexual assault on
college campuses.[9] Indeed, the one-in-five statistic has become nearly
ubiquitous in the discussion of sexual assault and college:

> If there's a conversation taking place about the prevalence of campus sexual assault in
> the United States, the phrase "one in five" is usually within earshot.
>
> "It is estimated that one in five women on college campuses has been sexually assaulted
> during their time there," President Obama said in January. Obama has cited the statistic
> multiple times throughout the last few years, as have Vice President Joe Biden and the U.S.
> Department of Education. Senators use the statistic when writing legislation or holding
> hearings. Pundits and columnists have opened many an editorial with it, and it's a favorite
> of student activists, frequently appearing on hand-written signs at protests and marches.[10]

The influential journalist and editor Ezra Klein has argued that whatever the
excesses of affirmative consent regimes may be, they are justified by the one-in-
five number. In an article titled "'Yes Means Yes' Is a Terrible Law, and
I Completely Support It," Klein paints a grim picture of life under an
affirmative consent regime:

---

[6] Glen Kessler, "One in Five Women in College Sexually Assaulted: An Update on This Statistic,"
  The Washington Post (May 1, 2014), www.washingtonpost.com/news/fact-checker/wp/2014/
  12/17/one-in-five-women-in-college-sexually-assaulted-an-update/?utm_term=.9815fe17913c.
[7] Id.   [8] www.nccpsafety.org/assets/files/library/Campus_Sexual_Assault_Study.pdf.
[9] Kristen Lombardi, "Biden Cites Progress on Campus Sexual Assault, but Says There's 'So Much
  Farther to Go,'" *The Center for Public Integrity* (April 24, 3015), www.publicintegrity.org/2015/
  04/24/17232/biden-cites-progress-campus-sexual-assault-says-theres-so-much-farther-go.
[10] www.pbs.org/newshour/education/critics-advocates-alike-doubt-oft-cited-1–5-campus-sexual-
  assault-stat.

It tries to change, through brute legislative force, the most private and intimate of adult acts. It is sweeping in its redefinition of acceptable consent; two college seniors who've been in a loving relationship since they met during the first week of their freshman years, and who, with the ease of the committed, slip naturally from cuddling to sex, could fail its test.[11]

He also rejects the position that innocent people won't be affected by affirmative consent:

Defenders of the bill argue that the lovers have nothing to worry about; the assault will never be punished, because no complaint will ever be brought. Technically, that's true. But this is as much indictment as defense: if the best that can be said about the law is that its definition of consent will rarely be enforced, then the definition should be rethought. It is dangerous for the government to set rules it doesn't expect will be followed.[12]

Nonetheless, he argues that all this dangerous excess is fully justified by the one-in-five number:

Every discussion of the Yes Means Yes law needs to begin with a simple number: A 2007 study by the Department of Justice found that one in five women is the victim of an attempted or completed sexual assault while in college.
    One. In. Five.[13]

For Klein, this number means that drastic remedies are needed to ensure that every man feels a "cold spike of fear" before he engages in any sexual act:

If the Yes Means Yes law is taken even remotely seriously it will settle like a cold winter on college campuses, throwing everyday sexual practice into doubt and creating a haze of fear and confusion over what counts as consent. This is the case against it, and also the case for it. Because for one in five women to report an attempted or completed sexual assault means that everyday sexual practices on college campuses need to be upended, and men need to feel a cold spike of fear when they begin a sexual encounter.[14]

Thus the question of the accuracy of this number has become a vital question. The following sections will argue that the one-in-five number is deeply misleading. It is based on studies that are not generalizable; suffer from low response rates and unrepresentative sampling; fail to account for other common methodological errors; and define sexual assault and coercion in ways that are far broader than the general understandings of those terms. Each of these will be separately discussed in the following sections.

Generalizability

For a survey to be generalizable it must "survey people who represent the population at large."[15] So, to use the CSA the way President Obama or Ezra Klein do, the CSA would have to be a survey of a population that resembles the college population at large. However, the CSA is no such thing. It surveyed

---

[11] Klein, "Yes Means Yes." [12] Id. [13] Id. [14] Id.
[15] www.iwh.on.ca/wrmb/generalizability.

students at only two universities: one in the South and one in the Midwest. It was administered only to seniors and was given only once.

The obvious question is how a survey of just two universities can possibly be representative of the nation's extremely diverse population of college students. The obvious answer is that it cannot be. In fact, the study's lead authors have made it clear that they believe their study is being used "inappropriately":

If you've followed the discussion about sexual assault on college campuses in America, it's likely you've heard some variation of the claim that 1 in 5 women on college campuses in the United States has been sexually assaulted or raped. Or you may have heard the even more incorrect abbreviated version, that 1 in 5 women on campus has been *raped*.

As two of the researchers who conducted the Campus Sexual Assault Study from which this number was derived, we feel we need to set the record straight. Although we used the best methodology available to us at the time, there are caveats that make it inappropriate to use the 1-in-5 number in the way it's being used today, as a baseline or the only statistic when discussing our country's problem with rape and sexual assault on campus.[16]

The authors could not be clearer that the survey is not nationally representative and was never intended to be presented that way:

First and foremost, the 1-in-5 statistic is *not* a nationally representative estimate of the prevalence of sexual assault, and we have never presented it as being representative of anything other than the population of senior undergraduate women at the two universities where data were collected – two large public universities, one in the South and one in the Midwest.[17]

When asked about this misuse of the CSA study, the Obama White House responded that the two other studies produced similar numbers:

A White House spokesperson, who asked not to be quoted, said that the one in five statistic was consistent with other studies, pointing in particular to two surveys: a 2000 Justice Department study that reported that, over a seven-month period, 2.8 percent of college women faced rape victimization (completed or attempted) and a 2014 MIT survey which found that 17 percent of female undergraduates experienced one or more unwanted sexual behaviors.[18]

However, neither of those two studies were designed to produce generalizable results. In fact, MIT cautioned that its study should not be used to generalize about the experiences of MIT students, much less the entire American college population:

But there are issues with both surveys. The 2000 report could be interpreted as suggesting that one in five women might face rape victimization over four or five years in college,

---

[16] Christopher Krebs and Christine Lindquist, "Setting the Record Straight on '1 in 5,'" *Time* (December 15, 2014), http://time.com/3633903/campus-rape-1-in-5-sexual-assault-setting-record-straight/.
[17] Id.   [18] Kessler, "One in Five Women in College Sexually Assaulted."

but the authors conceded in 2010 that "admittedly, these projections are speculative and await longitudinal studies that follow women throughout their college careers." Meanwhile, the MIT sample was based on self-selected responses, so its data could not be used as any sort of confirmation. The university itself warned that the numbers were not representative of all women at MIT: "Because the survey was not a random sample and was voluntary . . . it would be a mistake to use these numbers to generalize about the prevalence of unwanted sexual behavior in the lives of all MIT students."[19]

In terms of generalizability, a 2015 survey commissioned by the American Association for Universities (AAU)[20] is a bit better. It surveyed students at 27 universities. However, these universities were not meant to be a representative sample of American universities – they were the universities that happened to belong to the AAU. There are thousands of American universities, so 27 is not that large a number, especially for a sample that is not intended to be representative.

Further, the survey showed vastly varying rates of sexual assault, ranging from 13 percent to 31 percent that are difficult to explain as anything other than measurement error. Summarizing these results, as well as the results from the other surveys, the AAU warns:

Overall, these comparisons illustrate that estimates such as "1 in 5" or "1 in 4" as a global rate, across all IHEs [Institutions of Higher Education] is *at least over simplistic, if not misleading*. None of the studies that generate estimates for specific IHEs are nationally representative. The above results show that the rates vary greatly across institutions.[21]

Even Jennifer Freyd, who has written to defend the AAU study from its critics, cautions: "I agree with . . . critics that the AAU survey has limitations and we should be cautious about generalizing from it. We also should be promoting much better instruments."[22]

In sum, as things currently stand, the one-in-five number is a weapon of political rhetoric, not a generalizable finding. The CSA is being blatantly misused according to its own authors. The other studies cited by the Obama White House suffer from the same issues. The AAU is an improvement in terms of generalizability, but even its authors and advocates concede that we should be cautious about generalizing from it. At a minimum, before we demand that "men need to feel a cold spike of fear when they begin a sexual encounter," we

---

[19] Id. The other study referred to by the Obama White House is discussed later in this chapter.
[20] http://ias.virginia.edu/sites/ias.virginia.edu/files/University%20of%20Virginia_2015_climate_final_report.pdf.
[21] AAU Executive Summary (emphasis added), www.aau.edu/sites/default/files/%40%20Files/Climate%20Survey/Executive%20Summary%2012-14-15.pdf, xiv.
[22] Jennifer J. Freyd, "Examining Denial Tactics: Were Victims Overrepresented in the AAU Survey of Sexual Violence on College Campuses?," *Huffington Post* (December 6, 2017), www.huffingtonpost.com/jennifer-j-freyd/examining-denial-tactics-were-victims-overrepresented-in-the-aau-survey-of-sexual-violence-on-college-campuses_b_8216008.html.

should wait for a survey of a nationally representative set of institutions using the best survey instruments available. Further, there are other compelling reasons to doubt the accuracy of the one-in-five figure. The next section discusses the issue of response bias.

Response Bias

For any survey to produce useful results, the population answering the survey must be representative of the overall population being studied. This means at least two things. First, the population that is being *asked* the questions must be representative of the overall population. That issue is discussed in the preceding section. Second, it means that the people who choose to *answer* the questions must be representative of the overall population as well. Even if a survey were administered to every college student in the country, if students who were sexually assaulted were significantly more likely than other students to take the time to answer the survey, then the survey results would not be representative of the general population of college students. This problem is called "response bias," and it has plagued most of the survey research in this area.

Recall that President Obama and Vice President Biden relied upon the CSA in making their claims about sexual assault. However, by the admission of its own authors, the CSA has a clear response bias problem, and it is not possible to determine how large the bias is:

[A]nother limitation of our study – inherent to web-based surveys – is that the response rate was relatively low (42%). We conducted an analysis of this nonresponse rate and found that respondents were not significantly different from nonrespondents in terms of age, race/ethnicity or year of study. Even so, it is possible that nonresponse bias had an impact on our prevalence estimates, positive or negative. *We simply have no way of knowing whether sexual-assault victims were more or less likely to participate in our study.*[23]

The survey took about 15 minutes to answer, which is a great deal for busy college students. Quite possibly, someone who was sexually assaulted would have a stronger motivation to make the time to take the survey. Statistical analysis indicates that a survey of sexual assault is exactly the kind of survey where a low response rate strongly correlates with a heavy response bias. According to a meta-analysis of 59 methodological studies, "We know from statistical expressions that influences on survey participation that are themselves measured in the survey will show the largest nonresponse bias."[24] That is exactly the case with the sexual assault surveys – the fact that a person

---

[23] Krebs and Lindquist, "Setting the Record Straight" (emphasis added).
[24] R. M. Groves and E. Peytcheva, "The Impact of Nonresponse Rates on Nonresponse Bias: A Meta-analysis," *Public Opinion Quarterly* 72, no. 2 (2008), 167–189.

has been sexually assaulted is likely to affect their motivation to fill out the survey and is also the variable that is being measured.

The AAU survey had an even lower response rate than the CSA study – just 19 percent. Perhaps the most thoughtful defense of that survey comes from Jennifer Freyd. There was a great deal of variation in the response rates from different campuses and also much variation in how many students said they were sexually assaulted. Freyd points out that schools with the lowest response rates do not report the highest rates of sexual assault, which is what we might expect if students who were sexually assaulted were the most likely students to fill out the survey. That makes sense, but it is undercut by the fact that the AAU study cannot explain the very significant variation among campuses in either response rates or reported rates of sexual assault. In short, everybody is just guessing here.

Freyd also speculates that response bias could run in the other direction. Students who have been traumatized by a sexual assault may be *less* likely to respond to a survey about sexual assault. However, that guess is directly contradicted by the AAU's own analysis:

The report provides the results of three different assessments of nonresponse bias. Two of these three analyses provide evidence that nonresponders tended to be less likely to report victimization. This implies that the survey estimates related to victimization and selected attitude items may be biased upward (i.e., somewhat too high).[25]

So, we see that not only are the surveys at issue being administered to populations that are not representative of the overall student population, but only a small, probably nonrepresentative, subset of those surveyed are responding. Therefore, we are looking at a nonrepresentative subset of a nonrepresentative population.

In addition to all this, there are serious questions about whether the surveys are getting accurate information even from the students who are filling out the survey. This issue is discussed in the next section.

Time Frame and Telescoping Issues

The surveys of sexual assault do not just ask *what* happened to students. They also ask *when* sexual assault happened. This has several important implications. We need to keep in mind that these surveys are being used by politicians to justify special regulation of student sexual behavior. That means that they ought to be studying victimization rates of people who were attending college at the time of the assault. If all the reported assaults occurred while the survey takers were still in high school or were away on summer vacation, for example, this would hardly justify special affirmative consent rules for college students.

[25] www.aau.edu/sites/default/files/%40%20Files/Climate%20Survey/Executive%20Summary%2012012-14-15.pdf, 6–7.

An early survey, the "Sexual Experience Survey" (SES) of 1982 asked students if they had "ever" been sexually assaulted, which obviously captures experiences going back to high school and beforehand.[26] The revised SES of 1987 asked about experiences since the age of 14.

Most subsequent surveys focused on post–high school experiences but were still not limited to what happened in college. The CSA asked about experiences "since entering college," so it covers students that were home for vacation or weekends and off-campus incidents that may not have involved an assailant who is a college student. Indeed, more than 60 percent of the reported incidents were off campus and were not necessarily perpetrated by college students.[27] Affirmative consent would not apply to nonstudent perpetrators, so these sexual assaults cannot logically be used to justify restricting the sexual autonomy of college students.

There is also the issue of "telescoping": the tendency of people to misremember when something happened, usually in the direction of thinking it happened more recently than it did.[28] So if you ask someone if they were sexually assaulted in the past year, they may say yes even if they were assaulted longer ago than that. There are survey techniques for reducing this problem such as focusing respondents on "landmark events" to create a point of temporal reference.[29] The various sexual assault surveys discussed in the preceding text do not appear to have used these techniques. This is especially concerning because "research has suggested that traumatic events, such as rape and sexual assault, may be particularly prone to telescoping."[30]

Further, the way that some of these studies derive their overall estimates of sexual assault are likely to seriously exacerbate this telescoping problem. For example, a 2000 study commissioned by the US Department of Justice, "The Sexual Victimization of College Women" (this is the other study referred to by the Obama White House), concluded that between one in four and one in five college women are sexually assaulted during their time in college.

However, their conclusions rest upon some very questionable extrapolation. In response to their survey, only 2.8 percent of college women reported that they had been raped or that someone had attempted to rape them during that college year. The authors of the study acknowledged that "one might conclude that the risk of rape victimization for college women is not high;

---

[26] Lecture by Callie Rennison, Professor and Director of the Office of Equity and Title IX Coordinator, School of Public Affairs, University of Colorado–Denver, www.youtube.com /watch?v=wZuODobgCYk.

[27] CSA, 5–16.

[28] Paul J. Lavrakas, *Encyclopedia of Survey Research Methods* (Thousand Oaks, CA: Sage Publications, 2008), http://sk.sagepub.com/reference/survey/n579.xml?term=telescoping.

[29] Id.

[30] Sinozich and Langton, "Rape and Sexual Assault Victimization among College-Age Females, 1995–2013," 15.

'only' about 1 in 36 college women (2.8 percent) experience a completed rape or attempted rape in an academic year."[31]

The authors of the study argued that the numbers were really far higher than that. The average period that a responding student had been in school that year at the time they took the survey was 6.91 months. So, they nearly doubled the figure of reported incidents to extrapolate it to a 12-month year, even though the academic year is usually far shorter than 12 months. They then assumed that it usually takes five years to graduate and therefore multiplied the number again, this time by five, to calculate their nearly "one in four" estimate:

> The figures measure victimization for slightly more than half a year (6.91 months). Projecting results beyond this reference period is problematic for a number of reasons, such as assuming that the risk of victimization is the same during summer months and remains stable over a person's time in college. However, if the 2.8 percent victimization figure is calculated for a 1-year period, the data suggest that nearly 5 percent (4.9 percent) of college women are victimized in any given calendar year. Over the course of a college career – which now lasts an average of 5 years – the percentage of completed or attempted rape victimization among women in higher educational institutions might climb to between one-fifth and one-quarter.[32]

There are numerous problems with this approach. The authors concede that their numbers are only "suggestive," which is very different from how politicians have been using them. They lump together assaults that occur off campus and over the summer with assaults on campus and during the school year. They assume that all the survey takers will be in college for five years even though nearly half of all college students attend two-year colleges.[33] They assume that students face the same risk of sexual assault throughout their college careers, which is not supported by the evidence.[34] Further, they amplify the problem with telescoping. If a student misremembers a sexual assault as occurring within the past six months when it really occurred, say, eight months ago, that distorts the survey results. But when the researchers multiple those numbers by two (because they count a college year as 12 months) and then again by five (because they assume that it takes five years to graduate), they are multiplying this distortion by a factor of 10.

None of this is intended as broad criticism of this study's researchers. As noted, the authors of this study conceded that their results were only suggestive, just as other authors have conceded that their results are not

[31] Bonnie S. Fisher et al., "The Sexual Victimization of College Women," US Department of Justice (2000), 10, www.ncjrs.gov/pdffiles1/nij/182369.pdf.

[32] Id. at 10.

[33] www2.ed.gov/about/offices/list/ovae/pi/cclo/ccfacts.html. While it is true that many of these two-year college students will transfer to four-year colleges, it is also true that many will not stay in college until graduation.

[34] Molly Redden, "Welcome to the Red Zone: What Is Wrong with Sexual Assault Training on Campus," *The Guardian* (August 26, 2016), www.theguardian.com/society/2016/aug/26/campus-sexual-assault-training-red-zone

meant to be generalizable and that there might be a response bias issue. The problem occurs when journalists and politicians used these studies to claim that there is an "epidemic" of sexual assault and to justify major policy decisions without acknowledging the studies' limitations and flaws. Of course, politicians are free to argue that a 2.8 percent rate of sexual assault is indeed an epidemic because the ideal rate is obviously zero, but that is very different from what they have been saying and they certainly could not use it to justify special rules for college students.

However, for all the issues discussed so far, there is an even more significant reason for caution in using these studies to justify public policy. They define terms like *sexual assault* far more broadly than those terms are generally understood by the public, creating an unjustified sense of panic. This will be discussed in the next section.

Issues of Terminology

There are no universally accepted definitions of terms such as *rape* or *sexual assault*.[35] Therefore, survey designers have great leeway to define these terms as they see fit. There is nothing wrong with researchers defining these terms broadly enough to capture all the behaviors that they wish to study. But, if the terms are defined very broadly, this leads to at least two distinct problems. First, if the surveys do not disaggregate the data sufficiently, we do not find out how much reported sexual assault is the result of things like force or incapacitation and how much of the reported sexual assault is the result of things like a student feeling verbally pressured to engage in unwanted sexual conduct. Regardless of where one personally draws the line on what constitutes sexual assault, this sort of information would certainly be useful.

Second, where the survey's definition of *sexual assault* is sufficiently different from the popular understanding of sexual assault – for example engaging in any type of sexual touching after having had a few drinks – this lends itself to abuse of the data by political actors and to easy sensationalization by the media. This is exactly what has been happening.

As will be discussed in the following text, almost all the major surveys on college sexual assault use behaviorally specific questions rather than asking students if they have been raped or assaulted. This approach has advantages and disadvantages. In its favor, it means that we are not asking students to play lawyer and respond to legal terminology. As discussed in Chapter 1, these terms are defined in divergent ways in different states and require various legal elements. We cannot necessarily expect students to accurately define these terms or to correctly understand those definitions even if supplied in the

---

[35] Charlene L. Muehlenhard, Terry P. Humphreys, Kristen N. Jozkowski, and Zoë D. Peterson, "The Complexities of Sexual Consent among College Students: A Conceptual and Empirical Review," *The Journal of Sex Research* 53 (2016): 4–5, 457–487.

survey. However, it often means substituting inherently vague terms for legal terms. Students have to decide for themselves what *pressured, drunk,* or *expressed displeasure* mean.

Many of the survey questions indeed use terms that are broad, vague, and well beyond the popular understanding of what it means to be raped or assaulted. While society may be undergoing an important shift in its understanding of these terms, students are being asked questions about behaviors that are very far from legally defined assault. For example, in several surveys, students are deemed not to have effectively consented to sex if their sexual partner threatened to end a relationship over lack of sex or even if their partner expressed "unhappiness" about lack of sex:

Consider, for example, the National Intimate Partner and Sexual Violence Survey (NISVS; Black et al., 2011) sponsored by the Centers for Disease Control and Prevention (CDC). This survey includes "threatening to end your relationship" as a type of pressure associated with sexual coercion (Black et al., 2011, pp. 17, 106; to clarify, in the NISVS, sex after this type of pressure is not considered rape; it is considered sexual coercion, a broader category). Other studies have also included threatening to end the relationship as a verbally coercive technique for obtaining sex (e.g., Kanin, 1967; Koss et al., 2007; Koss et al., 1987; Livingston, Buddie, Testa, & VanZile-Tamsen, 2004; Struckman-Johnson, Struckman-Johnson, & Anderson, 2003; Zurbriggen, 2000) . . ..
Similar questions could be asked about other verbally coercive behaviors. For example, "wearing you down by repeatedly asking for sex, or showing they were unhappy" is another type of coercion included in the NISVS (Black et al., 2011, pp. 17, 106). Other studies have also included repeated requests for sex and continual verbal pressure as coercive techniques for obtaining sex (Koss et al., 2007; Koss et al., 1987; Livingston et al., 2004; Struckman, Johnson et al., 2003).[36]

Asking students if they have felt pressured by repeated requests is also a problematic question. Recall that affirmative consent regimes require students to ensure their partner's consent for each escalation of sexual activity, probably through a "stop and ask" approach. That means that they are "repeatedly asking for sex." While this is probably not what the researchers had in mind in designing the question, there is no way to know how students are interpreting the question.

Surveys also ask students if they have ever engaged in sexual activity as a result of "lies" or "false promises":

Some authors (e.g., Muehlenhard, 1995–1996; Tuerkheimer, 2013) have argued that this concept is also important in considering sexual consent. Consistent with this idea, the NISVS (Black et al., 2011, p. 17) and other surveys (Koss et al., 2007, p. 368) include using lies or false promises to obtain sex in their definitions of sexual coercion.[37]

Society can debate about whether telling lies or falsely promising gifts or other things of value should be formally punished by college authorities. But these

---

[36] Id. at 466.   [37] Id. at 466–467.

things are very far from what most people probably imagine when politicians tell them that one in four or one in five women are sexually assaulted in college.

Other definitions commonly used in surveys are open to debate. The AAU survey, among others, includes "rubbing against [you] in a sexual way, even if the touching is over the other's clothes"[38] This question is very likely to capture student experiences at college dance parties where "grinding" is common:

> Grinding is also known as "freaking," "freak-dancing," "dirty dancing," "bumping," and "booty-dancing." This style of dancing is associated with club culture and hip-hop, the type of music commonly played at mainstream college parties. When using the word "grinding," I mean to capture a common set of dancing behaviors that may nonetheless differ slightly across regions. Though different terms exist to refer to grinding, the sexualized nature of the dancing, and accompanying explicit gestures, are the defining characteristics.[39]

Here again, reasonable people can disagree on whether grinding without clear prior consent is sexual assault. "Central to an analysis of grinding is the question whether grinding is just a style of dance or a meaningful and intentional sexual act."[40] However, because grinding is common, including it in a survey is likely to greatly inflate the rate of reported sexual assault, and the public is likely to be misled unless its inclusion is explicitly discussed by politicians, academics, and the media.

Other decisions by survey designers lead to high estimates of sexual assault. One very important example is the AAU survey, which explicitly incorporates the affirmative consent standard into its questions. Question G-19 asks: "Since you have been a student at [University], has someone kissed or sexually touched you without your active, ongoing voluntary agreement?" The question explicitly "Incorporate[s] affirmative consent as a tactic from the AAU and COFHE [Consortium on Financing Higher Education] schools affirmative consent policies."[41]

Recall, though, from the beginning of this chapter that the authors of California's affirmative consent law specifically cite the AAU study as evidence that "'no means no' has proved ineffective" and we therefore need "yes means yes" – affirmative consent. This is a paradigm case of circular reasoning; they use a survey that defines lack of affirmative consent as sexual assault to produce the very numbers that they claim justify affirmative consent.

Many surveys also treat the question of alcohol consumption in a way that likely inflates sexual assault statistics. In the NISVS "Rape is defined as any completed or attempted unwanted vaginal (for women), oral, or anal penetration ... and includes times when the victim was *drunk, high,* drugged,

---

[38] www.aau.edu/sites/default/files/%40%20Files/Climate%20Survey/Survey%20Instrument.pdf, G-3.

[39] Shelly Ronan, "Gendered Scripts and Sexualized Dancing at College Parties," *Gender and Society* 24, no. 3 (June 2010), 355–377, at 356.

[40] Id. at 363.   [41] AAU survey at 29, n. 18.

or passed out and unable to consent."[42] While it should not be controversial that sexually imposing oneself on a passed-out person is rape, note that the terms "drunk" and "high" are listed separately from "passed out," so they are meant to capture a lower state of alcohol or marijuana consumption. The question of how much consumption means that the survey taker was "unable to consent" is left entirely to the individual. The *New York Times* reported on a mandatory lecture/discussion at Trinity College where the students expressed confusion over questions such as, "[W]hat if a student has just one beer – or even just a sip?"[43] We can assume then that students are interpreting the NICVS definition of *rape* in widely disparate ways. The CSA also asks students about being "drunk" apart from asking them if they were passed out, incapacitated, or asleep, which invites them to interpret the word *drunk* as something short of incapacitated or unconscious.

How do we know how much of the sexual assault reported in these surveys was different from the type of incidents the public generally thinks of as rape or sexual assault? The students give us a strong indication. As will be discussed in the next chapter, only a small percent of sexual assaults are reported. According to the AAU survey, "The most common reason for not reporting incidents of sexual assault and sexual misconduct was that it was not considered serious enough."[44] The same is true for the Sexual Victimization of College Women study[45] and also for the CSA, even when the survey takers indicated that there had been a physical assault: "Of the victims who did not report the incident to law enforcement, the most commonly reported reasons for non-reporting were that they did not think it was serious enough to report (endorsed by 56% of physically forced sexual assault victims and 67% of incapacitated sexual assault victims)."[46]

One possible way to interpret this is to assume that the self-esteem of college women is so low that they do not consider forcible sexual assault a crime serious enough to report. However, given the very broad and vague wording of the survey instruments, the more likely possibility is the surveys were capturing many behaviors that these adult, college-attending women, using their own judgment, did not consider to be particularly serious.

In sum, even apart from the methodical issues discussed in the first three sections, the terminology of the surveys is often so broad and vague that the one-in-five estimates of rape and sexual assault are probably greatly exaggerated. The question then, is what is the real prevalence of rape and assault on college

[42] www.cdc.gov/violenceprevention/pdf/NISVS-StateReportBook.pdf, 17 (emphasis added).
[43] Jessica Bennet, "Campus Sex … with a Syllabus," *New York Times* (January 6, 2016), www.nytimes.com/2016/01/10/fashion/sexual-consent-assault-college-campuses.html?_r=0.
[44] www.aau.edu/key-issues/aau-climate-survey-sexual-assault-and-sexual-misconduct-2015.
[45] Fisher et al., "The Sexual Victimization of College Women," 23. "Thus, the common answers included that the incident was not serious enough to report and that it was not clear that a crime was committed." https://www.ncjrs.gov/pdffiles1/nij/182369.pdf.
[46] www.nccpsafety.org/assets/files/library/Campus_Sexual_Assault_Study.pdf, xvii.

campuses? Based on current data, it is impossible to know for sure, but there is one study that helps us estimate it. This is discussed in the next section.

The Bureau of Justice Statistics Survey

In 2014, the Bureau of Justice Statistics (BJS), an arm of the U.S. Department of Justice, published a report on the prevalence of sexual assault of college students. It was based on a study that had an impressive 88 percent response rate; a large, nationally representative pool of survey takers; and specifically used methodology to account for telescoping issues.[47] Its findings were very different from the studies expressed in the preceding text. It found that, between 1995 and 2013, an average of 6.1 for every 1,000 female college students were raped or sexually assaulted each year. Not every student remains in college until graduation or takes five years to graduate, and the survey included students at two-year colleges, but even assuming that all the survey takers remain in school for five years, this means that about 3 percent of college women are sexually assaulted during their time in college. Any amount of sexual assault is too high, but this number is far lower than the "epidemic"-type numbers found in the surveys discussed previously.

Of course, the BJS survey, like any survey, is open to criticism. Its definition of female college students is quite broad: "females ages 18 to 24 enrolled part time or full time in a post-secondary institution (i.e., college or university, trade school, or vocational school)."[48] However, as noted earlier, the survey found that noncollege students are at greater risk for rape or sexual assault, so this broad definition would only have the effect of *raising* its estimates because it was including a higher-risk population in its sample.

Also, the BJS study used in-person and telephone interviews to collect data. This likely accounts for the high response rate, but it is also possible that survey takers may not have wanted to reveal traumatic or personal information in this context, which would suppress positive responses. The BJS study used a two-stage approach to minimize this problem as best as possible:

The [BJS study] uses a two-phased approach to identifying incidents of rape and sexual assault. Initially, a screener is administered, with cues designed to trigger the respondent's recollection of events and ascertain whether the respondent experienced victimization during the reference period. The screener questions are short and worded specifically about experiences with rape and sexual assault. For instance, "Incidents involving forced or unwanted sexual acts are often difficult to talk about. Have you been forced or coerced to engage in unwanted sexual activity by (a) someone you didn't know before, (b) a casual acquaintance? OR (c) someone you know well?" The screener is then followed by an incident form that captures detailed information about the incident,

---

[47] Sinozich and Langton, "Rape and Sexual Assault among College-Age Females, 1995–2013," table 12, 14.
[48] Id. at table 2, 5.

including the type of injury, presence of a weapon, offender characteristics, and report-ing to police. Even if the respondent does not respond affirmatively to the specific screeners on rape and unwanted sexual contact, the respondent could still be classified as a rape or sexual assault victim if a rape or unwanted sexual contact is reported during the stage-two incident report.[49]

Nevertheless, it is impossible to say how effective this approach is, and it is possible that there was some degree of underreporting. Another potential problem with the survey is its use of legal terminology: "The [BJS survey] definition is shaped from a criminal justice perspective and includes threatened, attempted, and completed rape and sexual assault against males and females."[50] It is possible that, as a psychological defense mechanism, some victimized women will refuse to apply that label to themselves, which would result in underreporting.

The survey does take measures to address this. It defines *rape* and *sexual assault* fairly broadly by including verbal threats and coercion:

Rape is the unlawful penetration of a person against the will of the victim, with use or threatened use of force, or attempting such an act. Rape includes psychological coercion and physical force, and forced sexual intercourse means vaginal, anal, or oral penetra-tion by the offender. Rape also includes incidents where penetration is from a foreign object (e.g., a bottle), victimizations against males and females, and both heterosexual and homosexual rape. Attempted rape includes verbal threats of rape.

Sexual assault is defined across a wide range of victimizations separate from rape or attempted rape. These crimes include attacks or attempted attacks usually involving unwanted sexual contact between a victim and offender. Sexual assault may or may not involve force and includes grabbing or fondling.[51]

Of course, it is still possible that some survey takers will not want to self-identify as a rape or sexual assault victim even if the description in the survey fits their experience. As the authors of the report concede, "Because of the sensitive nature of the topic, measuring the extent of these victimizations is often difficult, and best practices are still being determined."[52]

So what to make of all this? Obviously none of these surveys are perfect instruments. The only fair answer is that we just do not know the rate of sexual victimization on college campuses. It could be even lower than the 3 percent indicated by the BJS survey because many students do not attend college for five years. (The survey found that .61 percent of students are assaulted in any given year, so the 3 percent estimate is based on multiplying that number by five.) It could be significantly higher if students have a strong resistance to acknowledging that they are rape or sexual assault victims.

It seems unlikely though, that the 20 to 25 percent estimates are more accurate than the 3 percent estimate of the BJS survey that, of the major surveys, suffers least from problems of generalizability, response bias, and

[49] Id. at 2.   [50] Id.   [51] Id. at 11.   [52] Id.

telescoping issues. While using legal terms might suppress responses, it seems more likely that the very broad terminology of many of the other surveys capture a significant amount of behavior that is well beyond the popular understanding of sexual assault.

It is important to be clear that the argument here is not that a 3 percent rate of sexual victimization is somehow acceptable. Indeed, the next chapter suggests how to lower the rate regardless of what it is. The argument here is simply that the evidence does not suggest that sexual assault has reached "epidemic" levels and that we should not respond in panic to these survey results.

Another panic-inducing term that has been oft-used is *predator*. The idea is that most college sexual assaults are committed by repeat offenders, so anytime we fail to expel a student accused of sexual assault we are exposing the student body to countless new attacks. This is addressed in the next section.

ARE MOST SEXUAL ASSAULTS OF COLLEGE STUDENTS COMMITTED BY SEXUAL PREDATORS?

The word *predator* is loaded with emotional meaning and has a history of being used to justify unwise policies.[53] It often leads to overheated rhetoric. Danielle Dirks, an Occidental professor and a leading advisor to the student antirape movement, has argued that the great majority of men who don't get verbal consent are sexual predators. As quoted in *New York Magazine*, she stated:

"There are people out there who want to say that survivors today are feminism gone wild, railroading men for power ..." says Dirks, the Occidental sociologist. "And they can rely on talking about kids and alcohol, saying what happened was just drunk sex – and, you know, we've all had great drunk sex!" Research, she says, shows that only a small percentage of college guys truly don't know where the line is – "and, for them, if you tell them to get verbal consent, they don't push so hard." She pauses. "But the rest of them – and I know it's hard to think of our brothers, our sons, like this – are calculated predators. They seem like nice guys, but they're not nice guys."[54]

As the widely cited researcher David Lisak said at a speech at Harvard University in 2013, "College presidents don't like to hear this, but these are sex offenders ... Every report should be viewed and treated as an opportunity to identify a serial rapist."[55]

---

[53] An example of this would be the invocation of "super predators" by the Clinton administration in the 1990s to justify policies of mass incarceration that the Clintons would come to see as mistaken. See Anne Gearan and Abby Phillip, "Clinton Regrets 1996 Remark on 'Super-predators' after Encounter with Activist," *Washington Post* (February 25, 2016), www .washingtonpost.com/news/post-politics/wp/2016/02/25/clinton-heckled-by-black-lives-matter -activist/?utm_term=.c12ed74f9fb0.

[54] Vanessa Grigoriadis, "Meet the College Women Who Are Starting a Revolution against Campus Sexual Assault," *New York Magazine* (September 21, 2014), http://nymag.com/thecut/2014/09/ emma-sulkowicz-campus-sexual-assault-activism.html.

[55] Quoted in Yoffe, "The College Rape Overcorrection."

The idea that most campus rapes are committed by a "serial predators" who commit one undetected rape after another has been highly influential. Senator Kirsten Gillibrand has argued: "These are not dates gone bad, or a good guy who had too much to drink. This is a crime largely perpetrated by repeat offenders, who instead of facing a prosecutor and a jail cell, remain on campus after a short-term suspension, if punished at all."[56] As we saw from the University of Montana example, sometimes students at college fraternities do indeed behave in a way that can be described as predatory. But this is a far cry from the claim that the majority of sexual assaults are perpetrated by predators.

The leading exponent of the serial predator theory is David Lisak, whose work is frequently cited by government officials and others arguing for a "get tough," anti–due process approach to sexual assault on campuses:

> At a meeting last fall of several hundred university administrators who were gathered to discuss campus sexual assault, a Department of Justice official repeated a frightening statistic. "We know that the majority of rapes are committed by serial rapists, and those folks are very unlikely to be reached by any prevention messages that we're going to be sending out, or education about rape," said Bea Hanson, who works in the DOJ's Office of Violence Against Women and served on a White House task force on the issue of campus rape.
>
> Hanson was referring to an influential study, published in 2002 by David Lisak, then a professor of psychology at the University of Massachusetts Boston, and Paul Miller, then a clinical psychologist at Brown University School of Medicine . . . . Over the past few years, the data from Lisak and Miller's 2002 study has become ubiquitous, cited in countless news reports and advocacy briefs, and even appearing in a report by the White House Council on Women and Girls. Recently, it has been used to argue for harsher punishments – and even jail time – for student rapists, whose cases have traditionally been handled through university judicial systems.[57]

The image of the "serial predator" is a frightening one and, as indicated in the preceding text, it has been cited by sources as high as the White House and Justice Department and by countless media reports. It has also been at the center of much of the student-organized anti-rape movement. At the "heart of the movement" is the belief that "[n]o one should talk the way activists did in the '90s – no more date rape. Focus on college men as serial predators, and cite a study that claimed that 6 percent commit three or more undetected rapes and attempted rapes each."[58]

The study referred to in this quotation is from the 2002 article by Lisak and Miller referenced previously. However, there is surprisingly little research on this important question, and the Lisak and Miller study is generally the only

---

[56] Gruber, *Consent Confusion.*

[57] Amelia Thomson-DeVeaux, "What If Most Campus Rapes Aren't Committed by Serial Rapists?" (July 15, 2013), https://fivethirtyeight.com/features/what-if-most-campus-rapes-arent-committed-by-serial-rapists/.

[58] Grigoriadis, "Meet the College Women Who Are Starting a Revolution against Campus Sexual Assault."

study cited in support of it. But that study has extremely serious methodological problems and in a less charged environment would be unlikely to be as influential as it currently is.[59] To begin with, the entire sample for the study is taken from a single university. To quote from the study:

> Participants in this study were 1,882 students at a mid-sized, urban commuter university where students are diverse both in age and ethnicity. The mean age of the sample was 26.5 years (SD = 8.28), with a range of 18 to 71. More than 20% were over age 30, and nearly 8% were over 40.[60]

Given the highly diverse nature of the student bodies at various American universities, there is no possibility that a sample from a single school can provide nationally representative results. Furthermore, the study did not rely upon its own sampling or survey data. Rather it combined the results of four different studies, taken during different years over a seven-year period, all with sample sizes too small to produce statistically significant results on questions of sexual assault:

> The total sample consisted of four separate studies (n = 576; n = 587; n = 123; n = 596), conducted between 1991 and 1998. The three largest samples each represented 10% to 12% of the total male student population of the university at the time. The four samples were combined to provide a large enough subsample of rapists to permit the proposed analyses.[61]

Further, these four studies were not principally concerned with the issue of sexual assault on university campuses, and the questions were not oriented toward ascertaining the specific information that would be necessary to draw reliable conclusions about the nature of sexual assault on college campuses. Because this was a commuter campus consisting of largely part-time, adult students, there is no way to tell how many of the sexual assaults admitted to in the survey data were committed while the survey subjects were college students, whether they victimized other college students, or whether they occurred on or near the college campus or at college events.[62] These are extremely serious problems for a study that has been so influential.

Just as concerning, is that the study did not even attempt to use a random sample of students. Rather, it relied upon a convenience sample of students who happened to be passing by tables that were set up for purposes of the survey.

---

[59] My thanks to Loyola Marymount University Visiting Professor of Political Science Jennifer Jones for her help in analyzing the studies discussed in this section.

[60] David Lisak and Paul M. Miller, "Repeat Rape and Multiple Offending among Undetected Rapists," *Violence and Victims* 17 (2002): 73–84, 77.

[61] Id. at 76.

[62] See Linda M. LeFauve, "Campus Rape Expert Can't Answer Basic Questions About His Sources: The Problem with David Lisak's Serial Predator Theory of Campus Sexual Assault" (July 28, 2015), http://reason.com/archives/2015/07/28/campus-rape-statistics-lisak-problem.

Simply put, this is not a process that has any chance of producing a representative sample of even the one university involved in the study.

Finally, it should be noted that a 2015 study published in the prestigious journal *JAMA* (Journal of the American Medical Association) *Pediatrics* analyzed the situation very differently than Lisak and Miller: "Although a small group of men perpetrated rape across multiple college years, they constituted a significant minority of those who committed college rape and did not compose the group at highest risk of perpetrating rape when entering college."[63] The *JAMA* study is not perfect either. It has a relatively small sample size and defines a serial rapist as someone who has committed rapes in more than one college year, and therefore does not define someone who commits multiple rapes in a single year as a serial rapist. Nevertheless, it is more methodologically sound than the Miller and Lisak study and casts serious doubt upon that study's findings.

Of course, even if the Lisak and Miller study were perfect instead of deeply flawed, it would be unreasonable for any serious policy maker to place too much reliance on a single, unreplicated study. Yet, as we saw at the beginning of this chapter, the authors of the California affirmative consent bill state "that perpetrators are most often repeat offenders" as though this were established fact.

IS AFFIRMATIVE CONSENT THE MOST EFFECTIVE STANDARD FOR PUNISHING SEXUAL ASSAULT?

The third reason for "yes means yes" given by the authors of California's law is that "while 'no means no' has become a well-known slogan it places the burden on victims, making it their responsibility to show resistance." As we will see, this statement is very misleading.

One of the most common standards in the American legal system, both criminal and civil, is the "reasonable person" standard. I am guilty of stealing your bicycle rather than borrowing it if a reasonable person in my position would not have believed you were lending it to me. The same is true for a sexual encounter. "Most scholars would say that B is permitted to have sex if he has a *reasonable* belief that A is willing."[64] This view is the "prevailing view in contemporary American case law."[65]

However, too many states, including New York State, require active refusal or resistance:

Finally, some laws make sex a rape only when the victim expressly refuses or resists. These refusal laws, like New York's felony provision requiring that "the victim clearly

[63] Kevin Swartout et al., "Trajectory Analysis of the Campus Serial Rapist Assumption," *JAMA Pediatrics* 169, no. 12 (2015): 1148–1154.
[64] Gruber, *Consent Confusion*, 427 (emphasis in original).
[65] Id. at 428, n. 58 (citing Model Penal Code Draft no. 5).

expressed that he or she did not consent," differ substantially from laws that punish any unconsensual sex. Refusal laws might not criminalize a situation where the victim was clearly unwilling but did not openly protest.[66]

There is no question that the New York approach is foolish and fails to sufficiently protect rape victims. But affirmative consent is not the only alternative to this narrow approach, nor is it the best alternative. As law professor Aya Gruber notes: "[T]he alternative to a presumption of willingness in the absence of explicit refusal does not have to be a presumption of unwillingness in the absence of explicit affirmative agreement."[67]

The reasonable person standard, common across the American legal system, is the middle ground between the New York approach and affirmative consent. It does not presume consent in the absence of explicit refusal or resistance. But, unlike affirmative consent, it does not assume lack of consent in absence of overt words or actions. It asks the fact finder to determine what a reasonable person in the situation would have believed. It can take context into account.

"No means no," properly applied, adds an extra layer of protection to the reasonable person standard. It means that if someone says no, the law will presume that a reasonable person will understand this not to mean yes. The person who does not want a sexual encounter can avoid any ambiguity by saying no. But, crucially, under a "reasonable person" standard they do not *have to* say no. If they are asleep, a stranger cannot break into their house and credibly claim that they reasonably believed they had consent. If they stay silent because an attacker has threatened them with violence, a fact finder would not be likely to see that as a reasonable belief in consent. "No" is a sufficient, but not necessary, way to deny consent.

So which standard is more protective of unwilling victims of sexual aggression: "Yes means yes" or the reasonable person standard augmented by "no means no"? Interestingly, there is some empirical evidence on this, and it does not favor "yes means yes." A 2010 study by Yale law professor Dan M. Kahan examined the impact of various legal instructions on fact finders' determination of sexual consent. The study centered on a highly controversial case, *Commonwealth v. Berkowitz*,[68] in which the Pennsylvania Supreme Court unanimously overturned a rape conviction due to lack of evidence of forcible compulsion. The facts of the case are as follows:

At roughly 2:00 [i]n the afternoon . . ., after attending two morning classes, [the alleged victim] returned to her dormitory room. There, she drank a martini to "loosen up a little bit" before going to meet her boyfriend, with whom she had argued the night before. Roughly ten minutes later she walked to her boyfriend's dormitory lounge to meet him. He had not yet arrived. Having nothing else to do while she waited for her boyfriend, the victim walked up to appellant's room to look for [her boyfriend] Earl . . . . She knocked on

---

[66] Id. at 439.   [67] Id.   [68] 641 A. 2d 1161 (Pa. 1994).

the door several times but received no answer. She therefore wrote a note ... which read, "Hi Earl, I'm drunk. That's not why I came to see you. I haven't seen you in a while. I'll talk to you later, [victim's name]." She did so, although she had not felt any intoxicating effects from the martini, "for a laugh." After the victim had knocked again, she tried the knob on the appellant's door. Finding it open, she walked in. She saw someone lying on the bed with a pillow over his head, whom she thought to be Earl .... After lifting the pillow from his head, she realized it was appellant. She asked appellant which dresser was his roommate's. He told her, and the victim left the note. Before the victim could leave appellant's room, however, appellant asked her to stay and "hang out for a while." She complied because she "had time to kill" and because she didn't really know appellant and wanted to give him "a fair chance." Appellant asked her to give him a back rub but she declined, explaining that she did not "trust" him. Appellant then asked her to have a seat on his bed. Instead, she found a seat on the floor, and conversed .... ["(D)uring this conversation she ... explained she was having problems with her boyfriend." After a few minutes, the defendant] moved off the bed and down on the floor, and "kind of pushed [the victim] back with his body. It wasn't a shove, it was just kind of a leaning-type of thing." Next appellant "straddled" and started kissing the victim. The victim responded by saying, "Look, I gotta go. I'm going to meet [my boyfriend]." Then appellant lifted up her shirt and bra and began fondling her. The victim then said "no." After roughly thirty seconds of kissing and fondling, appellant "undid his pants and he kind of moved his body up a little bit." The victim was still saying "no" but "really couldn't move because [appellant] was shifting at [her] body so he was over [her]." Appellant then tried to put his penis in her mouth. The victim did not physically resist, but rather continued to verbally protest, saying "No, I gotta go, let me go," in a "scolding" manner. Ten or fifteen more seconds passed before the two rose to their feet. Appellant disregarded the victim's continual complaints that she "had to go," and instead walked two feet away to the door and locked it so that no one from the outside could enter. ["The victim testified that she realized at the time that the lock was not of a type that could lock people inside the room."] Then, in the victim's words, "[Appellant] put me down on the bed. It was kind of like – he didn't throw me on the bed. It's hard to explain. It was kind of like a push but no .... " She did not bounce off the bed. "It wasn't slow like a romantic kind of thing, but it wasn't a fast shove either. It was kind of in the middle." Once the victim was on the bed, appellant began "straddling" her again while he undid the knot in her sweatpants. He then removed her sweatpants and underwear from one of her legs. The victim did not physically resist in any way while on the bed because appellant was on top of her, and she "couldn't like go anywhere." She did not scream out at anytime because, "[i]t was like a dream was happening or something." Appellant then used one of his hands to "guide" his penis into her vagina. At that point, after appellant was inside her, the victim began saying "no, no to him softly in a moaning kind of way ... because it was just so scary." After about thirty seconds, appellant pulled out his penis and ejaculated onto the victim's stomach. Immediately thereafter, appellant got off the victim and said, "Wow, I guess we just got carried away." To this the victim retorted, "No, we didn't get carried away, you got carried away." The victim then quickly dressed, grabbed her school books and raced downstairs to her boyfriend who was by then waiting for her in the lounge. Once there, the victim began crying. Her boyfriend and she went up to his dorm room where, after watching the victim clean off appellant's semen from her stomach, he called the police.[69]

This seems like a paradigm case in which we would want a legal definition of *rape* that guides the fact finder toward a finding that the accused student committed rape. The victim objected numerous times and was repeatedly overpowered by the defendant by, if in no other way, his weight over her while she was objecting. If the Pennsylvania Supreme Court correctly applied that state's law when it overturned the rape conviction, then the law should be changed.

But changed how? Advocates of affirmative consent would argue for a change to "yes means yes." This chapter argues that "no means no" with a reasonable person standard not only is less restrictive of personal freedom but is at least as protective of rape victims as "yes means yes." So who is right?

Professor Kahan designed an empirical experiment that tested this. He distributed a survey to "a diverse, national sample of 1500 Americans aged eighteen years or older . . . A demographic-matching methodology assured that the sample was representative of the general American population."[70] The survey takers "read a sixteen-paragraph vignette that consisted of a lightly edited version of the statement of the facts in Berkowitz as summarized by the intermediate appellate court."[71]

The survey takers were divided into groups that received different legal definitions of *rape*. The "reform condition" group was given a definition very close to what is now called affirmative consent: "Members of the reform condition were advised simply that:

"[a] man is guilty of rape if he (a) engages in sexual intercourse with a woman (b) without the woman's consent." They, too, were advised that "a mistaken belief that the woman consented is not a defense." In addition, "consent" was expressly defined: "'[C]onsent' means words or overt actions indicating a freely given agreement to have sexual intercourse."[72]

Another group was given the "no means no" condition:

Finally, members of the no-means-no condition were also advised that "[a] man is guilty of rape if he (a) engages in sexual intercourse with a woman (b) without the woman's consent." In this condition, however, subjects were also instructed that "sexual intercourse is 'without the woman's consent' if the woman communicates by actions or by words, including the uttering of the word 'no,' that she does not consent to sexual

---

[69] Dan M. Kahan, *Culture, Cognition and Consent: Who Perceived What and Why in Acquaintance-Rape Cases*, 158 University of Pennsylvania Law Review 729–813, 736–738 (2010) (quoting Commonwealth v. Berkowitz, 609 A. 2d 1338 at 1339–1340).

[70] Id. at 765. To be clear, Kahan was primarily interested in hierarchal attitudes impacted people's views of this case, but he also hypothesized that the legal standard was important as well and tested for that variable.

[71] Id.   [72] Id at 768.

intercourse." In addition, they were advised that "if [the man] knows that the woman has said 'no,' a mistaken belief that the woman consented is not a defense."[73]

Kahan analyzed the impact of the various legal definitions of *rape* on the likelihood of the survey takers concluding the defendant was guilty of rape. He used a method called "regression" that isolates the effect of a variable like "the legal definition of rape" on another variable such as "the likelihood of a survey taker concluding that the defendant was guilty of the crime of rape." He concluded *that only the "no means no" definition had a statistically significant effect*, and that it made survey takers more likely to conclude that the defendant had committed rape. The "reform condition" that resembles *"yes means yes" had no statistical impact.*[74]

As noted earlier, we should be careful about relying too much upon any single study, even one based on a large representative sample with no apparent response bias issues. But Kahan's results should not be surprising. "No means no" is empowering – it gives the victim an opportunity to put up a clear stop sign. "Yes means yes" is inherently vague. It allows for the sort of interpretation made by Camille Paglia, who wrote: "Oh please, she goes into the room of a man who's in bed and sits on the floor with her breasts sticking up: What are we teaching our girls? … When you go into a man's room and stretch on the floor, you are sending a signal."[75]

One might object that this example is loaded in favor of "no means no" because the victim in this case did say no, but a surprisingly large number of cases cited by advocates of affirmative consent as support for that policy also involve victims who said no. Amanda Marcotte, writing for *Slate* relies on this case:

Setting the bar for consent as "actually wants sex" will help prevent problems like what happened in this Seattle high school case in 2012. A 15-year-old accused another student of raping her, and while he didn't admit to rape, he did openly admit to having sex with an unwilling person … The alleged perpetrator was a classmate, who admitted that he had had anal sex with her. He acknowledged to law enforcement that she told him to stop several times but said he persuaded her to "roll with it" …. When asked if Emily said anything during the incident, the boy disclosed to the school district investigator, "I did not pay attention to her that much." The school determined there was "insufficient evidence" that she was a "victim of harassment." But under an affirmative consent standard, it's much harder to argue that a woman was consenting because she was bullied until she gave in or that it doesn't count as rape because he was too busy getting off to notice she was saying no.[76]

---

73 Id. at 769.   74 Id. at 773–780.
75 Nancy E. Roman, "Scales of Justice Weigh Tiers of Sexual Assault: State May Reform Rape Law," *Washington Times* (June 16, 1994), A8 (quoting Camille Paglia) (cited in Kahan, "Culture, Cognition and Consent," 741, n. 41).
76 Amanda Marcotte, "Don't Fear California's New Affirmative Consent Law," *Slate* (September 29, 2014), www.slate.com/blogs/xx_factor/2014/09/29/affirmative_consent_in_ca-lifornia_gov_jerry_brown_signs_the_yes_means_yes.html.

But as Kahan's research shows, there is little reason to believe that affirmative consent laws will help protect girls like Emily. Like the student in the Pennsylvania case, she repeatedly said no, which, under "no means no" is a red light.

Even in cases in which the victim cannot say no as a result of fear or unconsciousness, there is no reason to believe that affirmative consent is more protective than a reasonable person standard coupled with "no means no." In her thorough article "Affirmative Consent," Professor Deborah Tuerkheimer cites many examples of cases that she argues demonstrate the importance of affirmative consent. But all of them are cases in which a jury would be hard-pressed to decide that a reasonable person would believe he had consent. Tuerkheimer discusses the following case as an example where fear kept a woman from objecting:

In *State v. DeSautels*, the defendant became angry when he learned that the victim, his former girlfriend, had a male guest in her apartment. Uninvited, the defendant went to the victim's apartment, attacked her verbally, slapped her in the face, and punched her in the stomach. He then ripp[ed] her underwear off and shov[ed] his hand in her vagina to see if she had had sex with another man. He forced her to perform fellatio and have vaginal sex with him despite her verbal and physical protestations. The defendant left the apartment alone after trying unsuccessfully to convince the victim to come with him. Later that night, the defendant returned to the victim's home. As the court described the events that followed: The victim was afraid defendant would become violent if she did not let him in, so she instructed her children to open the door. Defendant was still angry and called the victim a whore. The victim then accompanied defendant into the bedroom, where they engaged in sexual activity. Throughout defendant's second visit, the victim was upset and crying. The victim testified that she was afraid of defendant, and did not think she could refuse him.[77]

This case, while tragic, hardly seems a compelling illustration of the need for affirmative consent. The perpetrator repeatedly used physical force. To be fair, Tuerkheimer is focusing on the second encounter where the victim never said no, but even here the victim was "upset and crying" and had been beaten and raped by the perpetrator earlier that very night. Any jury that would decide that the perpetrator reasonably believed that this was consensual sex would be unlikely to convict under any standard.

The same can be said for Tuerkheimer's illustrations of how a surprise attack can prevent a victim from saying no:

Another case to display the paralyzing effects of an abrupt assault is *State of New Jersey in the Interest of K.B.* On the day of the incident, the twelve-year old victim, D.J., was spending time after school with the fourteen-year-old defendant, K.B., along with their mutual friends. At one point in the afternoon, K.B. asked D.J. if she was a virgin, and she told him she was. A few hours later, one of the teenagers told D.J. that K.B. wanted to

[77] Deborah Tuerkheimer, *Affirmative Consent*, 13, no. 2 Ohio State Journal of Criminal Law 441–468, 459–460 (2016) (citations omitted).

talk to her. The court summarized what followed: "[D.J.] followed K.B. into the bathroom and sat on the sink. The door was closed. It was dark but she could see a little bit from a light coming from the kitchen. He then put [her] on the floor and he pulled [her] pants and panties halfway down her legs, a little below her knees. He then "put his dick in [her] pussy." She did not want him to do this and he hurt her; while he was doing this she did not say anything because he had his hand over her mouth, although she made noises that were like "moaning and screaming put together."[78]

Again, this case would be just as likely to result in a conviction under a reasonable person/"no means no" regime. A jury in a "no means no" regime that decided that a perpetrator could evade the "no" by clamping his hand over the victim's mouth and rendering her unable to speak seems unlikely to convict under an alternate standard. The same would be true of Tuerkheimer's "sleeping victim" cases – none of them involve situations remotely like the "kissing your boyfriend in his sleep" case discussed in Chapter 6. They are all cases in which no fair-minded jury would be likely to find that a reasonable person would have believed they had consent.[79]

The real problem for the victims in all these cases is the "force" requirement discussed in Chapter 1. They protect rapists who attack victims in their sleep, intimidate them into passivity, or hold them down by the force of their weight. The force requirement should be abolished in all states. But we should avoid false choices. The existence of some laws that do too little to protect victims does not mean that "yes means yes" is the only available alternative. There is no empirical evidence that affirmative consent would do more to protect victims than a reasonable person/"no means no" standard. According to the one significant empirical study on this question, "yes mean yes" had no statistically significant impact while "no means no" did. As a society we would be far better off, as a first step, ridding ourselves of the force requirement and enacting a "no means no" standard. This standard could be applied to all people, not just college students. "Yes means yes" is the worst of all worlds. It is so restrictive that the adult world is willing only to apply it to college students, yet there is no empirical evidence that it is the most protective standard against rape.

CONCLUSION

In sum, all the reasons given by the authors of California's affirmative consent standard are castles made of sand. The evidence that 20 to 25 percent of women are sexually assaulted in college is very flawed, and there is significant evidence that the rate of sexual assault is far lower. The talking point that sexual predators are stalking our campuses similarly lacks empirical support. The argument that "yes means yes" is the only alternative to laws that allow rapists to go unpunished is also unempirical and misleading.

---

[78] Id. at 462 (citations omitted).   [79] See cases discussed: Id. at 452–455.

Any argument that rests on claims that are either unsupported, exaggerated, or outright wrong is hardly likely to be the best approach. But as noted earlier, there is no "acceptable" level of sexual assault, whether those assaults are committed by "predators" or not. Colleges should do more to prevent sexual assault and to respond effectively when assault occurs. This book's suggestions for what exactly they should do, is taken up the next chapter.

9

Moving Forward

So far, this book has looked at the present state of things. It argues that colleges and universities are failing to respect the basic requirements of due process and are defining *sexual assault* in a way that violates the autonomy rights of students. This benefits neither male nor female students. This chapter makes some suggestions for how they can do better.

One of the great frustrations of the status quo is that it does not work well for anybody. The deprivations of procedural and substantive rights don't advance equal access to education as Title IX demands. The first section suggests that taking a more empirically driven approach would help everyone.

BE EMPIRICAL, NOT IDEOLOGICAL

The topics discussed in this book include sex, power, violence, gender roles, law, and punishment. These are all topics that often raise strong emotions. Politicians will be sorely tempted to use the issue of college sexual assault to press for their preexisting political agendas. The political right has done this as well as the political left. On the right, conservative legislators in many states have been eager to expand gun rights on campus and have used the current high level of concern about campus sexual assault to push their agenda. They have gone as far as stating that gun control advocates bear personal responsibility if an unarmed college student is raped:

"If you've got a person that's raped because you wouldn't let them carry a firearm to defend themselves, I think you're responsible," State Representative Dennis K. Baxley of Florida said during debate in a House subcommittee last month. The bill passed.[1]

---

[1] Alan Schwartz, "A Bid for Guns on Campuses to Deter Rape," *New York Times* (February 18, 2015), www.nytimes.com/2015/02/19/us/in-bid-to-allow-guns-on-campus-weapons-are-linked-to-fighting-sexual-assault.html?_r=0.

Along similar lines, a Arizona assemblywoman has suggested that "young, hot, little girls," should be empowered to shoot would-be assailants in the head:

> If these young, hot little girls on campus have a firearm, I wonder how many men will want to assault them. The sexual assaults that are occurring would go down once these sexual predators get a bullet in their head.[2]

Given how many of these cases involve heavy consumption of alcohol, adding guns to the mix seems unlikely to promote student safety.

Ideology has also played a strong role in how the political left has approached sexual assault. During the Obama administration, colleges rushed to implement anti-assault programs with little empirical data to support them or even clear theories of how the programs were supposed to work. "The best interventions from a policy perspective are based on theory and empirical evidence. Recent reviews and meta-analyses reveal that sexual assault prevention programs rarely meet this standard."[3]

As has been discussed throughout this book, sexual assault prevention in the college context has developed in a largely anti-empirical manner. Far too many claims about the rate of false accusations, the prevalence of assault, the dominance of predators, the gender balance of victims and assailants, and so forth have been made even when the evidence for those claims is poor, mixed, indeterminate, or, sometimes, even points in the opposite direction.

It should be emphasized that the practices criticized in this book, especially the lack of due process, are not supported by any sort of empirical study. There does not appear to any empirical research that purports to demonstrate that due process protections heighten danger to college students or that lowering such protections prevents sexual assault. "Unfortunately, little research has been conducted to examine what policies and investigative and disciplinary protocols are most effective at increasing student safety both among institutions and between campuses with different levels of regulative policies."[4] As a result, according to the *New England Journal of Medicine*, "[M]ost campuses use programs that have never been formally evaluated or have proved not to be effective in reducing the incidence of sexual assault."[5]

As discussed at length, there are enormous benefits to providing due process. The denial of due process is based on political calculations, not empirical research. "Limited research explores campus-based judicial procedures relating to sexual assault. Most of the research focuses on elements of due

---

[2] Id. quoting Nevada Assemblywoman Michele Fiore.

[3] Matt J. Gray et al., *Sexual Assault Prevention on College Campuses* (New York: Routledge, 2017), 75.

[4] Id. at 78.

[5] Charlene Y. Senn et al., "Efficacy of a Sexual Assault Resistance Program for University Women," *New England Journal of Medicine* 372 (2015), 2326–2335.

process with little published literature providing descriptions of the processes or their effects on students."[6]

Laura Kipnis has written about academia's antipathy to antisexual violence programs that teach women to effectively resist such violence. This antipathy stems from the position that we don't want to send the message that women are somehow blameworthy for failure to successfully resist. Bystander intervention programs are more popular because they do not put the onus of resistance on the victims and they show some tentative promise for changing attitudes about rape, at least in the short term.[7] But we should not allow ideology to trump empirical data. There is little data so far on whether bystander intervention programs are effective in reducing rates of assault and, because the great majority of these assaults occur in private, there is obviously a very limited upside to bystander intervention programs.[8]

The person who is always present, of course, is the target of the assault, so common sense tells us that resistance training is more likely to have positive results. This commonsense guess is supported by empirical research. In the *New England Journal of Medicine* article referred to previously, the researchers evaluated the impact of a very modest resistance training program in Canadian colleges. "The Enhanced Assess, Acknowledge, Act Sexual Assault Resistance program consisted of four 3-hour units that involved information-providing games, mini-lectures, facilitated discussion, and application and practice activities."[9] The results, in terms of actual reduction of sexual assault, were impressive:

The 1-year risk of completed rape was significantly lower in the resistance group than in the control group (5.2% vs. 9.8%; relative risk reduction, 46.3%; 95% confidence interval [CI], 6.8 to 69.1; P = 0.02), indicating that only 22 women would need to take the program in order to prevent one additional rape from occurring within 1 year after participation … The benefit of the resistance program occurred early, and its efficacy was sustained throughout the 1-year follow-up. The program also reduced the incidence of attempted rape (3.4% in the resistance group vs. 9.3% in the control group; relative risk reduction, 63.2%; P < 0.001).[10]

Furthermore, the positive results were also present for women who had previously been victimized:

[6] Angela F. Amar et al., "Administrator's Perceptions of College Campus Protocols, Response, and Student Prevention Efforts for Sexual Assault," in Roland D. Maiuro, ed., *Perspectives in College Assault* (New York: Springer Publishing, 2015), 168.
[7] Alison C. Cares et al., "Changing Attitudes About Being a Bystander to Violence: Translating an In-Person Sexual Violence Prevention Program to a New Campus," *Violence Against Women* 21, no. 2 (2015), 165–187.
[8] Caitlin Henriksen et al., "Mandatory Bystander Intervention Training," in Sara Carrigan Wooten and Roland W. Mitchell, eds., *The Crisis of Campus Sexual Violence: Critical Perspectives on Prevention and Response* (New York: Routledge, 2016), 170–175.
[9] Senn et al., "Efficacy of a Sexual Assault Resistance Program for University Women."
[10] Id. at 2326.

The 1-year risk of completed rape in the control group was nearly four times as high among previously victimized women as among women with no history of victimization (22.8% vs. 5.8%). Despite the elevated risk among previously victimized women, the resistance group had a lower 1-year risk of completed rape than the control group (relative risk reduction, 25.1%). The effect of the intervention did not vary significantly according to prior history of rape (P = 0.13 for interaction) or according to whether programs were on weekends or weekdays (P = 0.32 for interaction).

The concern that such programs might send the message that it is the victim's job to resist is not illogical, but it certainly is not the only way to look at it. After all, *any* program that empowers people to avoid victimization carries some risk of sending that message. But that doesn't mean that we don't offer the elderly courses on how to avoid fraud by retirement counselors or self-defense courses to women. What matters most is what has been demonstrated to reduce sexual violence.

As noted repeatedly throughout this book, we should be cautious about basing judgments on any single study, and this study has its limitations, including the fact that it does not study the impact of the program on sexual victimization of men. More research here would be very helpful. But, as the authors of the *New England Journal of Medicine* article note, the research on resistance programs is more promising than the research on more popular programs: "Other targeted programs for men and for women that have been evaluated for sexual assault outcomes have been disappointing, including interventions designed to decrease male perpetration of sexual assault."[11]

Beyond resistance training and bystander intervention programs, another area where ideology has often trumped empirical research is the question of alcohol. There is an overwhelming consensus that consumption of alcohol, by both victim and perpetrator, plays an outsized role in college sexual assault. As reported in the *Journal of Studies on Alcohol*: "At least half of [college] sexual assaults involve alcohol consumption by the perpetrator, the victim or both."[12]

Unfortunately, focusing on alcohol is often ideologically out of bounds. As the *New York Times* reports: "Some experts say women's participation in the culture of college binge drinking has made them more vulnerable, but advocates say it is a short walk from that to blaming victims."[13] Laura Kipnis, writing a bit more colorfully, reports that many funding sources refuse to fund research on alcohol and sexual assault:

Still if you're going to talk about the drinking in conjunction with the nonconsensual sex, tread carefully. One researcher studying campus sexual assault calls it "the 'third rail' of

---

[11] Id. (citations omitted).

[12] Antonia Abbey, "Alcohol-Related Sexual Assault: A Common Problem among College Students," *J. Stud. Alcohol* Supplement 14 (2002), 118–128.

[13] Richard Perez-Pena and Kate Taylor, "Fight Against Sexual Assaults Holds Colleges Accountable," *New York Times* (May 5, 2014).

the discourse, something no one wants to go near." Anyone who suggests that women should drink less to avoid sexual assault will be "disemboweled upon arrival into the gladiatorial arena of public discourse," as Hepola puts it. Those running sexual violence prevention programs (now mandatory on campus) often don't bring up drinking or dance carefully around it ... Agencies that fund sexual assault research, including the Justice Department, have told researchers that focusing on alcohol is "out of scope." Academics presenting reports have been told to take the word *alcohol* out of their presentation titles."[14]

Neither the first nor second reports of the White House Task Force to Protect Students from Sexual Assault discuss alcohol and the Department of Justice website "Not Alone" does not mention alcohol except in the context of saying that students are less likely to report alcohol-facilitated assaults.[15] As with victim resistance programs, the fear is that a focus on alcohol will put the blame on victims for their own assaults.

Here again, the resistance of many antirape advocates to focusing on alcohol is not entirely illogical. Those who are inclined to shame women can certainly use the alcohol issue to do so. In 2009, "a Baylor University regent and prominent Texas lobbyist Neal 'Buddy' Jones described female students who he suspected of drinking alcohol at parties as 'perverted little tarts,' the 'vilest and most despicable girls' and a "group of very bad apples.'"[16] In 2017 he conceded that his comments were "hyperbolic" and "too harsh" but coming from a man "who spent a decade as a Baylor regent, including two years as board chairman,"[17] they vividly illustrate the concerns of advocates who want to discourage discussion of alcohol in connection with sexual assault.

Nonetheless, the reality is that college students drink a great deal,[18] and alcohol makes perpetrators more likely to offend and makes victims more vulnerable. In terms of perpetrators, "Alcohol makes it even easier for men to feel comfortable forcing sex because alcohol myopia helps them focus solely on their desire to have sex rather than on the woman's signs of refusal and pain."[19] That same myopia too often leads victims to allow themselves to be led into vulnerable situations. "Being intoxicated allows women to let down their guard and focus on their desire to have fun and be liked rather than on their personal safety. Thus alcohol myopia may lead women to take risks they would not

---

[14] Kipnis, *Unwanted Advances*, 198. Kipnis does state that the damn might be beginning to break on this enforced silence.

[15] www.whitehouse.gov/sites/whitehouse.gov/files/images/Documents/1.4.17.VAW%20Event.TF %20Report.PDF; www.justice.gov/ovw/protecting-students-sexual-assault.

[16] Matthew Watkins, "As Baylor Regent, Top Austin Lobbyist Called Drinking Female Students 'perverted little tarts,'" *The Texas Tribune* (July 1, 2017), www.texastribune.org/2017/07/01/ emails-former-baylor-regent-powerful-austin-lobbyist-called-female-stu/.

[17] Id.

[18] See Beth McMurtrie, "Why Colleges Haven't Stopped Binge Drinking," *New York Times* (December 15, 2014), https://mobile.nytimes.com/2014/12/15/us/why-colleges-havent-stopped-binge-drinking.html.

[19] Abbey, "Alcohol-Related Sexual Assault."

normally take."[20] And once in that situation, alcohol reduces one's ability to effectively deal with a perpetrator. "Alcohol's effects on motor skills may limit a woman's ability to resist sexual assault effectively."[21]

It is understandable that some respond to this by arguing it not the woman's job to defend herself but rather the man's job not to attack her in the first place. That is an obviously true statement. However, as noted in Chapter 3, the situation does not always involve male attackers and female victims. More importantly, teaching students to avoid vulnerable situations is more likely to be empowering than disempowering.

While colleges have come under tremendous criticism for not preventing student drinking, research indicates that colleges cannot effectively address this problem alone: They need the support of local communities and law enforcement to achieve results. Research in California looked at the efficacy of community-based approaches to reducing alcohol abuse by college students:

The Safer California Universities study was designed to test the efficacy of a community-based environmental alcohol risk management strategy applied to college campuses (Saltz 2010). The intervention included nuisance party enforcement operations (i.e., "party patrols"), minor decoy operations, DUI checkpoints, social host ordinances, and the use of campus and local media to increase the visibility of these strategies. The investigators then used a controlled, randomized experimental design involving 14 public universities, one half of which were randomly assigned to the intervention condition and the other one half served as comparison campuses. Annual surveys of randomly selected undergraduate students assessed the student's drinking behavior in six different settings during the fall semester – that is, at residence hall parties; campus events; fraternity or sorority parties; and parties at off campus apartments or houses, in bars or restaurants, or in outdoor settings. The study specifically measured the proportion of drinking occasions during which students drank to intoxication in these settings, the proportion of students who reported any intoxication at each setting during the semester, and whether students drank to intoxication the last time they went to each setting.[22]

This community-based approached appears to be quite effective, including reducing heavy drinking at off-campus parties, which would obviously be extremely helpful in terms of reducing sexual assault:

Significant reductions in the incidence and likelihood of intoxication at off campus parties and in bars and restaurants were observed for the intervention universities compared with the control universities. Moreover, students at the intervention universities also had a lower likelihood of intoxication the last time they drank at an off campus party (odds ratio 0.81), a bar or restaurant (0.76), or across all settings (0.80) (Saltz 2010). The magnitude of these effects translated to approximately 6,000 fewer cases of intoxication at off-campus parties per semester at each campus and 4,000 fewer cases of intoxication at off-campus bars and restaurants. Nearly as important was the finding

---

[20] Id. at 223.   [21] Id.
[22] https://pubs.niaaa.nih.gov/publications/arh342/204-209.pdf, 205–206.

that no increase in intoxication (i.e., displacement) appeared in other settings. Furthermore, stronger intervention effects were achieved at the intervention universities with the highest intensity of implementation.[23]

This sort of approach requires significant resources and coordination between colleges, local police, media, business, and government. Such an investment would be well worth the effort. College alcohol abuse is associated with a host of serious problems in addition to sexual assault:

> More than 1,800 students die every year of alcohol-related causes. An additional 600,000 are injured while drunk, and nearly 100,000 become victims of alcohol-influenced sexual assaults. One in four say their academic performance has suffered from drinking, all according to the National Institute on Alcohol Abuse and Alcoholism.[24]

In sum, there is solid empirical research that points us in productive directions in terms of significantly reducing the incidence of sexual assault in college. None of it guides us toward the types of due process violations or unconstitutionally restrictive definitions of *consent* that have been critiqued throughout this book. There is a long history of politicians attempting to prove that they are tough on issues ranging from gang violence to domestic terrorism by advocating for punitive measures, broad definitions of *wrongdoing*, and swift justice. But by focusing on the evidence over political posturing it is possible to both reduce sexual violence and respect the rights of all students.

Finally, we should not stick our heads in the sand in terms of empirical research on racial bias. Given our nation's history of unfairly targeting minorities for sex crimes, at the very least the government should require universities to keep track of the race of students accused of and found responsible for sexual assault so that we can detect systematic biases. Given that universities are required to track many other racial statistics, this omission seems to be a case of willful ignorance.

DO MORE TO ENCOURAGE REPORTING

The first section of this chapter argues that colleges, in concert with local communities, governments, and law enforcement, could do significantly better at reducing sexual assault if they work together and pay attention to empirical research. But the rate of sexual assault will probably never reach the ideal rate of zero, so the question is what to do when such assaults do occur?

To begin with the obvious, there is very little anybody can do if the incident is not reported in the first place. Unfortunately, there is ample evidence that students often do not report sexual assault. According to a 2017 study of Clery Act data (the federal law that requires colleges to keep records of sexual assaults on campus), an astounding *eighty-nine percent of colleges reported*

---

[23] Id. at 207.   [24] McMurtrie, "Why Colleges Haven't Stopped Binge Drinking."

"zero incidents of rape" on their campus in 2015.[25] As discussed in the previous chapter, many accounts of "epidemic levels" of sexual assault are probably significantly exaggerated, but it seems even more unlikely that nearly 90 percent of colleges did not have a single case of rape in all of 2015. The obvious conclusion is students are not reporting significant numbers of criminal sexual acts.

To repeat the major theme of this book: This is a system that is serving everyone poorly. Significant numbers of accused students have been punished by unfair processes, but many serious offenders go unpunished due to lack of reporting. In too many cases, the lack of reporting is the fault of the university. According to a *United Educators* study, more than 40 percent of all "Title IX claims [by victims of sexual assault] alleged that the institution discouraged the victim from pursuing an internal complaint or reporting the assault to the police."[26] Examples cited in the study included:

• Allegations that a staff member told the victim that the perpetrator had been "punished enough."
• A college dean telling a victim that he would try to get the perpetrator to withdraw from the institution so she would not have to deal with the disciplinary process.
• When trying to manage expectations about the investigation and disciplinary process, a staff member told a victim to expect a "grueling" process if she wished to pursue her complaint.[27]

Colleges need to do a great deal better here. In a 2014 interview, Nicholas B. Dirks, chancellor of the University of California, conceded that Berkeley had only recently "corrected or set out to correct – confusing directions online about where and how to file a misconduct report or get counseling, too few workers in the office handling those issues, inadequate training for the people involved."[28] According to a federal investigation of the University of Montana, "[T]he university has eight policies or procedures explicitly or implicitly covering sexual harassment or sexual assault, their sheer number and lack of clear cross-references among them leaves unclear which should be used to report sexual harassment or assault."[29]

These do not appear to be isolated examples. According to a study by the Center for Public Integrity, institutional barriers were the obstacles most often cited by victim advocates:

Crisis counselors and service providers who work with college students described barriers as overt as a dean expressing disbelief. These counselors cited institutional barriers on campus more often than any other factor as a discouragement to students

[25] www.aauw.org/article/clery-act-data-analysis-2017/.
[26] www.ncdsv.org/ERS_Confronting-Campus-Sexual-Assault_2015.pdf, 15.   [27] Id.
[28] Pena and Taylor, "Fight Against Sexual Assaults Holds Colleges Accountable."
[29] Carrigan Wooten and Mitchell, *The Crisis of Campus Sexual Violence*, 121.

pursuing complaints of sexual assault, according to a Center survey of 152 on- and off-campus centers that provide direct services to victims.[30]

Bureaucracies can be very difficult to reform, but, at a minimum, universities should "do no harm" in terms of discouraging reporting. The law should, for example, forbid even religious universities from punishing students who admit to honor code violations in the course of reporting a sexual assault. A 2016 *New York Times* article about a rape at Brigham Young University provides a telling illustration of how such punishments can chill reporting:

> But after Brooke, 20, told the university that a fellow student had raped her at his apartment in February 2014, she said the Honor Code became a tool to punish her. She had taken LSD that night, and also told the university about an earlier sexual encounter with the same student that she said had been coerced. Four months after reporting the assault, she received a letter from the associate dean of students.
> "You are being suspended from Brigham Young University because of your violation of the Honor Code including continued illegal drug use and consensual sex, effective immediately," the letter read.

According to the *Times*, "The federal Education Department urges colleges to make sure their discipline policies do not discourage students from coming forward to report sexual assaults." Urging is not enough. The federal government should follow the example of the state of Maryland, which recently passed a law protecting students in Brooke's position.[31]

Colleges also discourage reporting through a mix of harsh punishments of offenders and the trend toward broad "mandatory reporting" laws that require even professors to break the confidentiality of students who tell them about sexual assault. In a classic example of good intentions gone wrong, research indicates that these policies appear to *discourage* reporting. As author and editor Caroline Kitchener writes in *the Atlantic*:

> Sweeping policies that crack down hard on perpetrators often have the unintended result of discouraging victims from coming forward. Administrators want to be seen as taking an aggressive stance toward sexual assault offenders. But that's not always the most effective method. Take this example: Regardless of the victim's preference, many schools (including Columbia and Barnard) have begun requiring faculty and staff to report all sexual assaults to the administration. While this will empower some victims to file formal complaints, many more who are unsure of what they want will inevitably keep their stories to themselves, afraid to share something they might one day regret. Another

---

[30] Kristin Jones, "Barriers Curb Reporting on Campus Sexual Assault," The Center for Public Integrity (March 26, 2015), www.publicintegrity.org/2009/12/02/9046/barriers-curb-reporting-campus-sexual-assault.

[31] http://mgaleg.maryland.gov/2015RS/bills/hb/hb0571E.pdf. The law does not, however, prohibit mandatory drug or alcohol counseling, which seems wise. Further, to discourage possible false reporting of a sexual assault to avoid punishment for drug or alcohol use, such immunity could be limited to prohibiting the use of the reporting student's statement against her, rather than a blanket form of immunity.

popular move by college administrators is to make expulsion the standard punishment for all perpetrators found guilty of sexual assault. Again, this will alienate a lot of victims. Many want to figure out how they're feeling but are not quite sure how and if they want to take formal action.[32]

Mandatory reporting and mandatory expulsions may sound like a "get tough" approach, but by taking decision-making power away from the injured student, colleges are making the problem worse, not better. According to the Obama administration's White House Task Force to Protect Students from Sexual Assault, mandatory reporting requirements were *"by far, the problem we heard most about in our listening sessions."*[33]

Once again, too many schools have proceeded in an unempirical manner, implementing policies that are ineffective and most likely counterproductive. According to University of Oregon Professor Jennifer Freyd, co-author of a study of 150 university mandatory reporting programs:

What we show in our study is that we lack evidence that mandatory reporting is safe and effective. In fact, the data point in the opposite direction – that many of the policies we that we reviewed are neither safe nor effective ... some evidence suggests that these mandates may carry negative consequences: silencing and disempowering survivors, complicating employees' jobs, and prioritizing legal liability over student welfare.[34]

This is another area where universities could benefit from help by the government. As Freyd mentions, mandatory reporting may be driven more by a fear of liability than by empirical evidence that the policy helps victims of sexual assault. The study suggests more effective alternatives such as allowing victims to report assaults solely for purpose of receiving support services and allowing them the option of seeking sanctions later. The Department of Education should clarify that this would not be a violation of Title IX.

PROVIDE RESTORATIVE JUSTICE OPTIONS

Campus sexual assault tribunals emphasize fact finding and punishment. They are tasked with making a yes/no determination of whether a sexual offense occurred and meting out punishment accordingly. This is not always the best approach for an educational setting. When a student reports conduct that amounts to a crime in the university's state, the university should help the student report that crime to the police. They should offer, if not an attorney,

[32] Caroline Kitchener, "Two Ways to Fix How Colleges Respond to Sexual Assault," *Atlantic* (January 29, 2014), www.theatlantic.com/education/archive/2014/01/two-ways-to-fix-how-colleges-respond-to-sexual-assault/283438/.
[33] www.justice.gov/ovw/page/file/905942/download, 11 (emphasis added).
[34] www.sciencedaily.com/releases/2018/01/180131133409.htm (discussing Kathryn Holland et al., "Compelled Disclosure of College Sexual Assault," *American Psychologist* [January 22, 2018]).

an experienced representative to go with the student to the police to advise and support the student throughout the process. Going to the police should not be mandatory but it should be encouraged and supported. Expelling a rapist protects the campus but exposes everyone else to danger. Only the police have the power to incarcerate a rapist rather than merely push that person into a new community.

Furthermore, colleges should encourage students to go to the police immediately because any significant delay makes it less likely that there will be a successful criminal prosecution. Police find it "difficult ... to pursue criminal action when they don't collect evidence from the victim early in the process."[35]

However, as we have seen in numerous examples throughout this book, many alleged campus sexual assaults do not clearly amount to criminal behavior. Many involve two intoxicated students and the sorts of ambiguities that "yes mean yes" advocates seek to classify as sexual assault for the purposes of college behavior but are not crimes.

What should happen in these situations – where there is no crime, at least not one provable beyond a reasonable doubt, but there is certainly hurt and injury? The current approach is for colleges to keep to a punishment model in which the accused student is found responsible or not responsible – the college equivalent of "guilty" or "not guilty." Even apart from the great many specific procedural problems with this system discussed in the book, there is a larger question. Is a guilty/not guilty, punish/exonerate model of sexual assault adjudication really the best approach for colleges? This section argues that it is not in many cases.

A very different approach, "restorative justice," should be offered as an option to the students involved. Rather than focusing on punishment as the primary goal, it focuses on reparation of harm, although it also can involve punishment, so long as that punishment is oriented toward rehabilitation and restoration. It provides for a much more active role for both parties:

While there is no one definition or method of restorative justice, its processes generally bring together victims, responsible parties and other harmed parties (including community representatives) to explore the harm done by the offense and collectively determine how best to repair it. It is undertaken voluntarily by both the responsible party and the victim where the responsible party admits to wrongdoing. Restorative justice provides both parties a more active role than the traditional adversarial process. It provides a victim with the opportunity to tell her story, describe to the responsible party the full impact of the harmful behavior, and shape the consequences that the responsible party will face. The responsible party has the opportunity to accept full responsibility for his actions, listen to the victim and other harmed parties discuss the consequences of his

---

[35] Eliza Gray, "Why Victims of Rape in College Don't Report to the Police," *Time* (June 23, 2014), http://time.com/2905637/campus-rape-assault-prosecution/.

actions, and collaborate with all stakeholders to determine how he can repair the harm he has caused and become a responsible and positive member of the community.[36]

Restorative justice often brings the students together. "It uses trained mediators to help the parties develop a reparative plan, though reaching an agreement is often secondary to the goals of communication and emotional healing."[37] As discussed in Chapter 5, most campus tribunals strive to keep the accused and accusing students apart to avoid further trauma. Restorative justice operates on the opposite assumption that, under the proper circumstances, it empowers the harmed student to confront the student who harmed her:

> For most victims it is satisfying to be able to express feelings about the offence directly to the offender and to explain fully its consequences. It is even more satisfying to see that the offender properly understands, sincerely apologizes for the offence and pledges actions to ensure s/he will never behave this way again . . . . [Victims and] others closely connected to the crime . . . usually desire as well some form of censure by the community, a recognition of the wrong as a wrong which is owed to the victim. They also need the offender to undertake a course of action that signals remorse and underlines the sincerity of the apology.[38]

The traditional punitive model strongly discourages the accused student from admitting any wrongdoing. If he is guilty, he is punished with the extremely severe consequences discussed in Chapter 2. Restorative justice requires the accused student to be forthcoming about exactly what happened. He will participate in the decision about what he needs to do to heal any injury he created. As we have seen throughout this book, there are many cases in which the students agree on many of the facts. But in a traditional tribunal, the accused student will have every incentive to argue with all his might that the other student was not so drunk that she could not consent. He will have every incentive to argue that she never said no or never gave any indication that she was withdrawing consent.

Furthermore, as noted previously, many students who have been harmed by the sexual behavior of other students do not want harsh punishments to be inflicted on those students. So, the punitive model can deter reporting. As Michelle Anderson, former policy chair of the National Alliance to End Sexual Violence, has argued: "Harsh penalties will deter reporting of routine sexual assaults, deter pursuit of such claims by administrators responsible for deciding when to pursue or close cases, and deter finding respondents responsible."[39]

---

[36] Margo Kaplan, *Restorative Justice and Campus Sexual Assault*, 89 Temple Law Review 702–745, 704–705 (2017).

[37] Id. at 715.

[38] Heather Strang, "Is Restorative Justice Imposing Its Agenda on Victims?," in Howard Zehr and Barb Toews, eds., *Critical Issues in Restorative Justice* (New York and Devon, UK: Criminal Justice Press and Willan Publishing, 2004), 95, 102, cited in Donna Coker, *Crime Logic, Campus Sexual Assault and Restorative Justice*, 49 Texas Tech Law Review 147–210, 188 (2016).

[39] Michelle J. Anderson, *Campus Sexual Assault Adjudication and Resistance to Reform*, 125 Yale Law Journal 1940–2005 (2016).

Restorative justice gives different incentives. In a process that emphasizes healing over punishment, a student can more easily concede that the issues of continuing consent and capacity were not as clear as they ideally should have been. He can recognize the harm his actions created and play a part in healing that harm.

The following real case well illustrates how much more appropriate and effective restorative justice can be than the traditional punitive model:

A male and a female student were part of a group of friends that regularly engaged in significant drug and alcohol use. The two students had had sex with each other before. The woman later went to the administrator for help with a sexual encounter with the male student that she found distressing. The sexual encounter started as consensual sexual intercourse. She had her back to him. At some point, she no longer wanted to have intercourse. She began crying and she said, "no," but she was not sure if he heard her. She was uncomfortable calling this sexual assault because she was not sure if he knew it was nonconsensual. She was hurt by his behavior because he "wasn't paying attention to her" during the sex. She did not want an investigation or a hearing, but she wanted him to know that she had been harmed by his conduct and that he should "pay attention" in future sexual encounters. The male student told the administrator that he felt badly, and he agreed that he should have been "paying better attention." He reported that not paying attention was a major problem for him in general, in part, because of his drug use and that he wanted to change his behavior. The female student said that she felt "heard" and understood by the student.[40]

Imagine this situation playing out in the traditional punitive university process. Seeking some form of justice, the female student would have every incentive to emphasize that she said "no" and was showing her lack of consent by crying. The male student would have every incentive to swear he never heard her and never saw her tears. He certainly wouldn't be admitting that he is worried that he might have a drug problem or that he wishes he could be a more attentive person. The panel would have to take an all or nothing approach – responsible or not responsible. If they found him not responsible, the female student would get nothing but a rebuke and new wound. If he were found guilty, he certainly would not be getting any help coming to grips with his drug problem and would likely join the ranks of young men who have anger issues with women. Because the male student would not be incarcerated, the danger he poses to other women would probably increase rather than decrease.

The restorative justice model can produce far superior outcomes. She can feel heard and validated. He can agree to drug counseling and is given an opportunity to acknowledge and apologize for the pain he caused her. There is no panel of professors and administrators deciding only whether she can prove he heard her say no.

Some might object that this is not justice – that the young man in this case is getting away with his crime. On this issue, it is probably best to listen to the

---

[40] Coker, "Crime Logic, Campus Sexual Assault and Restorative Justice," 206.

women (and male victims). One of the few restorative justice programs for sex crimes is RESTORE, a community-based restorative justice conferencing program that receives referrals from prosecutors. These referrals included both misdemeanor and felony sex crimes, and occur only with the victim's consent. The process takes place over four stages: (1) referral and intake, (2) preparation, (3) conferencing, and (4) accountability, reintegration, and monitoring.[41]

While the program is small and relatively new, a study showed that it has great promise:

[Women] demonstrated a high level of satisfaction with the process, reporting that they felt safe, listened to, treated with respect, and supported during the conference. They also uniformly agreed with the statement: "I did not feel blamed." All but one of the victims who participated in the conference agreed or strongly agreed that it was a success, and all strongly agreed that they would recommend the program.[42]

Restorative justice is particularly appropriate for universities. In terms of the offending students, it offers a true educational opportunity to learn from their mistakes and to grow into a more empathetic person. In terms of the complaining student, it enhances their sense of empowerment and safety:

Restorative justice processes may also reduce a victim's generalized fear of victimization. This is a particularly salient concern for sexual assault, which often causes a victim trauma and reduces her ability to trust others. In the university setting, victims often express trepidation at attending the same school as the responsible party or his friends and supporters. Restorative justice does not merely provide the victim with a supportive process, but also gives her the opportunity to confront both the responsible party and his supporters, as well as the ability to shape the reparation plan.[43]

Not surprisingly, "More than 90% of participants agreed or strongly agreed that they 'felt safe, listened to, supported, treated fairly, treated with respect, and not expected to do more than they anticipated [in the conference].'"[44]

As always, we must be careful about putting too much stock in any one study, particularly a small one. (The RESTORE study looked at only 22 cases.) But there is not more research here because the Obama administration warned schools off of mediation efforts, a policy that has been rescinded. If more colleges are willing to try restorative justice, more robust research can follow. There is much reason for optimism. While the RESTORE study is small, its results are in keeping with the positive results of larger studies of restorative justice programs dealing with other serious (but not sex-related) crimes,

---

[41] Mary P. Koss, "The Restore Program of Restorative Justice for Sex Crimes: Vision, Process, and Outcomes," *Journal of Interpersonal Violence* 29, no. 9 (2014), 1623–1660, 1628.

[42] Kaplan, "Restorative Justice and Campus Sexual Assault," 720 (citations omitted).

[43] Id. (citations omitted).

[44] Coker, "Crime Logic, Campus Sexual Assault and Restorative Justice," 193–194.

especially with regard to reducing recidivism. According to a rigorous meta-study of 22 studies of 35 separate restorative justice programs:

Arguably, one of the most important outcome variables for any form of criminal justice intervention is recidivism. The overall mean effect size for the 32 tests that examined the effectiveness of restorative justice programming in reducing offender recidivism was +.07 (SD = .13) with a 95% CI of +.12 to +.02. Although the effect sizes ranged from +.38 to –.23, more than two thirds of the effect sizes were positive (72%). In other words, restorative justice programs, on average, yielded reductions in recidivism compared to nonrestorative approaches to criminal behavior. In fact, compared to the comparison and/or control groups who did not participate in a restorative justice program, offenders in the treatment groups were significantly more successful during the follow-up periods, t (31) = 2.88, p < .01.[45]

Also, unlike traditional mediation, restorative justice can look beyond the two individuals involved and bring in members of the larger community responsible for the harm. This makes it ideally suited for a college environment where certain communities are overrepresented in terms of being accused of sexual assault. Although fraternities and sports teams do not always fall in this category, it is true that "some fraternity or athletic team members are more likely to commit sexual assault than males in the general student population."[46] In a restorative justice regime, fraternity presidents and team captains and coaches could be required to participate in the conferences. While it is impossible to know how this would play out, the potential for fraternity and athletic leaders, in the sober light of day and with a trained facilitator, to be confronted with the pain that their members have caused is enormous. There is a potential to bring reform to problematic campus institutions in ways far beyond what the current punitive system has been able to do.

For all its potential, restorative justice cannot work properly without cooperation from local police and prosecutors and/or state legislators. As noted, restorative justice requires students to be candid about their roles. In the example given earlier, the male student would have to be candid about his drug and alcohol use and the possibility that he didn't behave reasonably as a result of this use. Such candor is highly unlikely if the police can use these statements against him in criminal court.

Therefore, colleges would need legislatures to pass laws allowing for incriminating statements to remain confidential if they are made during the restorative justice process. Failing that, colleges can enter into memorandums of understanding with local prosecutors that could achieve the same result. As with the alcohol issue, this is something where universities would greatly benefit from cooperation from local or state government. Students would also

---

[45] Jeff Latimer et al., "The Effectiveness of Restorative Justice Practices: A Meta-Analysis," *The Prison Journal* 85, no. 2 (June 2005), 127–144, 137.

[46] Stephen E. Humphrey, "Fraternities, Athletic Teams, and Rape," *Journal of Interpersonal Violence* 15, no. 12 (December 2000), 1313–1323.

need to sign forms agreeing to hold any statements made during the process confidential and waiving any right to use such statements in civil litigation.

Restorative justice programs would, of course, have to be purely voluntary. Students should not be pressured into availing themselves of it. Quite the opposite, as discussed in the preceding text, universities should do everything in their power to help and encourage students to expeditiously report crimes to the police. But many students do want to go to the police. There is much to be gained by offering the students a restorative justice alternative to the highly flawed punitive process used on many campuses.

RESPECT THE PROCEDURAL RIGHTS OF STUDENTS

Obviously not all cases will be suitable for restorative justice and not all parties will agree to the process. And even when the complainant has gone to the police, there will be cases in which the college will need to adjudicate the complaint on its own, especially where it is in a state with narrow laws or in an area with an unsympathetic police culture. When colleges do resort to an adversarial, punitive proceeding it is imperative that the college respect the procedural rights of all students. Chapters 4 and 5 discussed the procedural rights that are essential for a fair hearing and, for each, gave examples of cases in which denying these rights produced an unfair process.

To summarize and recap, these rights are:

1) A Hearing. It is not enough to have a system where a single investigator talks to witnesses and reports to a committee that makes its decisions solely upon the investigator's report. The accused student is entitled to a hearing where he can hear the testimony against him and directly ask those witnesses questions unless there is clear danger of witness intimidation. The accused student should be able to directly speak to the decision-makers who control his fate. He should be able to present evidence and witnesses. Anonymous witnesses should not be allowed unless there is clear and convincing evidence that such anomimity is necessary to protect the witness's safety. The investigator should never be allowed to make the ultimate determination of guilt or innocence entirely on his or her own authority.

2) Notice of Charges and of the Specific Facts to Be Proved That Support Those Charges. It is not enough to merely tell the accused student what sections of the student handbook he is charged with violating. He should know the specific facts to be proved. Does the university believe he unduly pressured someone, touched someone without affirmative consent, or had sexual contact with a person who was too drunk to consent? Such notice should be provided prior to the beginning of the investigation. The hearing should not consider any factual questions or theories that are not included in the

notice of charges, although the notice can be amended in a timely manner. The notice should also clearly explain the process and the rights of both students.

3) Adequate Time to Prepare. A student needs time to consult with an attorney, speak with witnesses, and prepare a defense. A hearing should not take place less than two weeks after the student has been presented with a statement of charges.

4) The Right to See Evidence. Both students should see all evidence relied upon by the investigator or relied upon by the panel, including the investigator's notes. There should never be reliance upon secret evidence. Even in cases where anonymous testimony is allowed, both students should have access to the content of the testimony to the greatest degree possible while allowing for anominity.

5) The Right to Exculpatory Evidence. There should be an affirmative duty on the part of the university to reveal any exculpatory evidence of which it is aware. The university should never discourage students or other persons with relevant information from testifying.

6) Standard of Proof. A standard of proof lower than clear and convincing is acceptable only when all, or nearly all, of the other procedural protections listed here are in place. The burden of proof must always clearly remain with the university.

7) An Unbiased Panel. Non proprietary training materials for the panel should be publically available. Both students should be able to view, but not copy, proprietary training material prior to the hearing. No one with personal knowledge of the situation or of the students should sit on the panel except in a small school where this is not possible, even after good faith efforts have been made to assemble such a panel. The person who investigates the allegations should not serve on the panel or have authority over any person on the panel. Both students should be notified of who is serving on the panel prior to the hearing to allow them to object to any member they believe to be biased.

8) The Right to an Attorney. Both students should have the right to consult with an attorney throughout the process. The attorney should be allowed to fully participate during the hearing. If a student cannot afford an attorney, that student should be able to bring a representative of his or her choice who can also fully participate in the process.

9) Examination of Witnesses: Both students, or their attorneys or representatives, should be allowed to ask questions of witnesses unless the panel specifically finds, with a written explanation, good cause for not allowing such questioning. The accused student should not be allowed to personally question the accusing student. The accused student's attorney or representative may do so, subject to reasonable restrictions such as remaining seated and refraining from asking the accusing student any questions about her sexual history other than with the defendant.

The accusing student should also be represented by an attorney or other representative.

10) <u>Trained Panelists</u>. Legal training should be provided for panelists in alignment with the recommendations of the Association for Student Conduct Administration.

11) <u>The Right to Present Witnesses</u>: Both parties should be allowed to present witnesses, subject to reasonable limitations on the number of witnesses and the panel's determination of relevance.

12) <u>A Written Decision</u>: The panel should produce a written decision giving the facts, rules and reasoning justifying the decision. The decision should contain a clear acknowledgement that the university had the burden of proof on all relevant facts and state why the panel believes the university met that burden.

13) <u>Recorded Proceedings</u>: The entire proceeding should be digitally recorded.

14) <u>The Right to Appeal for Both Students</u>:

   a) The appellate decision maker should be limited to reviewing the initial hearing for errors, the appropriateness of the punishment, or new information that could not reasonably have been presented at the initial hearing. If the appellate decision maker determines that the initial panel made significant errors, imposed an inappropriate punishment or needs to consider new evidence, the case should be referred back to the initial panel.

   b) The appellate decision-maker may not rely on any evidence or any grounds not considered at the initial hearing or make a decision about the facts based upon its own weighing of the evidence. However should the appellate decision maker determine that the facts, as determined by the initial panel, do not amount to a violation of any school policy, the accused student should be found not responsible without further proceedings.

   c) The appellate decision-maker must not include any of the same panel members as the initial hearing panel nor any subordinates of the initial decision maker.

The American Bar Association has created a *Best Practices* document for college sexual assault tribunals.[47] Many of its recommendations are similar to the ones mentioned previously. The principle difference is that the preceding standards are not intended as just recommended "best practices." This book argues that for public universities these standards are *constitutionally required due process requirements*. They are each justified under the Supreme Court's constitutional balancing test from *Matthews v. Eldridge* discussed extensively in Chapters 2, 4,

[47] www.americanbar.org/content/dam/aba/publications/criminaljustice/2017/College_Due_Process .authcheckdam.pdf.

and 5. Chapter 3 argues that these standards should also be required of private institutions under Title IX and contract principles. The ABA document makes several recommendations that, while not constitutionally required, are excellent suggestions. For example the ABA recommends that:

Neither the complainant nor the respondent should be required to participate in the proceedings. However, the decision-maker(s) should not consider either party's personal account of what happened unless that party is available for questioning by the decision-maker(s) and the other party.[48]

On a few issues, the recommendations in this book differ from the ABA. The ABA states a "preference" for an adjudicatory hearing in which the evidence is presented directly to the panel as opposed to the investigative model where the evidence is presented through an investigator's report. This book argues that an adjudicatory hearing is a constitutional requirement. Also, the ABA concludes that the model in which the investigator is also the decision maker "carries inherent structural fairness risks." This book goes further, arguing that such a model is unconstitutional and should never be allowed.

Also, the ABA was apparently unable to come to a consensus on one of the trickiest issues: standard of proof. They suggest that a single fact finder should be held to a higher standard of proof but avoid legal terms like "preponderance of evidence" and "clear and convincing evidence" altogether.[49] This book also argues that the standard of proof should not be one size fits all but would not make the size of the panel the sole metric for deciding the burden of proof.

Finally, to repeat a point made earlier, none of the recommended procedures, either in this book or by the ABA, is designed to stand in the way of justice for victims of sexual assault. To the contrary, this book gives examples where it was the *lack* of fair procedures that prevented justice for the victims, as well as for the accused students. Cross-examination of the accusing student is the most difficult issue because the prospect of it might deter victims from participating. Chapter 5 recommends a number of steps to minimize this possibility. But the vast majority of what this book and the ABA recommend pose absolutely no obstacle to justice for victims. Nobody benefits from giving the accused student only a few days to prepare for a hearing, from an inadequate record of the proceedings, or from not allowing students, or their attorneys, to directly question the investigator or university detective, who are, after all, trained professional adults. As noted earlier, this is an area in which universities have been buffeted by political forces both externally and internally. The courts should step in and fulfill their essential function of enforcing basic procedural fairness when the university seeks to impose so significant a sanction as suspension or expulsion from a university for a sexual offense.

---

[48] Id at 5.
[49] www.americanbar.org/content/dam/aba/publications/criminaljustice/2017/College_Due_Process.authcheckdam.pdf, 6–8.

REPEAL THE FORCE REQUIREMENT FOR RAPE AND CREATE
A UNIFORM DEFINITION OF SEXUAL ASSAULT

As noted in Chapter 1, most states have retained the force requirement for rape. As we have seen, this requirement has protected home invaders who have attacked sleeping victims and men who have pinned victims with their weight. It is deeply disappointing that this cruel and foolish requirement is still the law in the majority of states. It serves no valid purpose and should be repealed in every state.

Meanwhile, affirmative consent is now the rule in an increasingly large number of states and individual colleges. As we saw in the previous chapter, it is justified by a series of empirical claims that range from contestable to demonstrably incorrect. As we saw in Chapter 7, it likely violates the constitutional rights of students and, at a minimum, stands in contrast to how consent is defined in almost every other legal context. It punishes sexual behaviors that are so widely practiced that it invites enforcement that is arbitrary at best and racially discriminatory at worst. Without justification, it creates one set of rules for college students and another for everyone else, including legislators that pass the laws but do not have to live by them.

The law should be harmonized and rationalized. As discussed in the previous chapter, the "reasonable person" standard is one of the most widespread, if not the most widespread, standard in both criminal and civil law. Rape and sexual assault should be evaluated by this standard for college students and everyone else. The question that should be asked is whether a reasonable person in the accused person's position would have believed that they had consent. Even in a murder case, where a defendant pleads self-defense, "fear is assessed according to the reasonable-person standard, which asks what an ordinary and reasonable individual would do under the circumstances."[50]

So a student who reasonably believes that he is engaging in consensual activity should not be expelled from college as a sex offender. That is not justice, and it does not make anyone safer. In or out of college, victims should not have to prove force or the threat of force. Sexual contact without a reasonable belief that the person is consenting should be considered sexual assault no matter who the victim is. And the law should recognize, for students and nonstudents alike, that reasonable people do not think they have consent when the other person says "no."

CONCLUSION

Society has been going through a period of rapid change in how it approaches sexual offenses. This is not the first time that this has happened. Generally, these periods of change have improved society. Marital rape is now illegal in all 50 states. The age of

---

[50] www.justia.com/criminal/defenses/self-defense/.

consent has been raised and child pornography laws have been strengthened. Rape complainants no longer need corroboration. The improvements have been many.

But periods of rapid change also can be dangerous. In our zeal to combat evil deeds, it can be easy to dismiss due process as protection for evildoers. Americans have made this mistake many times. It is easy to parody colleges as dens of sexual irresponsibility and young people as lacking the higher morals of their elders. These tropes often ride hip to hip with gender and racial stereotypes. It is all too easy for society to demand rules for students that they do not follow themselves and to turn a blind eye to the gender and racial biases that often come with regimes of sexual regulation.

It has been oft-noted that we are living in an era of "tribalism." It would be a mistake to reduce this debate to men versus woman, progressives versus conservatives, feminists versus traditionalists, or any other "us versus them" paradigm. It would be best to focus on principles that unify us, apply to all people, and have served this nation well for a very long time. Everyone is entitled to fair process. Everyone should abide by the same rules. Everyone has a right to feel safe. These are the principles that should guide us forward and bring us together rather than further apart.

Index

CPSIA information can be obtained
at www.ICGtesting.com
Printed in the USA
LVHW112104191119
637877LV00010B/278/P